T0365530

NOT ALL LUCK IS BAD

Bertha Newbery

Order this book online at www.trafford.com
or email orders@trafford.com

Most Trafford titles are also available at major online book retailers.

Note for Librarians: A cataloguing record for this book is available from Library
and Archives Canada at www.collectionscanada.ca/amicus/index-e.html

Printed in Victoria, BC, Canada.

ISBN: 978-1-4251-4168-4 (Soft)
ISBN: 978-1-4251-4169-1 (e-book)

*We at Trafford believe that it is the responsibility of us all, as both individuals
and corporations, to make choices that are environmentally and socially sound.
You, in turn, are supporting this responsible conduct each time you purchase a
Trafford book, or make use of our publishing services. To find out how you are
helping, please visit www.trafford.com/responsiblepublishing.html*

*Our mission is to efficiently provide the world's finest, most comprehensive
book publishing service, enabling every author to experience success.
To find out how to publish your book, your way, and have it available
worldwide, visit us online at www.trafford.com*

Trafford rev. 9/4/2009

 www.trafford.com

North America & international
toll-free: 1 888 232 4444 (USA & Canada)
phone: 250 383 6864 ♦ fax: 812 355 4082 ♦ email: info@trafford.com

Chapter 1

When the donkey nibbled her straw hat, Jane's future was sealed. The well ordered, comfortable life as daughter of a respectable dress maker – with prospects of marriage to a most eligible gentleman – was gone. The dark, handsome owner of the donkey enthralled her no matter what fate had in store.

George squatted beside his young daughter. In the candle light, her brown hair was like golden cobwebs drifting across her face. Soon it would be long enough for plaits, losing its crumpled beauty. She stirred beneath the rough blanket.

'Wake up, girlie.' He tickled her toes and she woke. Her face broke into a smile and she held her arms out to him.

'Come on. I'll help you put on your boots.' His fingers caressed the soft leather and his mind counted the coins he'd get if he pawned them. Just to tide them over.

But Jane would be angry.

'It's dark, Pa. Where're we going?' Laura's eyelids drooped. She was ready to crawl back under the blanket. In two months time she'd be three years old.

'We're going to Granny's place.'

'To see Sarah?'

'No. Sarah's with Granny Goult. We're going to Granny Stringer.'

Laura wrinkled her nose. There were nasty smells at Granny Stringer's house. She envied her sister, just eleven months older. Granny Goult even had a bed and sheets. Laura had seen them. She pushed her arms into the made-over coat and stood in the middle of the bare room. Father bundled their two cooking pots into one sack and pushed the rolled up bedding into another. Laura wasn't sorry to leave. It wasn't a nice room. There were no windows and it was frightening when the goat butted through the meagre brown paper pasted over the opening. Granny Stringer's house might be better than this. There was often a pot of strew bones simmering on the hob. She clutched her stomach. The thought reminded her she was hungry and she started to whimper.

'Shush!' Jane said fiercely. She scooped up five months old Georgie into her arms and walked out. As they went out into the sharp November air, Laura clung to her mother's skirts. They walked quickly along the back alley and kept to the smaller, darker roads of the east end of London. Laura couldn't under-stand why her mother was cross. Laura's heart grew lighter the farther they got from Angel Lane.

The Broadway was ahead. Jane paused at the corner. The moon came from behind a cloud and, as if destiny decided to play a cruel trick, illuminated a gold painted name on a glass window opposite: *Arthur Goult, Esquire. Photographer. Established 1890.* Seeing the studio, Jane remembered the last time she had seen her brother, seven month ago, when she was heavily pregnant.

It was hot. She shouldn't have hurried. She felt light headed. Then blackness.

'Mister!' a young woman rushed into the shop leaving the bell clanging loudly on its spring.

Arthur came forward and purposefully held the door.

'Mister. Young lady fell outside and...'

Before she had finished the prone figure was carried in.

Astonished, Arthur indicated the velvet covered couch where his customers posed.

'Got any brandy, Sir?'

Arthur held a small glass in his hand as the young lady stirred. He almost spilled the liquid as he recognised Jane. She opened her eyes.

He bent close. 'You've done this to embarrass me. Don't you dare have your baby here.'

Jane pushed away the drink and sat up. On first seeing her brother's face she had been happy such a coincidence had brought them together. But her smile vanished at his words.

'I want nothing, thank you, Sir. Nothing at all.' She looked blankly at Arthur. She willed herself to be steady as she stood up and walked out of the studio.

'What is it, Ma?' Laura whimpered.

'Nothing, child, nothing at all.' The moon slid behind another cloud and the shop sign was swallowed in darkness. 'No. I want nothing from you, Arthur. I have all I want in my husband, George,' she said to herself. The church clock chimed three. Jane hurried on dragging Laura behind her. Along the Broadway no hum came from the tram tracks, nothing moved. Past silent mills and quiet factories. Over Stratford Bridge and a couple of twists and turns brought them to Grace

Road and shelter in Granny Stringer's room. Grace Road! Whoever had named it so must have had a wry sense of humour. There was nothing gracious about it. Its dark, dirty buildings huddled together shutting out daylight and hiding its shame from the world that had created it.

'Done a moonlight, have you?' Granny stirred the cinders in the grate and bright sparks sent shadows across the room. She glanced slyly at Jane. 'Everyone told you he was no good,' she cackled showing her few remaining teeth blackened by tobacco.

Laura crept close to the side of the grate and its meagre warmth lulled her into sleep.

'It's not for want of trying, Ma,' George protested. 'Work's scarce all round.'

Jane lay the baby on the rag mat by the smouldering embers. A faint gleam illuminated her face showing a light dusting of freckles spilling down her nose onto her soft cheeks. Jane's light golden hair, soft as silk, lacked the unruly curl of her mother's fiery crown. It was drawn back into a bun adding severity to a normally sombre face. Except when she turned her gaze on her husband. Then a glow shone from behind her eyes bathing her face in a radiance.

She was tired. She wasn't going to rise to her mother-in-law's taunts, not tonight. Oh, it was true. Her friend said she'd married beneath her station. Whatever that was supposed to mean. Love didn't care about stations. Matilda Goult had tried to dissuade her daughter.

'You've had a good education, Jane,' her mother reminded her. 'Not something many girls get. You are working in a nice office with respectable people. And there is Oliver Steadall. Oh, I had hoped you'd marry him. What is George Stringer? Son of an Irish tinker!'

Oliver Steadall, although a second son, would still inherit some of his father's wealth. For three years Jane and Oliver had been close companions. Jane sometimes spurned him and took up with one of her other beaux but always came back to Oliver. Matilda was congratulating herself – James, her eldest son, happily married with two children and in steady employment; Arthur had his own photographic studio and Oliver soon to propose to Jane. and then George Stringer comes on the scene. Jane had met George when the tinker's donkey began to nibble Jane's straw hat as she stood at the edge of the road. In the effort to extricate hat from mouth, she'd fallen into George's arms and this dark, handsome man had stolen her heart. Jane was under age and Matilda refused to give her consent. But she ran off and married her beloved George on mid-summer's day June 1891. And the following February Sarah was born.

She tucked a shawl round Georgie and stood up beside her husband, linking her arm through his.

'He's a good man, Ma and he tries very hard. We've just had a bit of a bad luck lately, that's all.'

Granny Stringer stared at her. 'I'll never understand why you married my son.'

'I love him,' Jane replied.

Granny shook her head. 'Come on rest now. You can have that corner for yourselves.'

They spread their bedding on the straw convered stone floor. Jane scooped up the children and put them on the bedding then lay down herself. George covered then with sacking and a blanket and crawled in beside them.

Jane stirred as she heard Granny shutting the front door: she was off on her scavenging. Mrs Stringer had a nose for rooting out anything that might be worth a few coppers. She'd turn over every rubbish heap especially those near the shops or public houses. Bits of iron or wood; a piece of cloth, broken ornaments and, sometimes, even a coin might have been dropped. Her hands were ingrained with dirt. Jane shuddered at the thought and slid from under the covers. She poured water into the tin bowl and with a clean piece of linen rubbed her face and arms.

She turned to see George watching her.

'I'll get work, Jane. I'm sure tomorrow will be lucky.'

His sad face tore at her heart. She quickly knelt beside him and held him in her arms; his tears burnt her skin.

She forced a laugh and began scrubbing his face with her cloth.

'Come on. Wash!' she commanded. 'I'm not letting my husband go out unclean.' And she bathed away his sadness.

They spent the daylight hours walking the streets. Jane and George taking it in turns to carry the baby while Laura tagged along behind.

'Pa.' Laura plucked at her father's trouser leg. George turned and swept her high in the air.

'What my pretty one?'

She hugged her father's neck and he bubbled his lips on her cheek. He began to sing to her an old Irish folk song in a clear, melodious tenor voice until Laura tugged at him again.

'When is Sarah coming home, Pa?'

'Soon, girlie. We'll get a place of our own again and she'll be home for you to play with. Soon,' he muttered.

George went out early to the market but would be back within the hour when he wasn't hired and he and Jane would walk. They'd stay out until mid afternoon and return when they knew Ma would be making supper. A trivet perched over a few sticks and a couple of knobs of coal provided the means to cook. Unclean chimneys meant soot dropped down pushing acrid smoke into the room and covering everything with a fine ash. Granny Stringer was always quick to lift off the stew pot.

The room reeked of cabbage.

'I got some greens off Will. Your brother's stall in Abbey Road is doing well, George. Says he might take a shop. Stall's cold in winter.' She like to boast about her younger son who'd set up on his own.

Granny Stringer put the steaming pot on the upturned box. They sat on the floor and eagerly watched her serve a helping to them all with a chunk of bread. The hot liquid dulled their senses and they could rest.

Mist rolling in from the river and canals mingled with chimney smoke and created dense fog typical in November. It seemed to intensify the foul smells from the soap factories and tannery. Jane worried about taking Georgie out each day into the atmosphere but the rank air of the one room where they all lived, ate and slept seemed worse.

She was on her own today and decided to walk to the park. Laura was running ahead.

'Jane! Jane Goult.'

Jane turned to see her sister-in-law, Emily, hurrying towards her.

'Such a long time since we've seen you Jane. How are you? Silly of me to call you Goult. James was only saying the other day, we haven't seen Jane lately. And this is your son. What's his name?' Emily cooed at Georgie.

'He's named after his father, George Stringer,' Jane retorted.

'Names are important, aren't they?' Emily twittered.

Jane hadn't named the children for any special person, although George had been pleased she'd suggested calling their first girl Sarah, like his mother and he had added Matilda to please her. When their second child arrived, Aunt Laura was visiting Matilda, so Laura it was and George added Selina after his sister. Names weren't important to Jane. She couldn't be bothered to find new ones.

'James is doing very will, you know. There was a better paid job coming up at the works and he wasn't going to try for it. But I said he had to. James, I said, you must always try to better yourself. You must always strive for the next step up the ladder,' Emily smiled in a smug way. 'I have to bully my James now and again,' she simpered.

Jane almost felt sorry for her brother. She found it difficult to like Emily, such a scheming woman. Matilda was ambitious for herself and her family. May be that was why Emily go on with her mother-in-law. Perhaps James deserved Emily, too. Jane took her leave and wandered back.

George got up at three o'clock each morning and set off for Stratford Market. He stood in line waiting for hire as a porter. The other men were large and muscular but at twenty-six George still had the build of a youth although he was tall. Often he was passed over because they thought he wasn't strong enough. Foremen walked along selecting those they wanted for the day. Sometimes they would choose one as the gang leader and leave him to pick his own men. There were one or two bosses who did their own choosing.

'Give me a chance, Mister. Let me show you,' George pleaded. 'I'm fit as a fiddle and I can do anything they can do.'

Ernie Weston stopped in front of him. He'd seen the

man stand in line for the past five days and not be taken on.

'Got a family?'

'Yes, Sir. Two girls and a boy.'

'Where are you living?'

'Grace Road, Sir. With my mother. Just temporary, Sir.'

'I'll take you on today.'

'Thank you, thank you, Sir.'

'And if you're any good I'll keep you on – guaranteed work for four weeks. But you'd better be good.'

'I will be. I promise.' And he eagerly shook the hand Ernie held out.

Four weeks! Guaranteed! George took off his jacket and carefully folded it into a roll, tied it with a string and hooked it onto his belt. He followed Mr Weston through the large iron gates into the glass domed hall.

Jane heard the church clock chime six; seven. She waited. Eight. A tremor of excitement ran through her. George hadn't returned.

'Ma. Are we going out?' Laura asked.

Jane patted her head. 'No. We're waiting for father.'

Laura liked it when her Pa was there. He'd take her on his knee and cuddle her. He'd tell her stories to make her laugh.

Suddenly to Laura's surprise, her mother was laughing.

'Yes, we will go out. We'll go and see Sarah.'

Jane's heart beat quickened as she walked along West Street. So many memories. Unbidden, came the remembrance of her first kiss from Jack Nestor, his large hands holding her to him as his mouth pressed hard against her lips. He was the manager of the draper's where she worked and was ten years older. Matilda dealt with him promptly. Jane smiled. Her mother had dealt with all her beaux except Oliver Steadall and Jane had dealt with him.

'Hello, Mother.'

Matilda greeted her daughter cordially and bent to kiss Laura.

'Have you come to take Sarah home with you?'

'Not just yet, Mother. But we'll soon have our own place again.'

At the sound of voices, Sarah ran along the hallway to greet her mother and sister. Jane pushed the two girls ahead of her and followed her mother into the warm, cosy kitchen.

Jane sat down. 'George goes out each morning, and this morning he didn't come back.'

Matilda gaseped and stared at her daughter. Jane shook her head.

'I mean, George must've been taken on this morning.'

'He's not the man I would have wished for my daughter.' She held up her hand as Jane began to protest. 'All I ever wanted Jane, was your happiness.'

The two sisters were playing with a wooden doll. 'And a good home for your family. All of them,' she added.

'We will have, you'll see. Come on Laura, we're going home to wait for Pa.'

At half past two he came home.

'There! Three shillings.' He proudly gave the coins to Jane 'And I'll be working for the next four weeks. Until after Christmas.

Within the week, Jane had left her mother-in-law's place. She'd found two clean rooms in Marcus Street for four and sixpence a week. She brought Sarah home and they were a family again.

The bedding was put in the front room; Sarah and

Laura were allocated one corner. Jane and George were on the far side with the baby near to Jane. In the back room, a large upturned wooden box served as a table and apple boxes to sit on.

George, stripped off to his underwear, still sat on his box. Jane, too, was ready for bed. She stirred the last embers of the fire. The orange flames flickered across her face.

'It's almost midnight. Happy New Year, my husband.'

'You are beautiful Jane,' George murmured, 'Just as you were five years ago when we married. I wouldn't trade the gold of your hair for all the gold pieces in the world.'

Jane squatted on the floor and leant back against his knee. 'Why can't life be like this all the time,' she sighed.

His arms enfolded her and his lips tenderly brushed her eyelids and cheeks. He slid down beside her. His moist kisses became more ardent as he sought her mouth. Through the flannel night gown she felt the contours of his body harden. She lingered for a moment enjoying the smell of him then as she felt the urge rise within him, she quickly pulled away. Jane sensed his hurt and it almost broke her heart. If only it didn't end in babies.

She stroked his face. 'We have three children, my darling. Let us give each of them a chance. She stood up and held out her hand to him. 'Come to bed. Perhaps 1896 will be good for us.'

'We'll be able to take Sarah, Mrs Stringer,' she school master promised. 'But not Laura.'

'She'll be three on the nineteenth of this month, Sir. Only a few days.'

So Sarah and Laura entered into Bridge Road School.

The school room had a big stove in the centre and there were desks with fitted seats in rows on each side. Laura being the youngest and smallest was placed at the front. Sarah sat behind. They were each given a slate and a piece of chalk.

Mrs Maggs, the school master's wife, taught the youngest ones. Her dark black hair, plaited into coils at the side of her head, almost covered her ears.

'Now all copy as I write.' Mrs Maggs beamed a special smile at Laura.

As the letters and numbers were marked on the large board, the children's chalks squeaked across their slates. Laura liked going to school.

'Look, Pa. I'll show you.' Laura wrote a few wobbly numbers in the dry earth of the yard at Marcus Street.

George clapped his hands. 'What a clever daughter I have. Come and give your father a kiss.'

Sarah was slow to learn. She liked to gaze out of the window, until Mrs Maggs moved her to the far side against the wall.

Most days George was hired and every day, except Sunday, Jane worked as a laundry woman to Mrs Harris in Sandal Street. It wasn't long before Jane was again making her way to West Street.

She always approached the house with mixed feelings. Happy memories of childhood – games and romps with James and Arthur. They would swing her high in the air and pretend to drop her while she shrieked with laughter until father rescued her. But now, with only Matilda living there, it seemed a forbidding place. All the joy and laughter was stored away with the toys in the attic. And Arthur was ashamed of her.

She lifted the heavy knocker.

Matilda's welcoming smile faded a little as she saw only Sarah standing with Jane.

They sat in the parlour; Jane perched awkwardly on the edge of an over stuffed chair. The arc of the summer sun wouldn't touch the room until late in the afternoon so now it felt chill. Matilda listened as Jane unfolded the usual story of short time working making it hard to feed a family of five.

'How did you ever get into this situation, Jane?' Why are you having to do someone else's washing? It's not right.'

'Oh, Mother. What is the difference between doing my own family wash and another family's wash.'

'But with your education, you could work in a store. Even an office, anywhere,' she paused. 'You could work with me, Jane.'

'You know I'm no good with a needle, Mother.'

'I don't mean with the sewing. There are the orders to make up and the bills to send out. Accounts to do. All things you are qualified to do. And you would earn a decent wage.'

'George is the bread winner in our family. I just help out.'

'Help out!' Matilda's anger boiled over. 'He's not the bread winner, he...'

She broke off as Sarah came dancing into the room.

'I've smelled the sheet, Granny. Mmm, like flowers.'

'I've got some sweetmeats in a jar in the kitchen. See if you can find the right one, Sarah.'

They watched her prance out of the room.

'You've never understood, have you, Mother? I love George. I will do anything just to be with him and make him happy. And that's an end on it. I'm grateful you'll take Sarah for a few weeks while we get back on our feet. I'll come for her as soon as I can.'

Jane went into the kitchen and saw Sarah had found the right jar as she had a tell tale smear of chocolate on her lips.

As Matilda let her out of the front door, Jane looked resolutely at her mother.

'Even if I worked for you, it would still be charity. And that's something I cannot take.'

Working for Mrs Harris had drawbacks. Sometimes she'd receive cast off clothing instead of wages. But it was cash Jane wanted. Ada Green, Jean's neighbour gave her another address to try. A group of women were gossiping as she returned. They eagerly turned to her.

'Any luck with Mrs Smith?'

'Yes, she's taken me on as an out servant,' Jane replied. 'The pay is better than laundry woman to Mrs Harris.'

'Well, she's a real old skinflint.'

'Yeah,' Ada chipped in, 'Sometimes Jane didn't get wages, Mrs Harris give her clothes for the girls and baby. Cheek! It weren't new clothing, you know. All hand-me-downs,'

Jane smiled at her defender.

Ada carried on: 'Her Ma makes clothes. Proper dressmaking. Beats me, love, why you didn't go into 'er line of business. Must be a blessed sight easier that doing other people's laundry.'

Ironic, Jane thought, just what Matilda had said. 'I wasn't much good with a needle. It'll be good at Mrs Smith's. I can take the baby with me. There'll be other jobs to do as an out servant. And Paul Street is a nice area.'

She pushed open her front door. Laura a sturdy three and a half year old squatted on the floor beside her year old brother showing him the school book Mrs Maggs had given her. It consisted of rough sheets of brown paper stitched together with string.

'See,' she pointed, 'you've got to learn your letters, Georgie. Then you can make them in your very own book.'

Without Sarah as a school companion, Georgie was made to listen to Laura's lessons. When Laura came in from school Jane left her to mind the baby to go for her interview with Mrs Smith.

'Help me tidy up, Laura. Your Pa will be in soon. I got the job with Mrs Smith and she gave me some wages today. I want to make a special dinner.'

Excitedly, Laura picked up her school book and ran into the next room. She always placed it under her bedding by her head.

'Ma, will Sarah come home now?'

'We'll see. Bring me a stew pot.'

Jane unwrapped her purchases. The scrag end of mutton was a bit dry but with some liquid and a few potatoes it would make a wholesome meal.

She watched with pride as George wiped his mouth on the back of his hand and stood up.

'Jane, girl, you're a wonder. I don't know what I've done to deserve the likes of you. The Queen couldn't've dined better than us.'

He put his arm around her and first kissed her cheek; then his lips found hers. He pressed his body close to her, murmuring in her ear. For a moment Jane was limp in his arms before fiercely nodding toward the children.

Laura was surprised to see both her parents looking at her. Usually, it was only Pa who paid any attention to her: kissing her grazed knees better, dancing her on is knee and singing her to sleep. Now her mother was actually smiling at her. She repeated her plea for Sarah to come home.

'Of course,' George said. 'Mother will fetch her tomorrow.'

'And, Ma, as Mrs Smith is in Paul Street I could come from school to meet you. And we can walk home together, couldn't we?'

'Yes, yes. We'll see. Now, shush. I'm busy.' Jane turned back to clear the plates from their make shift table. There would be time later to fetch Sarah home.

Laura played a game with herself as she went to meet her mother. Leaving the school yard, she would walk slowly stretching out her little legs as far as possible to make long strides. Then, along Rokeby Street she'd run as fast as she could.

'Run, little girl, run,' a passer by called out.

Passing the end of Sandal Street she'd mutter Ma doesn't work for you Mrs Harris. Standing on tip toe, practising to be tall, she'd wait for her mother on the corner.

Mother and daughter walked along in silence while Georgie stumbled along in his reins until Jane gathered him up into her arms to walk at a brisker pace for home. The front parlour of a corner house had been converted into a draper's shop: Compton's. They also sold toys.

Jane paused and looked at the goods on display in the window.

Laura pressed her nose to the glass.

'You may choose a present,' Jane said.

Laura looked in astonishment. 'A present?' she echoed.

Coins jingled in her apron pocket as Jane nodded.

Laura's eyes darted between the dolly's stew pan

for a ha'penny or a wash copper for a farthing. She decided to push her luck and chose the more expensive toy.

It was a happy family life. Jane delighted in surprising George and it seemed there was a surprise almost every week. First of all, a table bleached white with repeated scrubbings and only one corner was chipped. Next, two chairs then two three-legged stools for the girls and Mrs Smith gave her a tall chair for Georgie. (Well, not exactly gave, let her have it for a shilling.) Knives and forks and, best of all, china plates. And at 'Old Moses', which was a jumbled treasure house, Jane bought a cupboard where she could keep them all.

The china plates were only used on Sundays. Laura laid the knives and forks on the table. Sarah was at the cupboard when her mother screamed:

'Don't touch those china plates. You're so clumsy, Sarah, you'll break them.'

Tears welled up Sarah's eyes. Laura took her sister's hand in sympathy. Jane turned back to the range and resumed cooking.

They were waiting for George to come home from the public house.

The baby began to grizzle and whimper.

'Georgie's hungry, Ma. May he have some broth?' Laura asked tentatively.

'We wait. Father always has the first serving.'

It was long past closing time. Sarah and Laura sat stiffly on their stools. Georgie was strapped into his tall seat. Jane sat mutely by the range. At last they heard him approach. The melodious Irish tenor voice was as beautiful when he was drunk as sober.

'Hello, me darlin' wife. Hello, me darlin' children.'

'Will you have something to eat now, father?' Jane asked calmly.

'I think I'll just have a nap first, darlin' Jane. Then I'll have me dinner.'

Laura gazed intently at her father. He could not ignore the pleading in her eyes.

'I think I will have a bite, Jane.' And he winked at Laura.

He would've collected four days wages yesterday. She should've looked then. Jane knew it was gone before she searched his pockets. No money for rent. Three weeks unpaid. He was snoring loudly, sleeping off the effects of the alcohol. When work was short George got depressed. And like the saying, drowned his sorrows.

Laura and Sarah waited on the corner of Paul Street. She was late.

'Should we go to Mrs Smith's house?' Sarah asked.

'No. Ma would be ever so cross. Look, here she comes.'

Jane's face was flushed. Georgie was straddled on her hip. She passed no word in greeting; the girls skipped along behind. The Smith's were giving a dinner party in celebration of the Queen's Jubilee and Jane had helped at every opportunity. Mrs Smith was pleased. Jane grasped the moment to ask for extra wages. It was a mistake. Mrs Smith merely said if she was unhappy in her situation, perhaps she should seek employment elsewhere. The past year had been good, she wasn't unhappy but pride wouldn't let her take back the words. She accepted dismissal money.

As they turned into Marcus Street, Jane smothered a cry and put Georgie down.

The girls had been chattering about the gay bunting and ribbons along the streets. Everywhere there were decorations to celebrate QueenVictoria's Diamond Jubilee.

'Isn't it pretty,' Sarah said. A light June breeze

ruffled the decorations. She tugged at her mother's skirt.

But Jane was rooted to the spot.

She was too late.

For several weeks Jane had missed paying the rent. Somehow, between George receiving his wages and his arrival at home, quite a tidy sum had gone; generous to everyone who told him a sorry tale. He would give Jane a sad smile saying: 'They were desperate, love.' As she'd lain in his arms last night, she'd told him they'd have to do another 'moonlight' only this time there was the furniture. They'd have to borrow a cart from George's brother, Will. But now it was to late.

Chairs, stools and the table were piled in the street. The bailiff's men were carrying out the small chest and banged it down, forcing open the two doors and Jane's patterned china plates smashed on the cobbles.

She held a fragment in her palm her fingers traced the torn petals of a rose.

Sarah and Laura stood silently behind their mother. Georgie still anchored by his reins, tugged forward treading on the fragments.

'It'll be the Poor House for you, Missis' the men said.

They nailed planks of wood across the door to prevent re-entry.

Queen Victoria was celebrating sixty glorious years on the throne. The world was celebrating. But not the Stringers.

'We couldn't stop'em,' Ada Green said. 'But I made sure they pinched nothing and slipped it in their pockets. What you going to do?'

Obviously the Bailiff's men had decided there was no value in the pieces. Jane stood up and balanced

Georgie on his feet. 'We'll decide what to do when Father comes home.'

'What about your mother? She could help you out, couldn't she? Or, your brother? Both have got a bob or two.'

Jane shook her head. 'Ada, have you got a bit of room out back to keep my sticks of furniture for a while? You can use the chairs and table if you like.'

'Course I have, Jane.' Ada agreed eagerly. In her mind's eye she already saw herself and Mr Green sitting on the polished wood chairs. Her own grubby chairs could stand out back.

Laura ran to meet her father as he approached.

'Here's a present for you, girlie.' He drew from his pocket a slightly crushed bunch of violets.

Her squeal of delight trailed into a sob as she remembered her mother's broken plates. She ran back to stand with Sarah as Jane emerged from Ada's to carry in the cupboard.

'I'm sorry, Jane. So sorry.' His voice was hoarse with emotion.

'Ada's keeping our bits for now. Come on, love. Let's go.'

She had thought naively they would give her some money as a loan, just to tide them over for a while. She thought that's what Parish Relief was about. Jane regretted overriding George's suggestion they should stay with his mother again. And now, they stood before the Workhouse Board of Guardians. After they were examined by the medical officer, they were taken to the bath house. Silently Jane watched her two small daughters and baby son being led into the children's section; just in time, she turned to see George go through the men's door. Her deep sob bounced off the tiled walls, increasing in volume forcing warders to cover their ears.

Matilda Goult stood before the Guardians.

'I am their grandmother. Surely I can take them home with me.'

'Sorry, Missis. You'll have to see the sheriff in the morning.'

'Please will you let me speak to my daughter. If she told you she wanted me to take the children, that would be all right, wouldn't it?'

The Guardians pondered. The girls could be used in the weaving room.

Jane was brought out from the laundry. Already her hands were bright red from the coarse carbolic. In her workhouse dress she faced her mother.

Through her tears, Matilda smiled brightly at her daughter. 'Will you let me take the children, Jane?' she pleaded. 'Just for now, until you...' Her voice trailed off into a silent sob.

'If you say it's all right,' the Parish Officer began, 'we could let the little'uns go with the lady. Course, the girls working in the weaving room could help reduce your debt.'

The summer night was hot and humid as Matilda walked through the streets with a little girl on each side clutching her hands. Jane kept two year old Georgie with her in the workhouse.

Chapter 2

'We get off here, children, 'Matilda said. She slipped off the back of the cart and then lifted down the girls.

'You were most kind. I'm much obliged to you.'

'Nothing to it, Missis. I was along this way myself. I reckon you must be Matilda.'

'Yes, I am,' she smiled. 'But I can't recall you.'

'Friend of your brother, Arthur. We were going to enlist together but father died and I had to work our bit of land. Much good it's done me with times so hard. Might as well have gone to Crimea and died along of Arthur. He was a good pal.' He touched his cap and clucked at his horse to move on.

At the mention of her brother, her memory darted back. If it hadn't been for Arthur giving a ride to a stranger when they went to the Great Exhibition she wouldn't have met James. Yes, Arthur was a good man.

A slight haze covered the sun, cooling the temperature of the past few days. In the old days, golden barley and corn stretched to the horizon. Now sharp outlines of structures punctuated the vista. From the yard, two dogs yelping fiercely rushed toward the approaching group. A figure strode into view from behind a barn to see the cause of the commotion. With her skirt hitched

NOT ALL LUCK IS BAD

up into her belt, displaying men's high leather boots, she stood akimbo glaring at the intruders.

As the dogs gained ground, the woman suddenly rushed forward to draw level and a curt command stilled them.

Sarah and Laura cowered behind their grandmother.

'Good Lord! It's Matilda.' Muscular arms wrapped about her sister's shoulder, crushing her in a warm hug. 'You are a sight for sore eyes.'

Matilda laughed loudly. And her sadness of the past few days eased.

'And who do we have here, then?' the big woman asked poking her head behind Matilda's back to squint at the two girls.

'One of them is your namesake. The taller one is Sarah – she's five and half and this one is Laura, she's four and a half. Children, this is your Great Aunt Laura and she's my sister.'

'Great Aunt! My! Doesn't that sound grand?'

The girls bobbed a curtsy but soon turned away to romp with the dogs in the dusty earth.

'I hope you don't mind us coming, Laura.'

'Don't be daft, Tilda. This is always your home.'

They left the children playing and walked into the large old kitchen. Great Aunt Laura poured cider from a round stone jug. Matilda ran her fingers over the ridged surface of the long-scrubbed table.

'Oh, Laura, I know you were only young but do you remember when all the family sat round this table? Mother at one end and father at the other.'

'Yes, and all the children spaced along one side, oldest next to father and me down by mother. Then father would get up and open the door and the farm hands would sit opposite us children. How many would there have been?'

'Well, eight in our family and a dozen or so hands at harvest time.'

Matilda looked out over the land. 'We had fields of barley and oats, we had milking cows, sheep, a couple of pigs, hens and the vegetable fields. But much of that had gone even by the time you were born, Laura.'

'There's even less now. I've got two cows, a few hens who don't give me enough to sell at market some weeks. And there's a couple of fields of turnips and cabbages. They've taken most of the land for building houses but not for the likes of you and me. As tenant farmers we have no rights. Not that I want the land. Most of the hands have moved on to other places. The only help I've got is Daniel Binder and he's as daft as a brush but such a loving boy. But you didn't come all this way to Barking just to hear my troubles.'

Matilda gazed into the golden liquid in her mug. 'Jane has got herself into such a mess, Laura, you just wouldn't believe it. She never has enough money to live on. In her short life, Sarah has lived more with me than with her own mother. And now,' Matilda stifled a sob, 'now she's in the Work House. That no good husband of hers. She could have had everything. Everything. If only she'd married Oliver Steadall.'

'But, Tilda, love, she didn't want Oliver Steadall. So there's an end on it.'

'She works as a skivvy for a woman hardly better off than her brother James and his wife, Emily. I said, if she had to work, why didn't she come and work for me. She's not clever with a needle but she could do the accounts and orders. But she won't. She says it would be charity. Oh, Laura, she won't let me help her.'

'Course not. Why should she?'

Matilda stared at her sister. 'What do you mean?'

Laura leaned forward and patted her hand. 'Now don't get bristly,' she smiled. 'She knows you don't like

George and whatever you do seems like another bit of disapproval. The best she can do to stretch out to you, is to ask you to have Sarah when times are hard.'

She held her sister's hand for a while. 'Now, Tilda. What about a bit to eat?'

'I'd best be getting back, dear. Thanks all the same. It's been nice seeing the old place again – and you. You're sure you don't mind having the girls for a few weeks, just until...'

'It'll be good to have someone to take care of again. I reckon Martha turned out all right after all the mollycoddling by her mother, God rest her soul. Our brother picked a wrong 'un when he married Mary and no mistake but love blooms in strange gardens.' She winked at her sister. 'So we must just accept folk as they are.'

'I'm glad I brought the children here. I'll be down again when I have some news.'

Young Laura thrived on the farm. Within days, her white face had acquired the tones of a russet apple. While Sarah sat day dreaming, Laura enjoyed helping Great Aunt.

'Take this down to Daniel, he's working in the first field. It's his meal tin. Don't say anything to him, 'cause he can't hear you. He'll say something to you but it'll be gibberish. Just smile and wave and come straight back.'

She ran across the yard and down the track to the field, delivered the box and ran back.

'My! But that was quick. You don't have to run all the time.'

'When I'm grown up and have long legs,' Laura replied gravely, 'I shan't have to run.'

'Well, don't run back when you've collected the eggs. Just walk.'

'Aunt, why is that little horse shut up in that shed'

'That's Queenie and she's a donkey. She usually pulls the market cart but she's in foal. Very soon she'll give birth.'

It was all very strange; no streets nor houses; no noise and clatter. Laura enjoyed it. But she missed her Pa. She'd sensed something was wrong but couldn't understand what it was. She missed school, too. Somewhere between leaving their home and going into that big building, Laura had lost her writing book. She tried to remember the shape of letters and would recite numbers and words as she ran around the farm. Sarah was content to listen to her sister.

Jane had seen him just once. She'd stood on a chair and managed to rest her chin on the window sill. Her gaze scanned the yard. The men stripped to the waist, worked in rows. The first gang split the large slabs of granite wielding sledge hammers; the next gang shovelled it forward; the third gang squatted on the ground and broke the pieces into small shapes with hand tools to make cobble stones to repair the roads. The inexperienced ones struck their hands more often than the stones.

George sat on the ground with his legs wide apart with a pile of stones between them. She saw him reach forward with bloody hands to take up a lump and with a feeble effort chipped away at the slippery surface until a prod from the overseer spurted him into faster action.

'Well, er...' The Guardian turned over a paper in front of him. 'Stringer, is it?

'Yes, Sir,' Jane answered.

'During your four weeks here, your record shows you have worked diligently in an effort to expunge your debt to the Parish. So, you may leave if you can show you have a place to go to and some form of employment. Do you have lodgings arranged?'

'Yes, sir. I have been promised employment in the Maryland Laundry and will lodge in the female hostel attached to the laundry.'

'Good, good. And, remember,' he stared at her through thick lens glasses, 'remember you must pay for what you have. You cannot live on credit, expecting someone else to cover your bills.'

Jane spent a restless night and at first light of dawn went to the children's room to collect Georgie. The heavy oak door of the Work House clanged behind them and she hurried away. The sky darkened threatening a storm and soon she felt the first drops of rain. Early morning workers scurried along, heads bent against the oncoming cloudburst. Trams hissed, dispersing water from the tracks. She looked longingly at the comfort of the coach as it rattled by but her pockets were empty.

Twenty-six women slept in the dormitory: ten truckle beds down each side and three at each end. Women with babies were allocated corner beds.

'Here! How old is he?'

Georgie, with great difficulty balanced on his frail legs. Since leaving the Work House, he hadn't made a sound. They had been soaked through walking the two miles to Maryland and Jane had taken off his wet clothes and wrapped him in the rough blanket from her bed.

'He was two last month.'

'He can't stay here,' the woman declared.

The other women in the room sensing the commencement of a fight gathered near the pair.

'My kid's two,' the woman continued, 'and I had to leave him behind in the Work House. So why is your kid here I'd like to know.'

A younger woman nursing an infant, stood beside Jane. 'Can't you see the little 'un's in a sick way. No use leaving him in the Work House. He's no use to them. What could he do in the weaving room 'cept be the shuttle.' She cackled at her own joke and several others joined in.

A young woman stepped forward. 'I'm Bessie. You and your babe may have this corner.' She guided them away and no-one else challenged Jane's right to keep Georgie with her.

Each woman took a turn sweeping out the room in an effort to keep it clean. It was the smell. You couldn't get rid of the smell. It was over the laundry and the years of steam rising to the room above dampened the wood flooring to give off a constant mustiness. Some brought up carbolic from the work place and sprinkled it round. Twelve hours of working in the laundry left them with scant energy to do anything else.

After paying the hostel fee for herself and Georgie, Jane stored every other penny of her wages. She bought food for the child but ate little or nothing herself. She had to find a place to live before George was released at the end of August. It would be two months since she had last seen his face.

After work in the laundry there was the clearing up and cleaning of the machinery before the women trudged upstairs to the hostel. Jane felt she had to have breathing space away from the close proximity of the other women. She asked Bessie to look after Georgie and stepped out in the cool evening air. The breeze dried the perspiration on her cheeks.

She had been wandering, oblivious of where she was. Women were bustling in and out of shops with brimming baskets getting last minute bargains or crowding round stalls along the kerb. The greengrocer was arranging a display of tomatoes on his barrow.

'Hello, Will.'

'Jane. It's good to see you. Heard about your bit of bother,' he glanced down at his feet. 'Are you managing all right now? You know, Ma is upset George hasn't been to see her. And she's so poorly. Not expected to last very long now.'

'I'm so sorry, Will. I didn't know about Ma. And George is still... hasn't... isn't home yet. I'll go and see her.'

A plan was forming in her mind. She knew Georgie would be safe with Bessie so she went straight away. Grace Road hadn't changed. Crumbling walls and peeling paint blurred the houses into one drab mass.

Jane pushed open the door and entered the gloomy space. In her usual corner Ma Stringer lay on her rag bedding. A woman squatted beside her.

'Ma, it's Jane. George's wife.'

Ma Stringer stirred; her head lolled to one side and opened her eyes to peer at the visitor.

'I'll come and take care of you, Ma.'

The other woman rose up from the floor.

'Now listen. I'M laying out the old lady, see. I promised her and she promised me half a crown, so don't you come poking your nose in now.'

'She's my husband's mother. I want to look after her.'

'Bit late for that, dearie. Where you been all these weeks?'

It was true. In all the good times of buying the chairs and the table and her pretty china plates, never once had she thought of her mother-in-law. After they'd moved into their own place, Jane had put Grace Road firmly at the back of her mind. Ma Stringer had been useful in the beginning after their flight from Angel Lane, now Jane intended to be useful to Ma.

'I shan't interfere with your arrangements. But I

shall move back here to do what I can to make her time comfortable.'

The plan was taking shape in her mind.

'Bessie, will you keep an eye on Georgie in the morning? I'm going out early.' A look of horror struck Bessie's face. 'Don't worry, I'll be back in time to start work.'

It was still dark as Jane let herself out of the side door. She ran as fast as she could. The men were slouched against a wall. As the gates opened, they straightened and formed a line. A group came out of the doors and Jane went forward.

'Excuse me, Sirs. Is one of you Mr Weston?'

'I'm Ernie Weston. Do I know you?'

'No, sir, but you know my husband, George Stringer.'

'Yes I do. Haven't seen him in line for a while. Has he been sick?'

'Oh, no Sir. He's as fit as a fiddle. He's just been out of the neighbourhood, Sir. But he's coming back tomorrow and I wondered if you could take him on, Sir.'

Some men at the start of the line overheard the conversation and guffawed loudly.

'Wouldn't have my missis getting a job for me,' one said.

'What she think she's doing interfering in men's business.'

Ernie Weston saw the intense pleading in Jane's eyes. He took her arm and led her to one side.

'Prison?' he asked.

'Oh, no, Sir,' Jane vehemently denied.

He looked at her lovely face. The freckles over her nose and cheeks had faded to a soft gold blurring into the whiteness of her skin. She stood tall and erect;

strands of her fine gossamer hair defied the ribbons and pins and went their own way.

'Your husband's a lucky man. Tell him to be here tomorrow.'

Jane grasped his hand and held it. 'Not tomorrow, Sir. Wednesday. He's not relea... he only comes home tomorrow.'

Ernie Weston felt distinctly uncomfortable standing so close to her. His palms were sweating.

'Wednesday it is,' he mumbled and broke away.

'You work record shows you were inclined to laziness. What do you say to that?' The guardian asked.

'It took me a while to get used to breaking the stones, Sir, that's all.' George replied.

'Hmm. I see from this paper, you have an address in Grace Road to go to and you are to work for a Mr Weston at Stratford Market.'

'Yes, Sir.' George's heart was pounding. Surely they couldn't stop him?'

'I am of the opinion you should remain here for a further two weeks but the other Board members did not share that view. I shall therefore sign your release.'

When Ma Stringer was finally laid out by her crony, the room was unrecognisable as the old scavenger's dwelling. Soon after Jane had moved in, she began bit by bit cleaning and clearing the room of the rubbish collected by Ma over the years and which hadn't fetched the penny she'd thought it might. The old lady, although paralysed, watched Jane's every movement.

'It's for the best, Ma.' She would say.

'Can't you leave some of it,' George had asked seeing his mother's distressed state.

'Some of it smells, which can't be good for little

Georgie. And we've got to make room to have the girls home, George.'

Jane dedicated herself to the clearance. George came home from work at three o'clock and would sit mutely beside his silent mother. Jane knew they were growing apart. Her heart was still full of love but it seemed unable to come out.

She expended her devotion on Ma, who against all odds, clung onto life until almost Christmas. The first snow fell as they walked out of the cemetery gates.

Laura wrinkled her nose. It wasn't the nasty smell she had remembered from her last visit. But it was strong. The carbolic almost make her eyes water.

'Come along, girls,' George pushed them forward.

With her hand still linked with Sarah, Laura purposefully strode along the passage to the room at the rear. As she opened the door, Georgie's gurgling laughter greeted her ears. She rushed toward to hug her young brother and gazed round the room, her eyes growing wide with each sweep of her vision.

'Where's Granny Stringer's things?' she asked. 'Did she take them to Heaven with her?'

'That's right, dear,' her father replied. He stroked her head. 'Took them to Heaven with her,' he repeated and his eye brimmed with tears.

They had a meagre Christmas, but Jane had determined they'd be together as a family once more. Each week, Jane set aside the rent money. The rent in Grace Road was three shillings, one and sixpence less than Marcus Street but still more than what Ma had paid. The upstairs rooms were derelict as well as the room at the front of the house as the landlord wouldn't spend money on repairs. But it suited. 'You're a new tenant, see,' the rent collector said, leering at her. 'But,' he squeezed her shoulder, 'we can always come to an arrangement, you and me.'

Jane had cast down her eyes so he would not see her fury. She didn't want to make an enemy of him. The memory of the Work House was too fresh. He mistook her reaction as acquiescence to his proposal and said he looked forward to seeing her next week. Even if all of them went hungry, the three shillings would be paid without fail. She collected the coins and tied them into her under petticoat so they should not be used for anything else.

It was a hard winter; the snow which had begun to fall on the day of Ma's funeral continued well into the first weeks of 1898. George had to rise even earlier to trudge through the deep snow to Stratford Market. Often, the men were told there was no work because farmers couldn't dig up vegetables buried under the snow. But Ernie Weston had made a promise to Jane, and gave George odd jobs to do around the sheds so he could take home some wages.

Sarah and Laura were entered into the Church of England school. It was the only one nearby and each pupil had to pay a penny a week. The necessary tuppence was also tied into Jane's under petticoat. Laura was happy to be back in a school room. Writing her letters on slate and reading them out in a clear voice. Sarah was less enthusiastic. The school was divided into one class for girls, one for boys and Sarah missed the boys. Even at six years old she knew how to use her feminine charms to get one of the boys to write her slate.

'Now girls,' Mrs Brandon said. 'Soon it will be Easter. Does anyone know what happened on Good Friday?'

'Please, Miss,' one girl ventured, 'was it when Jesus Christ was born?'

'Course, not,' said another, 'it's when he died.'

'But he was only born at Christmas. I always read he died an old man.' The first girl retorted.

'Girls, girls!' Mrs Brandon restored order. 'You are quite right when you say Jesus Christ died on Good Friday. And,' she turned to the other girl, 'you are right when you say he was born at Christmas. I'm sure you all remember our Nativity play at Christmas. When Joseph and Mary came to Bethlehem but there was no room at the Inn so Mary's baby was born in a stable with all the animals standing around.'

Laura was on her feet in excitement. 'Oh, Miss, I seen it when I was at my Great Aunt's farm. I was there when the donkey had her baby. It spread its legs wide, like this, see,' and she demonstrated with her short legs. 'Like it was going to do a wee, then out comes this mess like in a soft glass bag. But it wasn't a big job, it was her baby. Wasn't that wonderful. Just like Jesus.'

In the stillness, Laura sensed she had said something wrong. Her lower lip trembled as she hesitated for a moment.

'It was a baby girl donkey – not a boy like Jesus. Great Aunt said I could give it a name. I called her Rosie as she was so pretty.' Her voice trailed away.

Mrs Brandon at first nodded as Laura stood up. But as the narrative unfolded, her face drained of all colour. She froze on the spot. All the girls had turned to stare at Laura when she spoke, now their gaze turned back to Mrs Brandon. The silence remained for a few more seconds then Mrs Brandon strode forward, gripped Laura's wrist and marched her out of the room to the toilets. Most of the class had followed and watched as Mrs Brandon forced open her mouth. Vigorously, she washed Laura's tongue with soap.

Laura never cried.

Sarah couldn't stop laughing all the way home.

'Don't you dare tell Ma,' Laura turned on her sister. 'You say nothing, do you hear?' Although there was only eleven months between their ages, Sarah was gaining height while Laura still remained short but she presented a fearsome figure of determination.

'Course I won't tell.' Sarah walked ahead. 'But it was so funny to see teacher's face.' And her laugh rippled on the air.

Jane got up each morning at the same time as George. She would cut him two thick slices of bread to take with him for breakfast. Although she no longer lived in the hostel, the manager had kept her on at the Maryland Laundry. It was hard work but the money was regular, which was more than could be said for some of the so-called ladies who had employed Jane as washerwoman. And she got her food. She could still take Georgie with her but the girls were left to get themselves off to school. George met them as he was home from market at half past two. Usually, they were home before Jane unless it was nice weather, then they'd walk to look at the gulls sitting on the reservoir.

It was Friday night. Because of a fault in one of the machines, the manager closed the laundry early.

'We can't afford to lose an hour and half's wages,' one girl cried out.

'If you're all on time in the morning, it'll only be thirty minutes. All right?'

To get off work at five thirty just suited Jane.

'Bessie will you look after Georgie for me. It's my mother's birthday and I want to get her something. She wants all the family to visit her on Sunday after-noon for tea.'

'Coo, fancy that.' Bessie crooked her little finger and mimed drinking from a cup. 'You know I'm always happy to look after the little darling don't you worry Jane.'

'I may look in at home but I'll be back as soon as I can.'

'I'll make sure he's fed and watered.' Bessie winked.

Jane had found just the thing in Old Moses junk store: a pretty china pomander decorated with an exotic bird, its wings wrapped around the bowl. She was very pleased with it and made for home. She opened the front door and walked along the passage-way but no-one was home. She took off her bonnet and turned to hang it on the peg. A gasp escaped her lips.

'Now, my beauty. You've played games with me all these weeks. Hiding from me. Getting your neighbour or your kids to pay me. And then teasing me by stand-ing alongside your neighbour's gate. But not today.'

His hand gripped her wrist.

'I have the rent money, right here, Sir,' Jane tried to make her voice as normal as possible. 'Three shil-lings,' But it was tied into her petticoat! How could she get it with him standing by? She tried to wrench her wrist free.

His face pressed close to hers. His ale breath made her feel sick.

'Let go of me,' she demanded.

He released her arm and stood back a moment.

'I know your sort. Pretending you don't like it but just begging for it.'

She'd quickly turned away to undo the knot holding the coins. She had them in her palm as his arm wound about her waist.

'Told you! Didn't I? Lifting up your skirt, ready and waiting for me. You won't have to wait long, darling.'

He'd pushed her to the floor, sliding her forwards making her skirt and petticoats ride up above her knees, showing open fronted drawers. He quickly straddled her. He lent toward her, splashes from his slavering mouth dripped onto her cheek. She strug-gled and lashed out at him. Her loud scream dislodged pieces of ceiling plaster. Suddenly he was wrenched off. George's wiry arms gripping the collector's collar. They were locked together along the passage, each man trying to aim a punch at the other. Sarah and Laura ducked into the empty front room as the two men tumbled out onto the pavement. Within minutes the police were on the scene.

'Arrest him, Officer!' the collector pointed at George. 'He tried to rob me of today's takings. And he cut my face. I think he's got a knife.'

George remained silent. He stood with his arms at his side; his face bloodied and his right eye closing up.

Such excitement had drawn quite a crowd: all giving an opinion as to who started it. The chatter stopped as Jane appeared in the doorway: her bodice torn and her skirt hanging loose.

The office went close to her. 'Are you all right, missis?'

Jane nodded.

'We've heard about this bloke before. Tried it on with my brother's wife. Do you want me to charge him?'

Jane shook her head. She gave the officer the three shillings.

The officer spoke to the rent collector whose face darkened in fury. He produced his rent book and his leather pouch. He wrote in the book, showed the officer and put the money in the pouch.

The crowd dispersed.

'Sarah, go and get a mug of ale for your father while I bathe his face.'

'I'm all right. Don't fuss.'

'And bring back a bowl of pease pudding. That'll do us for supper.'

'Where's the young 'un?' George asked.

'He's with Bessie at the hostel. He'll be all right with

her till morning. I've got to be in on time as we shut down early tonight.'

The two girls were tucked down for the night. In the candle light, George prepared for bed.

'So, my husband,' Jane cooed at him. 'You still love me?'

'What's that you say?'

'You love me enough to fight for me?'

'I'll fight every man in the Realm. I love you Jane,' his voice was hoarse, 'I love you more than ever.'

Jane turned to look at him. She felt an overwhelming passion rising within her. He unbuttoned his combs and slid out his arms, dropping the garment to the floor. His slim frame was enhanced by taut muscles developed by hard labour. Facing him she removed her skirt and petticoats. Breathlessly, she undid her chemise. She pulled the pins from the bun at the back of her neck and her hair cascaded down over pearl breasts. Tenderly he took her in his arms and held her close. Her moist lips brushed his, as if in a dream. Still entwined, they slowly sank onto their bedding. George rolled over to blow out the candle. All fear of the consequences was swept away by the driving need of passion, and their frenzied excitement filled the darkness.

By Sunday morning, George had a real shiner. Jane had dabbed his black eye with lard and dusted on some flour but it still showed.

They paused at the bottom of the steps. Jane scrutinised each one. Sarah was dressed in a dark rose pink muslin dress which she'd found amongst Ma's bundles. A large bow pinned at the waist hid the tear in the material. The colour complimented Sarah's violet eyes and pale auburn hair twisted into a knot on her head. Laura had a hand-me-down of slate blue sateen. Her hair had darkened and lost its gold lustre as she'd grown older. It was drawn tightly back into plaits. Her flecked brown eyes gazed meditatively out onto a serious world. Georgie wore dark green velvet pants which Jane had bought in a second hand shop for sixpence as they were badly soiled but Bessie had worked wonders with the laundry steamer.

Yes, Jane was satisfied.

'Hello, children,' Matilda greeted them, then her vision made contact with George's eye but she said nothing. 'Come along in all of you. James and his family are here. We're just waiting for Arthur.'

James sat in an overstuffed armchair with fourteen year old James junior standing behind him. Eight year old Tobias stood behind Emily who sat on the couch holding her youngest, Benjamin, who had survived to three years old. Eleven year old Charlotte sat beside her mother. All stared intently at the new arrivals.

Jane smiled sweetly at her brother and Emily. 'How are you? It's good to see you both. Sarah. Laura. Come and greet your cousins.'

Sarah skipped forward showing the lace pantaloons beneath her dress. Laura walked sedately across the room behind her sister.

'How do you do?' she said in her clear voice.

Charlotte simply turned up her nose and poked out her tongue in response.

Matilda clucked a reproof at her and tried to retrieve the situation, by asking all tree girls to bring in dishes from the kitchen just as a knock came at the door.

Arthur strode briskly into the room ahead of his mother. His appearance caused a stir.

Matilda came into the room. 'How smart you are.'

'Latest fashion, you know. Call it a 'Norfolk' jacket.'

But it was the knicker bockers and fancy woollen hose that caught the attention.

'Happy Birthday, Mother.' And he briefly kissed her cheek. He turned and surveyed the room. His stare lingered contemptuously on George's black eye before turning to coolly greet his brother. He nodded curtly to Jane.

Matilda still looked at her son. 'Just for my birthday,' she said, 'Let's all have tea. Then I shall tell you my news.'

'I'm not staying, Mother. I have news, too,' Arthur said.

Matilda was excited. 'You're going to be married, aren't you?'

'Yes, Mother. Early next year.'

'Oh, Arthur. That's wonderful. I've been waiting such a long time to see all my children with families of own.' She dabbed her eyes with a lace kerchief. 'Why didn't you bring her with you today? Who is she? Do I know her?'

'Lor'! No! She is the Honorable Isabel Wells, daughter of Sir Francis Wells. He's a member of the Government. I certainly couldn't bring her here.'

Matilda's pleasure drained away.

'I'm moving up West. Taking a studio in Bond Street. Dare say I won't get down this way again.'

In the silence that greeted his announcement, Laura calmly set cups on saucers and laid out plates on the table.

Matilda looked at her three children. James, weak and docile, dominated by an ambitious wife who hadn't got the brains to see her schemes through. So unlike his father, what a pity she'd given him his name. Arthur, cold and calculating, distancing himself from his family: lacking the compassion of her brother, his namesake. And Jane, radiant, happy. 'And she's no right to be,' thought Matilda. 'She has a husband who can't provide for her; she works like a skivvy; they are poor and often homeless. And Jane is happy!'

She was bewildered by it all. Her news about moving

out of West Street to live above the shop seemed unimportant.

Chapter 3

George had quickly agreed; they must move away from Grace Road. By the end of the month, he'd found a clean front downstairs room in Victora Street off West Ham Lane behind the tramway depot. Far enough away from Grace Road but also too far from Maryland Laundry. Just why they had named it so, Jane could not fathom, as it was miles away from Maryland Point.

'I'll miss you, Jane. And little Georgie,' Bessie sniffled. 'But it's for the best I see that. You need to get away. I wish you all the best. God Bless you.'

Laura was quite happy to leave the Church of England school. After the incident of the donkey, she had been ignored by Mrs Brandon; never having her lessons marked, deliberately overlooked when it came to answering questions. The next school would be better, Laura was sure of it.

There were no opportunities to be an out servant so taking in washing was the only solution. Jane found a good used mangle going cheap and George borrowed a hand cart to bring it home. It had to be placed out in the yard and it was a struggle to get in along the narrow passage and round the corner through the side door. The upstairs tenants, and the back room tenants, were offered free use of the mangle.

'I'd rather you did my washing for me. I'll pay you.'

'So will I.'

Her first customers.

Laura and Sarah made new friends and, as well as taking in washing, Jane also took in two youngsters whose mothers worked at the soap factory so Georgie had playmates too.

While work was increasing for Jane, George had less.

'Mr Weston has been good, Jane. But he can't make work when there isn't any going. It was different in winter, because he knew things would pick up when the weather improved. He's thinking of packing it all in.'

'Won't someone else hire you?'

'They have their regulars for what's going. Most of the trade's been taken by Spitalfields Market. I heard they pay more for casuals than at Stratford.'

'Well then, why don't you try your luck at Spitalfields, George?'

'There'd be tram fare.'

'But if you were earning more, we couldn't be any worse off would we?'

It was turning out to be a scorching summer. In the back yard Jane had lifted a heavy sheet into the rollers and the next minute found herself on the ground. She'd felt giddy when she got up to see George off and had fallen back onto their bedding. The girls would be home from school soon, she'd have to get them to help her finish the day's wash. She felt sick and yet she had eaten nothing.

Suddenly she sat up. She began counting.

'Oh, no! Please, Dear God, no.'

Doctor Binns confirmed her fears. You're a strong, healthy woman. How old are you now? Ah yes, twenty eight. You should have no problem with your pregnancy.'

But she couldn't have this baby. Not now. George would be distraught. He'd blame himself. The new work at Spitalfields had given him a boost; he was lively and jolly. His jauntiness would go if they'd another mouth to feed.

It was strange to be walking in the vicinity of Grace Road again but she had to find the old crone who'd laid out Ma Stringer.

'Yes, I remember you, dearie. Someone else need laying out?'

Jane shivered. The old woman's hand weren't much cleaner than Ma's had been. But there was no-one else.

She plunged straight in. 'I'm pregnant and I want to get rid of it. Can you help me?'

The crone guffawed. 'That's plain talking and no mistake. How long?'

'Three months.' For a fleeting moment Jane remembered the passion of the night. George's lithe body pressed to hers. The intoxicating rhythm of their love. She blushed at the remembrance.

'It'll cost you three quid.'

'As much as that?'

'Well, seeing as you was related Ma Stringer, I'll say fifty shillings and half o' gin.'

Where was she going to find two pounds ten shillings?' But she must find it.

'When will you do it?'

'Come to me Friday night and bring a sheet. And some soap and a wash cloth. And, of course, the necessary coins.'

She'd picked up her boots and those of the girls.

'Don't very often see you at 'Uncle's' Mrs Stringer.'

Jane had taken a devious route to the pawnbrokers in the hope of being discreet and now she was faced by her upstairs neighbour coming out.

'Something special,' she said. 'Please don't mention it.'

'Mum's the word, Mrs Stringer.'

He passed quickly over the boots but held on to the brooch.

'I'll buy it from you if you like.'

'No, I'll redeem it as soon as I can. How much?' It had belonged to her grandmother and her father promised it to her for her twenty-first birthday. He hadn't lived long enough to keep his promise but Matilda had given it to her. It had lain in its velvet lined box through all the hard years as Jane was determined it wasn't going to be sold. Now she felt a coldness as the pawnbroker turned it back and forth in his hand.

'I'd like to borrow three pounds on it,' she said.

He cackled mirthlessly. 'You'd like to borrow three pounds! Oh, that's a rare one. I'll let you have two.'

'Two pounds ten shillings and half a crown on each pair of boots,' she countered.

He gently laid the brooch on its cushion of velvet and reached into his cash drawer. 'With a bit of luck,' he thought 'she'll never have a chance to redeem it.'

Most of the girls were perched on the low brick wall that enclosed the yard. Even the sun baked cobbles made a welcome change to the steamy heat of the laundry.

'Well, nice of you to visit us, Jane.'

'Where's Bessie?'

'In the lavvy. Here she comes.'

Jane took her arm and guided her to the far side of the yard. She listened in silence.

'Don't judge me too harshly, Bessie. We've only just got back on our feet. I've got to do it. You're the only friend I've got. I know I can trust you.'

'I don't want anything to happen to you, Jane, that's all. I'll meet you on the corner of Grace Road at half past seven.'

She had worked solidly all day to clear all the bundles of washing. She looked at George sitting with Laura on the front step. It was for the best, she was sure of it.

'Enjoy yourself with Bessie but don't come home drunk.' He joked.

Candle light threw grotesque shadows in the dingy room. Jane was on the makeshift bed: a layer of straw over wooden boxes, with her sheet placed on top. Knees bent and spread apart. The old crone's strong body odour almost made her retch. Bessie dabbed her face with a moist cloth.

'Breathe slowly and deeply,' she whispered.

A coarse hand roughly pushed down on her stomach. An implement was thrust inside her. The pain was intense and mercifully Jane fainted.

As she came round, her first thought was to get home.

'Jane, you can't get up yet.' Bessie bathed her face. 'it was terrible.' Tears still streamed from her eyes. 'Oh, why did you let her do it? She's a beast,' she hissed.

Blood was spattered in all directions, the palliasse saturated. Bessie turned her head and Jane's eyes followed the direction. The old hag sat in a battered rocking chair guzzling gin.

It was close to midnight when Bessie left Jane at her gate.

'I don't know how you managed to walk home, really I don't. You'll have to rest you know. Can't do any of that washing for other folks. I know,' Bessie said brightening. 'Why don't you come with us? Laundry shuts next week and there's a brake taking us girls to the fields, you and the children could come. You wouldn't have to do any hopping; we'll pick for you. But you'd be in the country air. You could have a good rest.'

'You've been a real good friend, Bessie. I'll never forget what you've done for me. I'll manage all right. Goodnight, love.'

She crept in beside George. His snoring ceased and he stirred.

'Have a good time, did you?' But he was asleep before she answered.

The hot summer was the excuse for her pallid complexion. George urged her not to work so hard. If it hadn't been for Laura, standing on a box turning the handle of the great iron mangle, Jane would have had many dissatisfied customers.

Matilda had packed most of her possessions. It had taken much longer to make the arrangements. She had hoped to be settled above the shop at the start of the summer. Now it was autumn.

'I wish Jane had come. You did tell her, didn't you James?'

'Yes, mother. But she looked very peaky. Lost a lot of weight, she's almost a skeleton.'

'Oh, my poor, dear girl. Why didn't you tell me that before? I must go to her.'

'No, mother. That's just what she doesn't want. She told me not to tell you how she looked.'

'But, why James? Why?'

'She's always so defensive if you say anything. Thinks you're having a go at her George. If you've cleared everything, I'll go now and be round first thing in the morning with the removal men.'

Matilda ignored James' warning.

'Here you are, lady. Last stop before the depot.'

Matilda walked along Victoria Street clutching several packages.

'Do you know where Mrs Stringer lives?' she asked.

'Ah, the washer woman,' the passer-by commented as she eyed the bundles.

'Along there on the left. Third house.'

She struggled to knock. There was no response so she pushed open the door and walked into the gloomy hallway. She put the bundles on the floor and walked through the side door into the yard. The sight of Jane, so thin, so pathetic, almost brought a gasp but she quickly fixed a smile on her face.

'Hello, dear. You didn't mind me coming in, did you? I've just brought over some things you might have a use for. Clearing out the house has been a painful task; so many memories of you children and your father but it's done now and I'll be content in the rooms above the shop. Not so far to go to work.' She laughed lightly but her heart was heavy.

'Can I do anything for you, Jane? Is there anything you need?'

'No, Mother,' she said curtly. 'Nothing.'

'Why won't you let me help you,' Matilda cried. 'Why must you be so stubborn?'

Jane gave a wan smile. 'Well, Mother. I'm independent because I inherited your spirit.'

Matilda sat on a box and wept pitifully.

'When you were all children, I could do things for you. Nurse you when you were sick, bathe grazed knees, find a coin from the tooth fairy, laugh with you. Now you are all older, and I am old, none of you share your lives with me. I'm shut out.'

There had been times when Jane wanted to pour her heart out to her mother. She would have welcomed a shoulder to cry on. Something always stopped her. A movement roused her from thought. Matilda was by the door, her hand reached for the latch.

Swiftly Jane was there before her. She took her hand and placed it around her. Instantly Matilda responded and they clung tenderly to each other.

'There is something you can do for me, Mother.'

Matilda smiled brightly through her tears.

Jane dipped into her bodice and took out a paper.

'Will you redeem this for me? It's for the brooch, the one father left to me. In all the bad times it was a talisman for me. But this time' – she shrugged. 'Anyway, I borrowed two pounds ten shilling on it. Don't let the old skinflint tell you it was more. If you get it back, will you keep it for me? I can always visit you to have a look at it.'

Matilda held the paper then put it in her purse. 'I'll be happy to do that for you daughter. And I shall keep it especially safe for you. I hope it will remain your talisman.'

She turned back at the door. 'And Jane. Although it is only small lodgings above the shop, there is room enough for me to have Sarah. And I'd like the company, if you wouldn't mind. You and George can bring Laura and Georgie on Sundays to see us.'

Sunday visits! Jane smiled to herself. They'd tried it before. It was all right when the rest of the family was there but if they were on their own, Matilda and George chafed against each other. But it was a nice thought. She nodded.

'I'll get Sarah's things ready. After George has had his supper I'll bring Sarah to you.'

As Matilda walked up the street, Jane noticed her drooped shoulders, the slow pace of movement. She said she was old. Jane thought back to the birthday party, how old was she? Sixty-something; yes, sixty-three. 'Yes, I suppose she is old,' Jane thought.

Gradually Jane's physical condition improved. Mentally she was still deeply scarred. The children made her irritable, and she was glad when Georgie began school with Laura. Her bruised flesh was changing from dark purple to yellow. She dare not let George see her naked flesh; worse, she could not bear for him to fondle her in case she was unable to resist him. At times she felt a nauseous repulsion of her beloved George. But it was as much her fault as his. In fits of depression she would sit in the corner of the yard and weep unceasingly.

'Can't you tell me what's making you so unhappy, my darling?'

Jane quickly wiped her hand across her tear stained face and stood up.

'I didn't hear you come in, George. I was just getting some fresh air. Bit stuffy inside.'

As she passed by him, his arm circled her waist and held her.

'There's so little of you to hold these days. Shouldn't you go to see the doctor, Jane. There must be something wrong with you.'

He held her at arms length and his frightened eyes stared into her face.

'Is that it, Jane? Has the doctor told you some bad news? What is it darling? Please, please tell me.'

She smiled at him. 'I've just been a bit down these past weeks, that's all. There's nothing wrong with me. Really there isn't. Everything is going to be all right.'

Much to the children's disappointment there was

no snow at Christmas. Sarah had come home and they'd gone to the canal but it wasn't frozen so no-one could skate. The next day they walked to West Ham Park and listened to the band. A fine end to a good holiday.

As they strolled back home, Jane linked her arm with George.

'It's been grand.'

'It's good to see you've got some roses back in your cheeks, Jane.'

Laura skipped back level with her father.

'Have I got roses, too, Pa?'

He lifted her up in the air. Singing at the top of his voice: 'You've got roses.'

Georgie tugged at his father's leg.

'Me, too! Me, too!'

'George put her down. She's too old for that,' Jane said.

George put her down.

'I'm not, Ma. I'm still only five I won't be six until...' She began counting the days on her fingers. She lost count and began again but gave up as she was lagging behind.

On New Year's Eve Jane took Sarah back to Matilda.

Although Sarah liked being with her sister, it was much nicer at Granny's place. Her own home was all right now mother had got some stools and truckle beds but her mother didn't have nice sheets like Granny.

Matilda was red eyed. 'I've just come from James. Emily lost her youngest. Little Benjamin. His throat seemed blocked and he couldn't breath. It's so hard. Why should such a little mite be taken? What were his sins. Poor Emily. She loses three babies before they are born then she has Benjamin and now he's taken.'

Jane bid her goodbye and walked back home. She

felt a moment's regret at what she had done to get rid of her baby while poor Emily lost hers. She shook her head; Emily's circumstances were quite different.

Bells peeled from the tower of St Stephen's. There had been a fine sprinkling of rain early in the morning but now the sun rose high and promised a fine warm day. Two lines of soldiers in bright red tunics stood along the path from the church door to the roadway.

'Who's getting married, do you know?' a woman asked.

'Dunno,' the crossing sweeper replied. 'I just know I was told to sweep thorough like. And that's what I done.'

'Doesn't she look lovely?' the woman said as the bride and groom stepped out.

The bride's oyster silk gown, drawn into the waist accentuating her slight figure, ballooned out to the ground. Her train of rich Brussels lace fell from her shoulders and was held by three bridesmaids and two pages. The groom's black swallow-tailed coat fitted his athletic figure to perfection and his hand held a black silk top hat.

Arthur smiled at his new wife.

'Happy, darling.'

'Of course. But I'm glad we waited until June. The weather was so awful at Easter.'

The guard of honour in the dress uniform of the Grenadier Guards stood to attention. One officer stepped forward and called: 'Hats off! And three cheers for Mr Grant and the Honourable Mrs Isabel.'

Sir Francis and Lady Wells followed. Sir Francis smiled at his eldest son who'd led the troop.

'Fine turn out, my boy. Your men do you proud. Grand for your sister's wedding.'

The carriages lined up as each group left the church. The ladies all finely dressed in muslin or silk in shades of lemon, pink, blue and the men in formal dress. With the flick of the whip, the coachmen sent the horses forward, their hooves clicking on the smooth cobbles as they headed for Buckingham Gate.

After greeting the guests, Sir Frances walked over to Arthur.

'I trust you will make Isabel happy.'

'I shall make every endeavour, Sir.'

'Lady Wells and I were opposed to this union, you know. But Isabel was determined. I think she likes defying her father. Trouble is we know next to nothing about you.'

'There is nothing much to know, Sir. I am an orphan, brought up by an aunt, a gentle woman I assure you. She died when I was fifteen. I'd read the up and coming thing was photography and by chance met Mr Alfred Harman who took me on as an assistant in the laboratory. The company flourished and was registered as Ilford Film. I set up my own studio. And as you know, that is how I met your delightful daughter.'

'I'm glad you changed your name from Goult. Not very British; Grant is much more acceptable.'

'I was very pleased of your advice in the matter, Sir. And I shall always look to you for guidance, especially in respect of some form of worthwhile employment on my behalf whether in the commercial field or political.'

Sir Francis smiled. 'You and I are going to get along I can see that. And I think I can persuade the committee to find a suitable Parliamentary seat for you in the not too distant future. I'll also introduce you so some fellows who'll be useful to you financially.'

'That is most generous of you, Sir and I am deeply gratified.' Arthur replied.

It was the same routine, winter or summer. First light the fire, boil the water, shave the soap into the tub, pound the linens up and down; leave to soak for a bit then hoist them out, carry the tub into the yard, empty it, put the laundry back into the tub, fill jugs and pour over the clothes, pound up and down up and down, empty the tub, fill the jugs, pound up and down, pass them through the iron rollers of the mangle. The only difference was in winter icicles clung to the mangle; shirts, stiff with frost, hung on the line like regiments to attention. In summer, if it was hot, the creases dried in them too quickly.

Jane could do it in her sleep.

'Are we going to Granny Goult on Sunday, Ma?'

'Don't bother me now, Laura.'

'We went at Christmas,' Georgie's voice piped up.

'That was months ago,' Laura said. 'We didn't go for my sixth birthday in January, we didn't go when Sarah was seven in February. Nor at Easter.'

Jane turned from the tub to the mangel. Holding the sheet high, she didn't see Georgie had crawled into the space and she tripped over him.

Her shriek brought the neighbours clattering down the stairs.

Laura was attempting to unravel the sheet which had wound itself around Jane as she tumbled.

Strong arms thrust Laura aside. 'Here, missis, give us your hand.'

Albert Graves, from top front, helped her on her feet and Laura lifted out her young brother.

Georgie wasn't sure about crying; his face wrinkled into a pout.

The tall man knelt down beside him and holding him tight waggled his arms and legs and tickled him, so he decided against crying.

'He's all right, missis, just had the breath knocked out of him a bit. But nothing broken.'

'Lucky my Albert was home,' his wife said. 'You've taken on a fair bit of weight, you have. Not like you were tail end of last year. You were like a ha'penny herring then,' she laughed.

'I thank you for your help, Albert. Sorry I had to disturb your day off.'

She scooped up the sheet and pushed it back into the tub then turned quickly to Laura and slapped her.

'That sheet's got to be done again, Miss. And it's your fault, with all your chattering about going to Granny's place. So there'll be no visit for you on Sunday.'

Laura silently took the box from behind the mangle and placed it by the tub. She methodically pumped the sheet up and down. Jane pushed her to one side and gathered up the folds of cloth. Laura moved her box back to its place behind the mangle and extended her arms to take the slack as it came from between the rollers.

'I couldn't go to Granny on Sunday, anyway, as Miss Billington is taking the Sunday school class to Wanstead Flats. That's what I wanted to tell you, Ma.'

They worked in silence. Georgie had crept quietly indoors. Laura didn't understand why it was her fault. She did chatter, she knew, for sometimes Mrs Gowrie punished her for chattering in class. Not real punishment like caning; just made her stand face to the wall in the corner without speaking. And then Mrs Gowrie would ask her to read a poem to the class as if she was sorry. It was very odd. Mrs Gowrie also hugged her when she had done something good. Her Pa hugged her and told her stories and laughed with her but Ma never did. But Ma didn't hug Sarah, either, and ever since Georgie began walking, he hadn't got a hug either.

'Don't day dream girl,' Jane's voice broke into her reverie. 'Hold up the sheet or this one will end up on the flags, too. And Mrs Arbuthnot's beady eyed maid will soon notice any dirty smudges.'

'Hello, my darlings,' George called through the open door.

Jane's grim countenance instantly changed to smiling rapture. What ever their problems, seeing his dear face always cheered her. Laura, too, lit up at her father's arrival. As she turned back to gather up the damp cotton, she looked at her mother's face. She does hug Pa, she thought.

'We'll finish for today, Laura,' Jane said, packing away the laundry. 'Laura was just telling me, Pa, she's going to Wanstead Flats on Sunday.'

'Is that so, my pretty one. Now you just come here and tell your Pa all about it.'

She climbed up on his knee and wound her arms round his neck.

'Miss Billington, the Sunday school teacher, says there's going to be races and things at the Flats on Sunday. And we're going. I wish Sarah was here, she could come, too. But Georgie could come. He wouldn't be able to run in any races, not like me, but he'd like the barley water. Miss Billington said there'd be sweet barely water. Georgie can come, can't he Pa?'

'Well, I don't know about that, my little missy.'

'Oh, please, Pa.'

'I suppose I'm going to have to say yes. I can never refuse my girlie.' He rubbed his stubbly chin against her cheek making her squeal. She tried to do the same to him, pulling her jaw in all directions. George laughed and cuddled her close.

Laura looked at her mother as she lifted the stew pan onto the range and began preparing their supper. Grown ups were really strange, Laura concluded.

Miss Billington moved her group forward at a steady

pace to the High Street. Early morning rain had left puddles along the gutters and Laura had to keep a tight grip on Georgie who was intent on jumping into every one he saw.

They met with other groups and were counted aboard the brake. There was still drizzle in the air but no-one minded. It was summer time, school was over and they were on a holiday. They set off with a cheer.

Laura ran in nearly every race. Her little legs thrusting like pistons kept her up with the rest but never out in front. Georgie tried to join in but was firmly discouraged by Miss Billington. At the end of a lovely day, they rode home.

Miss Billinton helped them down. As she held one small boy she frowned.

'Oh, dear, you are rather hot, Percy.' Her palm rested on his forehead. She eased his collar and saw the bright read rash.

She helped Georgie down then Laura.

'Can you get home by yourselves, Laura? I must get Percy home quickly. He seems to have a fever.'

'Oh, yes, Miss. I know the way. Come on Georgie.'

Laura skipped off clutching her brother's hand. She had a lot to tell Pa. Georgie was disappointed there were no puddles left to step in.

For different reasons, both Jane and Laura were glad school was starting next week. She needed Laura's help at times but to have her home all the time was exhausting with her constant chatter and Jane looked forward to a bit of peace and quiet. And it was good four year old Goergie went as well. Laura was anxious to get back to her writing and reading. There were a lot of books in the classroom. Mrs Gowrie had given her a dictionary, it's cover was lost and some words beginning with 'Z' had been obliterated by an ink blob. It was her most treasured possession even though nearly all of the words were unknown to her.

But each night, by the light of her candle, she would try to say five or six words. Not the meanings, yet, just the words.

'Bar. Barb. Funny one, that.'

Georgie whimpered beside her.

Jane and George sat on the back step. The full round moon bathed the yard in light, the iron mangle glowed like pewter. Jane heard the whimper.

'Put out your candle, Laura. You're disturbing Georgie.'

'Ma, he's ever so hot. He's on fire.'

A few hours later the doctor confirmed: 'Yes, it's measles. Keep him warm, he'll want to throw off the blanket but don't let him. At the moment your little girl is clear so keep her away from him but she mustn't go out.'

'But school is starting,' Laura wailed.

'No school for you for a while, I'm afraid.'

'I've got to go to work doctor,' George said.

'Of course, you're all right to go out.'

True, Jane was home but there was washing to do or else there'd be no rent money.

'Laura, just keep an eye on him. You don't have to touch him except to tuck in the blanket. You can read that book as you can't go to school. I'm only in the back.'

Laura was left to nurse her brother. Anxious days were followed by more anxious nights. Georgie had never been a robust child and his thin frame, covered in red blotches, looked so fragile. She hardly slept, except when her father lifted her away and cuddled her until she nodded off.

After ten days, the fever went down.

'How's the little one, now, Jane?' her neighbour

asked as she brought down Albert's thick shirts and under shirt.

'He's out of danger, thank goodness.'

'Picked it up at the outing, didn't he? I think there was about five or six went down with it. And what about Laura? She looks a bit pale, don't she.

'She would sit up with Georgie all the time, but once she's in the fresh air again she'll perk up.'

'Fresh air? Round here? Must be something the matter with your nose, Jane Stringer,' her neighbour laughed.

Jane lifted the pans onto the fire and began sorting the washing.

'I don't think I can go to school, Ma. I don't feel too good.'

'Oh, no!' Jane groaned. As soon as one is up and about another goes down.'

It was far more serious than Georgie's infection. The fever didn't break for over two weeks. For much of the time she was delirious.

'It's affected her eyes,' the doctor said. 'I'm afraid she may be blind.'

'Dear God, No!' George cried. 'No, doctor. There must be something. Can't you do anything?'

'We'll have to wait and see. I'll bind her eyes but she must be kept in a darkened room and kept still for a month or two. Then, we'll know if the eyes have recovered. But expose the eyes to light and it will burn out the cornea and she'll be blind.' George cuddled the limp form. His tears ran freely down his face.

Chapter 4

Great Aunt dipped her hand into the bowl and vigorously punched and pounded the dough.

'I'm making bread. When I've set it to rest, I'll be along.'

A slim beam of sunshine brightened the dull autumn afternoon.

'I'll have to get the lamps going before I come to you,' she shouted over her shoulder.

Four neat rounds were laid near to the range. She rinsed off her hands in a bucket and with her tinder box lit a candle and then an oil lamp.

'Here I am, dearie. Are you comfy, Laura? Not cold are you?'

'No, aunt. What is this room? I don't remember this place.'

'It's a narrow bit at the far end of the pantry. It was where we stored barrels of cider in winter time ready for the summer when we'd need to quench the thirst of the farm hands. Nowadays, I just make enough to keep me going. We were able to get a little bed in here for you.' Great Aunt tucked the thick woollen cover over Laura's feet.

'Will you read now, aunt?'

Great Aunt kissed her forehead. 'Yes, dearie. I'll just

put my chair by the doorway so as I can see but not to get no light near you.'

She cleared her throat. 'Cloth – C L O T H. Cloud – C L O U D. Clover – C L O V E R.'

'Oh, aunt, you must have missed some out. I'm sure there were more words in between.'

'Yes, dearie. But I can only read to you the words I know. And there are lots I can't say.'

'I'm sorry, aunt. I must be an awful bother to you.'

'Course, you're not. No bother at all. I really like you being here. It's nice to have a bit of company.'

'Granny says she likes having Sarah to live with her.'

'That's right. I know Tilda tells me she doesn't know what she'd do if she didn't have Sarah visiting regular. Shall I go on reading or shall we just have a gab?'

Laura didn't answer.

'Have you gone to sleep, little one?'

'I don't think Ma likes Sarah or me.'

'What's that you say?' Your Ma and Pa love you ever such a lot.'

'I know Pa loves me. But Ma's always cross with me.'

Great Aunt pulled her chair into the small cubicle.

'Now, you listen to me. Your Ma really does love you. It's just she can't always show you how much she loves you. She holds her feelings back like. Tilda says so. Even your granny don't get a hug and a kiss from your Ma but that doesn't mean she doesn't love her. Course she does. And she loves you and Sarah and Georgie.'

'She loves Pa best of all.'

'Ah well. A wife and husband is different. You'll know when you grow up and have a sweetheart. Now I must get the bread baked. You stay quiet and then I'll get supper.'

During the day time, Great Aunt was busy feeding the stock or working in the fields and Laura was left alone. She would recite words or snatches of poems she remembered or songs:

> *The holiday's all over; Money is all spent*
> *Wish I'd never gone a-hopping down in Kent.*

Great Aunt laughed as she came in from the yard. 'Now wherever did you learn that?'

'Bessie taught it to me. She went hopping. She asked Ma to go. Said we could, too. But Ma was very poorly last year.'

'Now I know you can't see, but you can hear. What do you think this is?'

Laura cocked her head on one side. There was a tapping sound on the kitchen flag stones. Then a snort.

'It's Rosie,' Laura cried. 'Oh, Please, may she come close?'

The donkey shuffled forward, prodded by Great Aunt. Laura rubbed Rosie's rough coat and softly stroked her moist nose. Great Aunt squeezed round the other side of the bed and put something in Laura's hand.

'Oo, it's a carrot, isn't it?' she whispered. 'Here, Rosie.'

The donkey crunched loudly. 'Hasn't she grown. She's taller than the bed.'

'Naturally, she's grown. She's not going to stay a midget for all of an eighteen months is she? Do you remember seeing her born, do you?'

'Yes, I do,' Laura replied excitedly. 'It was wonderful and...' Her words dried up as she remembered Mrs Brandon. 'When we were at our old school, the teacher was talking about Jesus being born and I described seeing Rosie born. She took me to the sink and washed out my mouth with soap then I had to stand in the corner.'

'What a horrible creature to do such a thing,' Great Aunt exploded.

'I still don't understand why. I only said exactly what I'd seen. Someone said it was because nice girls don't talk about such things. But she didn't say what things. Why shouldn't I have said I saw Rosie coming out of her mother's backside in a sort of glass bag?'

Great Aunt was glad Laura could not see at that moment or else she would have seen a huge grin on her face. She could just imagine someone from the town being aghast at what went on with nature in the country.

She came close and took Laura's hand and stroked it.

'There are some folk who don't like the truth, dearie, that's all. Maybe she herself had never seen the miracle of creation and she couldn't understand what you were describing. So for people like that it's best not to tell them too much. Keep it to yourself.' She kissed the girl's cheek.

Rosie stood still at the other side and then there was a rumbling noise and an odious gas filled the small cubicle.

'Cor! What a pong!' Great Aunt exclaimed. 'Come on, Rosie, you get out quick, we don't want a mess on the floor. Off with you.'

Rosie was pushed and pulled out into the main room and hurried out to the yard. Laura was left holding her nose which was difficult as she was laughing so much.

She was still laughing when Great Aunt returned.

'I'll have to put some carbolic down to clear the air. I suppose she got a bit frightened in the small space. But we got to her in time. What is it dear?'

Laura strained her ears. 'Aunt! The dogs are barking. Someone's coming.

'Who is it?'

'Well until I go and have a look I shan't know, shall I?'

Laura listened as Great Aunt's boots trod across the kitchen floor.

'Now it won't be your Pa, as it ain't a Sunday,' she called back. 'Today's Tuesday.'

The kitchen door was opened and the sound of the dogs was louder until they were hushed by the visitor.

'It looks like your Granny, child.'

Matilda was glad to step into the comfort of the warm kitchen.

She could hear their voices but Laura couldn't hear the words.

'This weather finds its way into all my old bones.' Matilda complained. 'How is she today?'

'She's fine. She's always fine. Doesn't stop chattering from morn till night. Wants me to read words to her from that book so she can remember them. So I sit at the pantry door and yell my head off so she can hear in the still. I tell you, Tilda, I'll be worn out before Christmas.'

Matilda looked at her sister. 'Has it really been bad for you? I am sorry. I didn't mean you to be burened.'

Great Aunt laughed. 'Do I look as though I'm burdened? Course not. She's a treasure and no mistake. I do sometimes send Daniel in to sit with her. And she talks away to him though he can't hear her.'

'Well it won't be for much longer. Jane sys the doctor will see her week after next so I expect George will be down to fetch her next Sunday.'

'How does the doctor know her eyes are all right?'

'He doesn't. Not until he takes the bandages off. But there's no point waiting any longer.' Her gaze was far away. 'Nearly three months. What a trial it must have been for the child. Shut away in darkness. Kept in her bed. She was always running everywhere.' A sob escaped her lips. 'If she's blind she won't be able to run, will she?'

Great Aunt took her sister in her arms and rocked her gently.

'Don't fret. I'm certain she'll see. Certain I am. My namesake isn't going to be beaten at the first obstacle in life.'

'Granny!' Laura called. 'Why are you staying out there? Haven't you come to see me?

Matilda dried her eyes. 'You're right, sister.' She smiled.

'I'm coming child.'

She eased herself onto the edge of the bed and took Laura's hand.

'How's Sarah, Granny? Have you seen Ma and Pa. And little Georgie. Is he all right? I'm glad his eyes are good. They are, aren't they?'

'My goodness! You don't give a body a chance to speak. Yes, Sarah is well. She's doing her lessons well but finds counting hard.'

'When shall I go home, Granny?'

'That's what I came to tell you. Your Ma and Pa will come on Sunday.'

Laura clapped her hands and gave a joyous squeal.

'And the doctor will come to see you on Tuesday night. That is a week from today.'

Fog rolled in from the river, blended with chimney emissions and spread its sulphuric haze over the streets and houses.

'It's not the sort of day we should have brought her back.'

George sat hunched on the plank, peering into the opaqueness. He gripped the reins but the tapes were slack over the horse back. The animal's feet were firm on the cobbles as it pulled the wagon.

'Is she all right, Jane? Is she warm enough?'

'Yes, Pa, I'm warm. But I expect you are cold sat high up there. Where are we now? When will we be home?'

'Don't talk so much, Laura,' Jane said.

The wagon jolted across a pot hole, Jane lost her balance and tumbled onto the base of the cart.

'And your father has got to keep his mind on getting us home in one piece.

The fog lifted on the next day but gathered in again on Tuesday. Jane's washing hung limply on the line and refused to dry.

They had moved Laura's truckle bed into the corner of the kitchen to give her warmth. Georgie came in from the yard and ran straight for her. He tried to scramble up on top of her. Laura laughed as she heard him fall off with a thump.

George sat quietly by the range reading an old newspaper.

'Shush, Georgie,' Laura said. 'Pa said the doctor will be here at six o'clock so I must listen for the church clock.'

It had chimed six, then seven, then eight.

In the warmth of the range, Georgie had fallen asleep at the foot of her bed. Laura was fidgeting nervously with the bed covers. Her tears were absorbed by the bandages. Jane and George stood silently by her bed.

'Why hasn't he come, Pa?'

His voice was as emotional as his daughter's. 'Well, girlie, it is terrible bad weather out there. He might not be able to find his way. I'll go up to West Ham Lane, shall I? Just in case I can catch sound of his trap.'

Laura lay waiting. Listening. Then she heard footsteps along the passageway. There was someone with her father.

'... absolute chaos by the Town Hall in the Broadway. Horses tangled up with trams. And damned cold with it. Beg pardon, Ma'am.'

The doctor took off his great coat and warmed his hand on the grate then he wiggled Laura's toes.

'Bring the candle close, Mrs Stringer,' the doctor said. 'And you, father, prop up her head a bit.'

Gradually he unwound the bandages. With dampened lint he bathed her eyelids and then smoothed on boric acid ointment. He held his left hand over her eyes. His other hand reached into the depths of his black medical bag.

'Now, miss, open your eyes and tell me what you see.'

Her young brother, woken by the arrival of the visitor, crept close to the bed. Laura sucked in her breath. She screwed up her eyes tight puckering her face. Jane, too, drew in a sharp breath and George started to speak but the doctor silenced him. Slowly the creases smoothed from her face and she lifted her lids just a slit; then she opened them wide and a smile spread across her face.

'It's a fairy doll,' she cried. 'Such a pretty fairy doll with a silver cape.'

He handed her the small doll. 'Well, your focus is good, young lady.'

'She's so light, she really is a fairy.'

Georgie reached out to grasp the doll.

'It's celluloid,' the doctor said. 'So be gentle with her, else she'll crack. Now, Laura, the bandages stay off while you are indoors for the next three or four days. And, Mrs Stringer, you'll have to rub her legs with camphorated oil as she has been immobile for some time. After a few days, she can go out for an hour or so but be careful of bright lights and sunlight – not that there's much chance of that until next spring. Just take the precautions for a few weeks and then let her have her head. It will be necessary, Laura, to bathe your eyes in clean water as soon as you wake. They will be crusty along the rims so wash downwards toward you cheek. Do you understand?'

'Oh, yes, Sir. I'll take good care of my eyes, Sir, for there are lots of books I want to read when I'm older. May I keep the doll, Sir?'

'Yes, it's an early Christmas gift for you.'

George put the doll on a box where Laura could see it. She had wanted to keep it in bed until she remembered it might crack.

It was funny when she tried to get out of bed. Her legs were all wobbly and she couldn't stand. Jane massaged them back to strength and soon Laura was able to get her own bowl of water and bathe her eyes. First of all she'd pour some into a tin basin and rub her fingers clean. Then with the forefingers she would dab her eyelids and smooth her fingers down her cheek. Sometimes the icy water made her shiver but she never stopped until she'd done it ten times.

The doctor had been right, there was no bright sun. Each dull, dreary day, Laura would walk to the corner of the road and back marching up and down to strengthen muscles weakened by inactivity.

Soon she could walk with Georgie as far as school, just to see classmates and teachers. She wasn't to start school until the New Year when her eyes would be strong enough to study text books. The bubble of her excitement burst when she was told Mrs Gowrie had left at the end of the summer term to teach at a new school. Laura couldn't hide her disappointment when taken to her class and introduced to the new form mistress.

Miss Pinge had large staring eyes and a hooked

nose which was reddened from sneezing. She waved Laura to a desk and continued reading to the pupils in a high pitched monotone.

Laura couldn't bear it. 'I cannot stay today, Miss.'

Miss Pinge didn't pause in her nasal reading, simply waved her out of the door.

'We're all going to West Ham Park to see the bonfires,' George said. 'Now wrap up well because it'll be cold standing in the open. You see it's a special New Year. It's the start of a new century, the Twentieth Century.'

There were three huge mounds of kindling wood positioned in the park. In the blackness around the outer edges people gathered. The torch bearers stood ready, sparks were whisked by the breeze and for a fleeting moment soared toward the skies but were extinguished before they could join the stars.

'Listen!' someone shouted.

The chimes of the church clock rang out. A few began counting the hours then the whole crowd was chanting:

'EIGHT, NINE, TEN, ELEVEN, TWELVE.'

The torches were applied and soon the bonfires were blazing; flames of brilliant red and orange leapt from side to side, illuminating the faces round about. Children joined hands and danced round the fires to link up with others to make a complete ring. Laura and Sarah with Georgie between them were swept along in the current of celebration.

'Another year, my darling,' George said as he stood close to Jane.

'Happy New Year, my husband. Perhaps this year, this new Twentieth Century will bring many good tiding for us and for everyone.'

She rested her head on his shoulder and George

turned her face toward him and pressed his lips on hers.

For a moment, Jane closed her eyes then pulled away. 'George! We're in a public place.'

'But you're my wife and I love you and I want the world to know.'

He cleared his throat, took a deep breath and was about to holler but Jane put her hand over his mouth, which he promptly kissed.

Jane laughed. 'You're a caution and no mistake. Let's find the children. It's time they were in bed.'

It had been a good evening. They'd met James and Emily, who was expecting again, the third time since Benjamin's death; the two previous times she had lost the unborn child.

'But this time I know it will be all right,' she'd said. 'I'm taking care of myself properly, as James wants me to, put my feet up every afternoon. You know we have an out maid, don't you? She also does the cooking, so there is really nothing for me to do.'

Emily had proceeded to list all their new purchases and boast about the cleverness of their children. Jane was only half listen and turned gratefully when hailed by someone calling her name.

'Bessie!'

They'd hugged each other.

Bessie held her at arm's length. 'My it's been an age since I've seen you. How are you getting on?'

A delighted Jane walked off with Bessie to find the children, leaving George to the mercy of his sister-in-law.'

'Come and give, our father a kiss, girlie, and your Pa may give you something. Now, what's today? Oh, yes, Nineteenth of January, I think it is.'

'Where are they, Pa? Where are the violets?'

'How d'you know it's violets. And not until I've had my kiss.'

George stooped down and Laura clung to his neck and smacked kisses all over his face. He reached into his back pocket and brought out a stiff brown paper tube. Protruding from the open end were bright purple heads of violets.

'I knew you'd bring me violets. You always do on my birthday.'

He rested his hand on her shoulder. 'It's a very lucky thing to be aged seven in the round years, like nineteen hundred.'

'It's funny when we write the date. I keep putting one, eight nine, then have to rub it out and put one, nine, nought, nought. Pa, why is seven lucky?'

'I dunno. But everyone says so, so it must be so.' He paused and sniffed. 'My! That's a good smell coming from the pot, Jane.'

Jane stood at the range slowly stirring the liquid. She was startled when George came beside her.

'I said it was a good smell but you must have been across the ocean.'

'I was thinking. But we'll have supper first and then I can put something to you.'

'Put what to me?'

'We'll have super first.'

'With a hangman's noose above my head, how can I do justice to supper Out with it Jane.'

'I want to move.'

George roared with laughter. It was several minutes before he could stop. He wiped his eyes. 'Jane! It's my family were tinkers, not yours. My grandfather and his before him travelled up and down Ireland and then my Da came to England and still we never settled. But you, you had never moved in all your life until we wed.' He shook his head. 'Why, Jane, why do you want to move again?'

'Bessie was telling me about some houses in Stratford New Town, near the Crownfield Road. They have a sink with water inside from a tap. It would be so much easier in winter. They are a bit bigger. Two rooms from the front and one back with a scullery. Of course, the rent's more.'

'How much more?'

'Six shillings a week.'

'What!'

'But, George, we'll manage.'

'What do you want all those rooms for? The girls are still small enough for us to all share one room.'

'But that's what we will do, love. Laura and Georgie in with us as usual. Sarah can stay on with mother. We'll take in a lodger for the other room. He can take his meals with us in the back, and I can do his washing so we'll charge him rent for all found, see. We can furnish the room with a bed and may be a chair and table and give him a bit of kindling in the grate.'

'Whoa! Hold your horses! Give him a bit of kindling indeed. All of this is going to take more money than you and I bring in, love. We can't do it.'

'I've got enough put by to pay the first four weeks rent. I reckon we can charge three shillings for room and board, if we make it nice like. And a shilling if he wants his washing done.'

Goerge's face was taut with subdued rage. Sometimes his beloved Jane really tested him. Jane turned back to the range.

'Come and have supper, dearest. It's a nice pig's trotter.'

When Jane made up her mind about something there was no turning her. It fretted George to know how they were going to manage. Burgess Road, off Crownfield Road. One thing, it was nearer to the station for him to get to Spitalfields. So much more rent to pay. But he knew he was beaten.

Through the scullery window she gazed onto the small back yard covered with snow. First week of March and it had snowed! Jane was actually humming as she stood soaking the washing in the sink. The big iron mangle had fitted nicely into the recess at the back. There was no need to hang out the washing, she had secured a rope across the room to take the damp laundry.

She was very pleased at her efforts in preparation for a lodger. A bed, table and chair furnished the small second room. On the shelf above the grate were china candle holders. By the grate was a skuttle full of wood chippings and at the foot of the bed was a chamber pot cupboard. Everything was ready.

'Ma! Shall I go?'

'No, Laura. I'm coming.'

Jane smoothed down her clean apron and anchored a wayward wisp of hair.

A large, broad shouldered man stood on the step.

'Mrs Stringer? My name is Reg Packard. The railway union said you would be expecting me. Is that correct?'

'Yes, do come in.' She led the way down the hall to the second door. 'This is the room, I've got it ready for you.'

'Oh, very nice, Mrs Stringer. Real homey. I can say it will suit me just fine.'

'Did the union man tell you it was three shillings a week, board and lodging?

'And extra if you want washing done.'

'Yes, missis. And I would be obliged for the washing. Mind you some of it is a bit grubby. Being a wheel greaser means lying flat underneath the couplings.'

Jane was frowning.

'Beg pardon, missis. Of course, women don't understand a man's work.'

'I'll be putting supper on the table just after six, Mr Packard. The door straight ahead of you.'

It was several weeks before Laura and Georgie started at the new school. Not that Laura minded; her enthusiasm for learning had waned a little but she still read her dictionary at home. Before the move, she'd gone back to her old class as soon as it started in January but the pupils were inattentive and began chattering. Miss Pinge seemed oblivious to the disruption. She continued intoning the English lesson in a nasal whine punctuated by frequent sneezes. Her browned fingers and nostrils explaining the cause.

'She takes snuff,' the other girls told her when Laura had blessed the teacher for the tenth time.

English literature no longer held her spellbound and she became as the others, inattentive and lazy. Laura was glad when her mother declared they were to move. She made the excuse at school she had to help her mother with the arrangements.

Before the actual move Jane planned what she wanted to buy and was glad to have Laura along when she went in search of pieces to furnish the second room for the lodger.

They browsed through the second hand junk shops in West Ham Lane.

'I like those four chairs, Laura.'

Being small, Laura could crawl among the pieces and examine undersides of tables and chairs.

'I'll take a shilling each those chairs, missis.'

Jane looked across to where Laura stood. She shook her head but put up three fingers.

'I'll give you three shillings for the lot,' Jane stated.

'Have a heart lady. I got to live as well.'

Laura was examining a cupboard. It reminded her of the one her mother had had for the pretty china plates. There was a deep scratch mark across the top but it wouldn't notice if a lace cloth was spread over. She came to her mother's side and whispered.

'I'll give you four shillings if you throw in that piece.'

'That's good mahogany, missis. That's worth a packet.'

'It's damaged all it's fit for is the fire,' Laura piped up. 'All I want it for is to put my toys in. Come on, Ma. I saw something better at Izzie's place.'

'Why do you want the cabinet, Laura?' Jane whispered.

'I thought you might like it. Perhaps you will get some pretty plates again.'

Jane had forgotten about the plates; so much had filled her mind since then. But she was touched Laura should remember. She made to move away and then passed her hand along the back of a chair. He was no match for the combined forces of mother and daughter. The four chairs and the cabinet were sold for four shillings; he delivered them that night.

Even after they'd moved into the half house in Burgess Road, Jane delayed entering Laura and Georgie into school. Although Laura was short, she was sturdy and helped arrange the new possessions. And in her best writing, Laura had printed a letter about the room for rent and how much it would cost. George had said the landlord of the *Thatched House* pub might know someone who wanted lodgings but Laura said they should ask at the Town Hall. It was a clerk there who suggested the rail union.

When there was no more excuse to keep the children at home, Jane took them to Ellingham Road School. Laura liked living in Burgess Road; there were other children to play with and walk along together to school.

Reg Packard settled into the family routine as well as he could but working shifts often meant he had his meal alone.

'I'll take it in my room, Mrs Stringer. I don't want to take up time in your kitchen.'

'It's better to see here with the gaslight.' Jane was proud to show they had the new gas lighting. 'You've only got candles in your room. And I'll make sure you get a bit of peace and quiet to eat without Laura battering you with questions.' She turned a stern face to her daughter. 'Mind what I say, miss.'

Laura liked talking to Reg. He told her exciting tales about far distant places.   'My brother worked on the railways with me. But he wanted to see the world and managed to get a passage to North America. He's working on building a railway right across the country. Says the track will stretch for thousands of miles. They have to blast through whole mountains. He says it's dangerous with all the wild animals.'

'Are there really wild animals?'

'Yes, and wild Indians. But they don't let it worry them.'

Laura tried to imaging riding in a train surrounded by wild animals but she couldn't see them in her mind. What were wild animals? She remembered the goats that butted through the papered windows in Angel Lane. They were wild. She was about to ask Reg if the wild animals were goats when she was packed off to bed. She would ask at school tomorrow.

With Sarah not living at home, Laura had had no close companion. Now she had Vily Walters. For the first time in her life, Laura had a friend. The Walters lived at Number Nineteen Burgess Road, right opposite. Laura could stand at the front room window and wave across to Vily and it was nice to walk with a group to school. Of course, Georgie had to tag along as well and he grumbled when they spoke so low he couldn't hear what made them laugh.

At the school gates they parted, boys and girls entered through separate gates. The assembly areas were segregated, too but the brick wall was low enough for Laura to hand Georgie his bread and jam at midday. The younger girls block was at the far end. They were walking along the corridor when Laura suddenly turned back.

'What are you doing, Laura?' Vily was horrified to see her friend put her ear to the door. 'These are the junior classrooms. Come on Laura. Oh, No!' She fled as she saw Laura turn the handle and walk in.

'...now we've reached the part in the play where Antony addresses the citizens.'

The teacher was aware the attention of the class had moved from her to an intruder. Her gaze turned toward the door.

'Mrs Gowrie! How wonderful to see you,' Laura exclaimed.

The pupils began tittering as they looked at this strange creature in a faded green woollen dress with a large, badly stitched patch on the side. A cloth bonnet, far too large, tipped off the back of her head. The startled teacher frowned and was about to rebuke such behaviour then as she recognised the child, she got down from her high stool and went to her smiling.

'It is good to see you, Miss Stringer.' Mrs Gowrie inclined her head and Laura bobbed a curtsey. 'Are you a pupil at this school now?' Laura nodded. Mrs Growie purposefully stared back at her class and they were silent. 'Then I shall have the pleasure of teaching you when you come up into the junior class.'

She opened the door and Laura walked out into the corridor.

Laura began to skip along, looping from side to side until a voice boomed from somewhere:

'Behave, girl!'

Jane pinched Laura's ear and began pulling her away.

'Now go to bed. I'll not tell you again about bothering Mr Packard.'

'But I want to tell him...'

'NO! Bed!'

Laura brought her candle close to her bedside and drew her dictionary from her box. Through tears, she began to recite the words. Georgie crept beside her.

'What's up, Laura?'

'I wasn't really bothering him. I only wanted to tell him about the animals. We learned about Africa today and there are wild animals there.'

'Tell Pa. He'd like to know about them.'

Laura used to tell Pa what she'd learnt at school that day but Pa went to the *Thatched House* when it opened and she was nearly always asleep when he came home. Sometimes she would hear him stumbling through the front door and Ma would hiss him to be quiet. And there'd be a strong smell of ale in the room when he came to bed.

Reg changed shifts at the weekend. There was plenty of time before Jane would put supper on the table.

'Will you tell me what you've done at school this week?' he asked, giving a big wink at Luara.

She eagerly told him about the wild animals and asked him if they were the ones his brother had seen.

'Lor' bless you, no. Elephants and lions don't live in

America and that's where he is. As you learnt, those animals are in Africa. Do you know, there's a new museum opened in London that has all manner of wild animals.'

Laura's eyes widened. 'Wont they eat the people?'

Reg laughed. 'No, they've stuffed'em. But they look very life like. I went there last year. Tell you what, would you like to see them?'

'Oh, yes, very much.'

'We'll ask your Ma and Pa if you can go. I shan't be working next Saturday. May be we can go then. And what about asking your friend to come.'

The days didn't go fast enough for Laura but at last Saturday came and she and Vily went up West with Reg. It was such a big building. Inside, the roof was almost as high as the sky and there was such a big staircase Laura wondered how long it would take them to climb up.

'This place is called the Natural History Museum and they've brought animals here from all parts of the Queen's Empire,' Reg told the girls.

Some were in a fierce, striking pose it seemed they would lunge forward at any moment. It could be terrifying but Laura and Vily were too absorbed in the size, colour and features of the animals to be scared. Laura stood on tiptoe by the hippopotamus and peered into his gaping jaws.

'That creature has such a tender skin he has to stay in the water when the sun is high.'

'Have you seen it in the water, Reg?'

'No but I hope to go to Africa one day.'

They arrived home tired by very happy. At Number Nineteen, Vily thanked Reg with a hug and skipped off indoors waving to Laura.

'I've a pot of broth on if you're hungry, Mr Packard,' Jane said. She never used his first name. She handed a mug of warm milk to Laura who was almost asleep on her feet. 'I keep it warm in case Mr Stringer wants anything when he comes in.'

Reg looked at Jane. Her beauty wasn't dimmed by the hardship she endured. Her eyes seemed to hold a shimmering silver pool where he could drown and enjoy sinking beneath the surface. She charmed him. At last, he lowered his eyes and broke the spell that bound them.

'I'll turn in, if you don't mind.' His voice was a hoarse whisper.

Chapter 5

It was s scene of domestic bliss. Jane, sitting in her newly acquired rocking chair, with her mending basket on her lap and awkwardly darning a hole in a sock. Laura, with head resting on elbows on the table, intently listening. Reg, his strong arms stretched forward to the table and holding a book and nestled against his chest and dozing, young Georgie.

'...and the young lad set off for London.' He put a twist of paper in as a marker and closed the book.

It was several minutes before Laura realised he'd stopped reading.

'But I want to hear more.'

'We'll have more tomorrow night, Laura,' Reg promised.

'When I was at school, I wasn't interested in reading at all,' Jane said. 'My mother believed girls should have as good an education as boys and sent me to Clark's College in the city. But literature and history didn't hold my attention. I liked doing sums and can add up in my head. But, hearing you read, I'm sorry now that I didn't pay attention to my lessons.'

'You have many other talents, Mrs Stringer, that reading is of little importance.'

Jane smiled and blushed at the compliment. 'Now

then, Laura, time for bed. Oh, and look at Georgie. He must be a dead weight on your legs, Mr Packard.'

'It's a joy to have him on my knee. And Laura is such a good listener; I like to use my voice. You are lucky to have two such lovely children.'

'I have a sister, Sarah,' Laura said. 'And she is ever so pretty.'

'I should like to meet her.'

'I've been thinking about having her home.'

'Oh, Ma! It'd be ever so lovely.' Laura ran to her mother's side and looked at her. 'Sarah will come home won't she Ma?'

Jane kept her promise and Sarah was reunited with Laura. Matilda had seemed off-hand when she called. 'Perhaps it's for the best,' she'd said curtly. It was true Jane hadn't visited her mother for several months. She'd tried to talk about family but Matilda seemed anxious for her departure. As she was leaving, Matilda asked her to wait a moment. She returned and held out her hand. Jane took the brooch. Matilda had smiled and placed her hand over Jane's. 'Keep your talisman safe, my daughter,' she'd said.

Jane had got a nice bit of offal from the butcher and was simmering the hearts and kidneys with potatoes and swedes. She replaced the lid and walked along the passageway.

She tapped at the door. 'It'll be ready in abut ten minutes.'

'Thanks. I'll be along.'

With her back to the room, she didn't hear Reg come into the kitchen.

He stood looking at her until she sensed his presence.

'Would it be all right if I had a wash in the scullery? I like to get some of the grime off before sitting at table.'

The splashing of water drew her attention. Her gaze

rested on his body, naked to the waist, and blazing bronze in the brilliant sunshine that flooded through the window. In the middle of his broad back a narrow band of black hairs ran from his shoulder and disappeared into his trousers. His muscles rippled as he raised his arms and lathered chest and armpits. Jane felt an ache in her stomach and palpitations so strong she could hardly breathe. He was moving, turning; she must look away but she hadn't the strength to move. The children's voices as they came in the front door broke the spell.

'But it's mine,' Laura said.

'I was only borrowing it,' Sarah replied.

Jane recovered her senses. 'Now then, you two. What are you squabbling about?'

'It's my ribbon, Ma. I found it and now Sarah wants it.'

'I only wanted it for a while. I wanted to tie my hair up on top.'

'And prance in front of the boys,' Georgie said but quickly dodged out of the way as he saw Sarah's hand coming in his direction.

'If you children are home, what must the time be? And where is father?'

George was always in by three o'clock. The market closed at one o'clock and there'd be the swilling down to do before he got the tram home. He'd have his supper and then lie down for a bit before going out for a drink at the *Thatched House* when it opened.

Jane had removed the pan from the heat and sat waiting. Reg sat at the table with the children and listened to their tales of goings on at the school but his eyes kept seeking Jane's face. There was such proud resignation.

'Shall I go and look for him? I can go to the tram stop.'

'No,' Jane said. 'Don't want supper going to waste, we'll have ours.'

They ate in silence and the children crept away to bed. Reg couldn't bear her anguish.

'I think I'll look for him. He might have had an...'

He stopped as a slurred voice cried: 'Mafeking's been relieved.' His shuffling gait forced him from one side to the other and he banged against wall and doors along the passageway. He stood framed in the kitchen doorway.

'All London celebrating...streets crowded with folks mad with excitement.

'Mafeking relieved. Baden-Powel safe. Had to celebrate such a victory.'

Jane stared at her husband, ashamed of his drunken state. Reg touched her arm.

'Best let him sleep it off,' he said as he helped George to bed.

Jane was standing by the range, the gas mantle shafting a fan of light about her shoulders. Reg hesitated in the doorway. Her gaze was into the far distant future, or was it into the past? He drank in her beauty: her slender neck, her firm rounded figure. His feelings overcame him. He was by her side, his arm turned her to him and he held her in a warm embrace. Jane was aware of a coldness inside her. Had she lost George? How had they drifted so far apart? When had it happened? They'd endured much yet it was hardship which had bound them closely together in the beginning.

She felt utterly alone and lonely. Arms about her body drew her back from the edge of desolation. She didn't want to think any more. She rested her aching head against his warm, pulsing chest and took comfort from his strong arms pressing her to him.

'Jane, I love you. I've loved you almost from the first

day I came here. I want to take care of you, I want to sooth your sorry and worn heart. Let me, Jane.'

He held her head in his hands, gazing into her eyes. His lips kissed her forehead, her cheeks, her soft white neck. His lips sought Jane's. Her arms reached up round his neck and she responded to his embrace. They were locked together, lost in their own emotional world.

Jane pulled away. 'No! It's wrong. Please, please go.'

'But, Jane, I want to make you happy and I know I can. I can make a fine life for you and the children.'

'No! Go! Please.'

The fierceness of her voice, the wildness in her eyes, was like a knife cutting through him. Reg started toward her but she flung out her arms in a anguished plea. He slowly turned and walked away.

Jane had tossed and turned most of the night. It was almost time to get up yet she found herself drifting into sleep. Suddenly her senses were alert. There was a movement in the room. Their double bed was fitted into the recess beside the chimney and the wall adjoining the next room. George slept on the side into the room and Jane on the side near the wall; there was sufficient space for a box where she placed garments removed at bedtime. Someone was almost beside her. For one terrible moment she feared it was Reg. Under the covers her hand slid toward George and she touched vacant space.

In the thin early light of dawn, she saw the figure lift her petticoat from the box. George's slim wrists twisted and turned as his fingers felt for the knots.

Jane swung her feet out of bed and was beside him. Her hand grabbed his wrist and held it tight. George released the petticoat and slumped down onto the bed.

'I'm sorry, Jane. I need the money.'

'Did you drink on tick yesterday?'

'It was the ganger said he'd make a loan of it to me. But it was more than what my wages would be by Saturday. If I don't pay him, he'll see I don't get taken on. Ever again.' George was snivelling; he rocked himself backwards and forwards.

This pathetic creature was her husband. Jane's anger subsided.

'Oh, George, why do you do it? Why do you turn to drink?'

'I dunno, Jane. It helps me to forget.'

'Forget what? Your family? Your home? You want to forget US?'

'No, Jane! Not you and the young ones. Just to forget I can't give you what you really deserve.'

Jane began untying the knots.

'Is this what we deserve?' she asked quietly.

The coins jingled into her hand. 'How much do you need?'

'Two and ninepence ha'penny.'

She sucked in her breath. 'There'll be no wages coming into the house on Saturday, as well as owing two and ninepence ha'penny, is that right?'

His head nodded on his drooped shoulders.

'How many did you have?'

'We was buying for each other to celebrate.' He lifted his head in defiance. 'It was a great victory for England.'

'The Boer war is thousands of miles away. Victory for England my foot! The war is about gold and diamonds: the British want the mines and the Boers want them. The working class are fighting a war right here in England, a war against poverty, sickness, ignorance and...'

Jane stopped abruptly. She realised she was repeating words Reg had said. He couldn't abide politics of Government but he believed workers deserved something better. She, and Laura too, would listen attentively to him. But what had it to do with the here and now? She silently gave George the money.

Laura had woken at the sound of voices. She listened. Her heart went out to her father; he seemed such a broken figure crouched on the bed. She pulled the covers over her head and quietly wept.

Since moving to Burgess Road and taking in a lodger, Jane had managed by taking on just three or four washing customers. Now she would have to find more. It wouldn't be easy as most women here about did there own. There were tenants upstairs but they were a queer lot. Five or six men, she couldn't be sure how many. Shadowy figures who came and went silently, only the front door clicking announced there arrival or departure. Or, glimpsed from the scullery window as they went to the privy at the bottom to the yard. Once Jane had crept up the stairs, on the pretext of looking for Georgie, but a swarthy skinned foreigner waved his arm and said: 'Not here.' She asked her existing customers if they knew anyone wanting washing done and got an extra three loads on a regular basis.

George kept his promise to Jane; he had no funds to do otherwise. When he came in from market he would ask Jane if there were any errands she wanted doing; after she'd refused his help with the mangling he'd sit morosely at the table until the children came in from school. He would romp on the floor with Georgie and sing a comic song to amuse Sarah and Laura but Jane could see he was deeply unhappy. There was no way to understand his grief, she had asked him time and time again to talk about things as they did in the old days but he would give her a sad smile and shake his head.

With George at home, there was no place in the

kitchen for Reg. He would take his meal with them then retire to his room. Since he had declared his love for her, Jane contrived not to be alone with him. To be so close to her and yet not to have her for his own was a great torment. He endured it in the hope one day she might need him. If George went off the rails, she would need someone and he would be here. He would lay on his bed in the darkness and imagine such a situation. He found himself longing for George to get drunk.

'But what is it, Mr Packard?' Jane asked.

'It's a month's rent in lieu of notice.'

'I don't understand.'

He stood beside her in the scullery. He'd left the house as usual, but had waited at the corner, watched until the children left for school and then he'd returned. He looked at her lovely face, the freckles dancing across her nose as her lips lifted in a smile.

'I can't stay here, Jane. Loving you as I do, I cannot face another day when it is not me sitting across the table from you. When it is not me whom you greet with compassion and feeling. When it is not me sharing your bed.'

She reached up and put her fingers on his lips.

'Hush. You mustn't say such things. It was a rash moment on my part that night and I pray forgiveness if it seemed an encouragement to you.'

'No, Jane. You have nothing to reproach yourself for. I think it's best for me to go and leave you in peace. I'll try my luck in America, same as my brother. I've booked passage and sail on Saturday. The rent money is to cover the time until you take in a new lodger.'

There was an emptiness in the house after Reg left. Laura missed him reading books to her. She was glad her Pa was home more now but often he wouldn't speak for hours. And then he'd do a silly jig and instead of laughing there'd be tears in his eyes.

Jane glanced up under her lashes. The children had gone to bed and it was quiet. Dusk had given way to darkness and in the gloom she studied this man, her husband. The man she had loved – no, the man she still loved with a fierce passion – had travelled such a long way from her. She moved out of the rocking chair and stood beside George. She touched his hand and he leapt as if from a flame.

'What is it, dearest George? Can't you tell me? We've shared everything together in the past, won't you share this trouble with me?'

'You just startled me, that's all, Jane.'

'I don't mean this moment. What has happened to you?'

Deep inside her she felt the same wretchedness as when she had seen him walk through the doorway at the Workhouse. The sob came out involuntarily. Her arms folded abut his neck and she sank on the floor beside him.

'Oh, my beloved Jane, I don't want to make you unhappy. I've tried to do the best but it turns out wrong. I love you so much, my darling. And...and I've kept my promise about the drink, Jane, haven't I?'

His voice held such pleading. Jane raised herself off the floor and touched his cheek with a kiss.

'Yes, my dearest, you have kept your promise.'

The new lodger, Cecil Styles, had been in residence for almost a week. He was a thin faced man with a sharp beaky nose. His lank pale blond hair touched his collar. He spoke very little and wolfed his food down, belched, then retired to his room. But he had paid two weeks rent in advance and came recommended from the rail union so Jane was satisfied.

She was standing at the front room window. She had taken to watching for George to come home from the market. Morning time passed quickly as she was occupied with washing, wringing and cooking. And then she'd become anxious. For George's sake more than anything she wanted him to come straight home. He walked along the opposite side of Burgess Road as for as Vily Walters' and then crossed diagonally to No. 26.

Jane was relieved and quickly moved back to the kitchen to wait for him.

Something puzzled her.

'I'm home, mother,' he called as he came through the door. His voice was firm and clear as if to reassure her.

By the time he'd stepped into the kitchen the front door opened again the lodger came in.

George turned round. 'Hello there, Styles. It's good to get in out of that wind, isn't it?'

Cecil Styles merely grunted in reply and scuttled into his room.

George chuckled. 'He's a rum one and no mistake.'

'I don't know why you bother to address him; he never responds. He only says yes or no.'

Jane had turned to look at him. George was standing framed in the doorway. Clothes hung loosely on him as he had to have big sizes to accommodate his height but his lithe figure couldn't fill the width. His head almost touched the top of the frame. She knew now what had puzzled her as she'd watched his approach. His shoulders weren't drooped; he held his head high. A surge of happiness swept through her.

Late on a Saturday afternoon, the market stalls knocked out goods very cheaply. Jane walked to the Broadway and along to Angel Lane to get a few bargains for the table. You had to be quick but it was difficult to know how low it would go. Sometimes you might buy at one price but the stall holder could've gone lower. She walked the length of the street market gauging which butcher's meat looked best. At the end, on the pavement, were the Laskars with bundles of old clothes or a few pots, it was a mystery why they offered them for sale or who would ever buy them. She gazed at them, curious to see if she could recognise any of them as the upstairs neighbours. She had turned to walk back.

'Jane! Jane! Wait!'

She was making up her mind: the second stall from the top looked like the best one to try today.

'JANE!'

She was gripped by the shoulders and spun around.

'Oh, Bessie. How good it is to see you.'

'I've been shouting and hollering at you but you're as deaf as a post.'

'I was concentrating on what to buy.'

'Come and have a little tipple, just to keep the cold out, so we can talk comfortable like.'

'Let me make my purchases first. Don't want to miss a bargain. Then we can sit and gossip.'

Jane got a nice piece of shin of beef for fourpence and scrag end of mutton for thruppence and, passing the greengrocer's, 'helped him out' – as he said – by taking a cauliflower off his hand for tuppence. She was very pleased with herself.

In the warmth of the public house, her cheeks glowed.

'You're looking well, Jane. Are things going right for you?'

Jane laughed. 'Well, not all luck is bad, and that's a fact. But I'm so very glad to have met you again, Bessie. It's good to have a friend,' she paused and looked clearly at her companion,' a good and steadfast friend. I'll never forget your kindness over that, you know, that matter.'

'Get along with you, Jane. You'll have me blubbering in a minute.' She reached out and clutched Jane's hand. 'Is there anything I can help you with at this minute, my dear?'

'Oh, no, Bessie, I just mean it is nice to be able to talk to someone open like. I've had a few problems.'

It was true, it was good to tell her troubles to someone and Bessie listened, nodding now and again, shaking her head once or twice.

'I reckon George took to the drink because of Reg,' Bessie said.

'But there was nothing between me and Reg. We just had the one embrace and George was in bed at that time.'

'But he's got eyes, maybe saw the way Reg looked at you and probably felt he was losing you. But of course, with the new lodger, the way you describe him, George sees there's nothing to fear from him.'

'And when are you going to wed, Bessie? Why hasn't a man led you up the aisle?'

'I haven't had time to find one yet. I work at this theatrical boarding house and a right lark that is. Mrs Shipton runs the place.   It's all her own as well. When her husband passed on last year he left her the house and a tidy sum along with it. She always wanted to go on the stage but has no talent. Still, she likes all the stage folk and decided to fill her house with them. When we sit down for supper, we get potatoes juggled in the air three at a time or else they're majicked away. Sometimes I can hardly put away a mouthful of food for laughing.'

'What do you do there, Bessie?'

'I don't rightly know. I went there as a laundry hand. There are ten rooms in the house and most have two beds. So there was a lot of linen to wash. Then Mrs Shipton says it's too much for me to do as she wanted me to help her in the kitchen. So we took on a young girl to do the laundry in the basement. Next

Mrs Shipton says it's too much for me to do vegetables and washing up the dishes so we take on another girl. Now I just do the shopping. Well, I tell the butcher, baker, grocer and greengrocer what we want and they all deliver. It's a grand job and no mistake. I get paid well and I do enjoy Mrs Shipton's company, she's a very agreeable woman. She calls it *Gaiety* Lodgings and it's just off The Broadway in Great Eastern Road. If you should ever want me, you just call there.'

Jane promised she would. 'But not just if I should need you, Bessie. I hope we can meet now and again just for a gossip.'

There were times when George didn't work but not through any fault of his. Sometimes there wasn't enough produce in the market to warrant hiring more than two men and the ganger. When he did work regularly, all week, he brought home Twenty-one Shillings. Added to what Jane earned with the extra customers she managed to buy a bed for Georgie. Up till then, he'd slept on the floor between the two girl's truckle beds. And she bought proper bedding; instead of straw they each had a flock mattress.

One of her customers had brought in a double load and Jane needed to get it done before dinner time.

'I'll stay and help, Ma,' Laura said. 'Sarah you go along with Georgie.'

Feet planted firmly, she held the sheet while Jane turned the mangle.

'Just two more, love, and then we're done.'

Ten minutes later, Jane patted Laura. "You're a good girl. Now off you go,'

Her little legs flying out behind her, Laura sped along. She wouldn't be able to catch up with Sarah and Georgie but she didn't want to be late for the register. She decided to try a short cut and darted along back alleys. Up this one, down the next, turn the corner. Laura realised she was lost. She ran faster. She missed her footing on an uneven cobblestone. Her skirts flew up as she tumbled down. For a minute she just sat there in the road. Her knee hurt.

'Oh, you poor child.'

Laura saw someone approaching her. The lady was dressed in an elegant pale grey skirt and cloak trimmed with pure white fur. A stylish hat with a curling white feather sat on top of her coiled hair. Such a vision, Laura had never seen and here was this lady actually leaning down and help her stand.

'You'll get your lovely white gloves dirty, my lady,' Laura said with concern.

The lady's maid had caught up and she, too, shared Laura's concern about the gloves.

The lady ignored the comments. 'We must go back to the house. Quickly Louise. Prepare warm water; the child has grazed her knee.'

Effortlessly the lady lifted Laura into her arms. Laura's eyes widened still further as she was carried up the whitened stone steps, through a large wooden door, into a wide hall. On she was carried, up a broad staircase with carved panels etched in gold. Laura took in all the detail and thought she must've flown to Heaven. In the parlour, a servant was stirring the embers in the grate and leaping flames warmed the room. Her petticoats were raised to clean the cut knee and Laura felt ashamed of her tattered under garments.

Her gaze took in every aspect of the room. Pretty floral covered stuffed chairs; a small round table, its polished surface dancing with reflected firelight. A large vase with a swirling red dragon, stood near the long velvet curtained windows. It was like something out of a dream but her dreams hadn't aspired to such beauty.

'There child, it should heal well, now.' Lacking

a bandage, the lady bound the knee with a lace kerchief.

'How shall I know where to return it, my lady?'

'Nay, child, you may keep it.'

She solemnly shook hands with the lady and curtsied. The servant had told her the best way to get back onto the right road for school. As she turned the corner, Laura glanced back at the house. Such a magnificent house; with a staircase. In a pensive mood she arrived at the school gates. She made a vow to herself: one day she would have a big house.

It seemed no time at all since they had welcomed in the first year of the new century and now it was in its dying days. Although it had not settled there had been lots of snow showers making it damp underfoot. And there was a chill in the air. Laura's birthday on the 19th of January was a particularly dreary day.

George came in stamping his feet on the coir mat. Laura waited for him to produce the customary bunch of violets.

'The news from the palace is bad. The Queen is failing.'

'What about my flowers, Pa?'

'Ah, girlie, I forgot. Everyone was talking about the news, I didn't go back to the flower girl. I'll get you some tomorrow.'

'It doesn't matter, Pa. Tomorrow's not my birthday.'

Three days later the news came. Queen Victoria had died at her home in the Isle of Wight. All London, and England, mourned the loss of their Monarch who had reigned for over sixty years. The sadness felt by the people was so great it was almost tangible. The heir to the throne, the Prince of Wales was declared King Edward the Seventh.

George brought home a newspaper on Wednesday and sat at the table slowly reading every word. For a fleeting moment, Jane's mind went to Reg; he would have related how the Queen's death affected trade and commerce throughout the Empire.

'There has been talk that shops and businesses should close as a mark of respect,' George said.

'But not yet, I expected they mean the day of the funeral. In any case with all the processions and carriages, no-one could get to the shops.'

'Well, I'll get up as usual tomorrow, Jane. Thursday is always our busiest time.'

She had seen George off at half past three and crept back into bed for a couple of hours before getting up to prepare the children for school. Jane rummaged in a bundle of clothing and found comforter. She tied it round Georgie's shoulders.

'It's so cold and damp today, Georgie. You must keep well wrapped up. Laura, see he doesn't take it off. I don't want him to catch a chill, not with his weak chest.'

She shivered as she shut the front door. She was glad there was washing to do; the stove was regularly topped up for supplies of hot water for the tub which kept warmth in the kitchen. With sleeves rolled up and the heavy canvas apron tied around her waist, Jane began pounding the clothes. She was absorbed in thought and it was several minutes before she realised there'd been a rap on the front door. Hastily drying her arms, she hurried along the hall and opened the door.

'Am I addressing Mrs Stringer?' the man asked.

Jane looked at the tall stranger. He had raised his hat as he spoke revealing wavy silver hair.

'Jane Stringer?' he asked and a slight smile played about his mouth.

Jane nodded. Her curiosity made her speechless.

'My name is Lieutenant Colonel Bourne, Frederick Bourne.'

He watched her face as he spoke but there was no flicker of recognition. Foolish of him to have expected otherwise, he thought dolefully.

'I regret to say I am the bearer of sad tidings. May I step inside?'

Jane became aware of the cold on her damp arms. She held wide the door and signalled him in. After closing the door she walked ahead of him down the passageway. The coldness from the outside atmosphere penetrated her flesh as his words reeled around her mind: sad tidings...sad tidings...sad. In a trance she showed him to a chair at the table and sat mutely opposite him. She refused to let her brain say a name.

He reached across the table and placed his hand over hers.

'Your dear mother died yesterday.'

With relief she let out her breath; it wasn't George! And then she felt ashamed and guilty. It had been many months since she had visited Matilda.

'It is kind of you to come and tell me, er, Mr. I've forgotten your name.'

'Frederick Bourne.'

'Do you live near to my mother? How did she die? Was it peaceful?'

'I had hoped that perhaps my name may have been familiar to you.'

'No, it's not. Should I know you?'

'I am an old friend of your mother's. No, that is not strictly true. More than a friend. Your mother and I were to have been married in two months time. That is why I thought you may know of me.' He looked at Jane. 'It is good to see you are not outraged at the prospect. You would not have disapproved, I think.'

'I'm at a loss as to what to say. You must know

my mother and I were frequently in discord with one another. I am saddened at her passing more so now I have learned about you. I should have liked to have seen her married and happy again. I wish we had been close so she would have confided in me. How long have you known my mother?'

'I first met Matilda the day after she opened her shop in Leytonstone Road. I had taken a pocket watch to the watchmaker's next door. As I came out she was standing outside her shop looking at an arrangement in the window. My head was down adjusting the watch chain and carelessly bumped into her. A friendship began which awakened feelings in each of us.'

'But that was years ago. Mother must have had the shop ten or twelve years. Why did you take so long to get around to marriage?'

It was a minute or so before he replied softly, 'I already had a legal wife. She has been in an institution these past fifteen years. A fall from a horse rendered her incapable of reason. Mercifully, she was released from her torture and passed away last September. We believed six months was a respectable time to have elapsed before I remarried. God chose it to be otherwise.'

He tried to blink away the tears in his eyes but they nestled on his cheeks. Jane reversed their roles and found herself comforting Frederick Bourne. He wanted to talk about Matilda and their time together and Jane found it strange to realise the person he spoke of with such affection was her own mother.

'I have placed the sweet creature in the funeral chapel. I have already spoken with James, as head of the family, for there will be arrangements to be made for the funeral. He will come to Mrs Goult's premises this afternoon. Will you come too? And, there is Arthur. He should be told of his mother's death but I am at a loss as to his whereabouts. As you know he has had no contact with his family for some time now, much to Matilda's distress. James only knew he had married but could not remember the young lady's name.'

'Arthur told us about his marriage plans the last time we were all together as a family for mother's birthday. But that was all of three years ago.'

'He had told your mother his studio was to be in Bond Street. Matilda and I did go to look once but there was no proprietor named Goult and no occupiers of adjacent premises had any knowledge of such a person.'

'I'm trying to remember her name, the girl he married. Her father was Sir somebody. And he was something to do with the government, I believe.'

'It would be a good approach if I had the gentleman's name.' Frederick said pressing her to recall.

'Yes, if only I can remember.' Jane squeezed her eyes under her palms, casting her mind back, concentrating on the parlour at West Street. She pictured all the family in their positions and for a moment indulged in a slight smile at the remembrance of George's back eye.

'Arthur said he was marrying...Isabel Wells. That's it. Isabel Wells. She was the daughter of Sir Frances Wells who was something in the government at that time.'

'Excellent Jane, thank you so much. I shall go into town tomorrow. I shall probably be able to locate Sir Francis through the Carlton Club.' He looked anxiously at Jane. 'I presume you wish me to locate Arthur. I think it is right and proper all three of you arrange your mother's affairs but I do not wish to intrude. If you think it best not to pursue the matter of locating Arthur...'

Jane smiled at him. 'I think we should all be guided by you as to what is best. We may be her children but I do not believe any one of us has loved her as you have. You are truly her husband.'

'Thank you for those kind words. I, too, wish it could have been different, that we could have all known each other as family. I feel I know each of you as Matilda frequently spoke abut her children. I have no children of my own and wanted so much to declare myself a second father to you. Goodbye, until this afternoon.'

Chores forgotten, she sat on in the unlit room; her mind drifting on the flood tide of memory, leaping from one time log to another. Happy memories of her childhood; harsh memories of her young womanhood in arguments with Matilda. She smiled at something Frederick said. She had wanted Sarah to be there as it lent an air of propriety to their meetings! Sarah! Jane felt a surge of jealousy: Sarah had known of Matilda's relationship with Frederick.

When George came in she told him the news.

'I'm grieved for you dearest. I know because of me you didn't always see eye to eye but she was your mother and she was a good woman. God rest her soul.'

She had her bonnet and cape on, waiting for the children to come in from school. George had said he would tell them, but Jane said it was her task.

'I had a visitor today, Sarah. Frederick Bourne. You know him, don't you?'

'What a silly question! He's granny's friend. He's nice. He takes us out, sometimes in a carriage.'

Jane quietly told the children Granny Goult was dead.

Chapter 6

The bay window with the blown glass rings, curved toward the side alley and abutted to the heavy oak door. Its knocker was bound in black silk. How considerate of Frederick Bourne to have done that, thought Jane. She was surprised when Emily opened the door.

'Afternoon, Jane,' she said and turned and walked back up the rounded staircase leaving Jane to close the door.

Jane hesitated a moment, then opened the door to the left and strolled around the work room. On the cutting table lay pieces of soft checked wool with printed paper patterns pinned to them: a panelled skirt; disembodied sleeves; back yoke to an invisible cape. Her fingers followed the tracings of the flimsy paper. On a shelf in random order were stacked cards of lace trimmings, silk ribbons, velvet ribbons, embroidered cotton edges but no doubt Matilda knew exactly where to find everything. At the left side stood the solid Singer sewing machine which produced neat chain stitches much quicker than by hand. Jane had a clear recollection of how triumphant her mother had been when she acquired such a modern machine. It had held little meaning before but looking at this work now she admired her mother's artistry and skill in turning a simple piece of cloth into a dazzling creation.

In a desk drawer, Jane found the account book. In neat simple writing Matilda had listed the cost of materials, threads, trimmings. Postage for ordering patterns from Buttericks in Regent Street; purchase of Weldon's Magazine or World of Fashion to obtain free paper patterns. On the opposite page Matilda had written down the amounts she had received from customers: Mrs Pomfrey – cotton dress and petticoat 12/6d; Mrs Gregory – woollen costume 15/0d. But for those fashions borne out of Matilda's imagination were shown as S.I.D. – Special Individual design – and charged for accordingly: Mrs Ellory-Price – dress with silk ribboned bodice £2.12s 6d.

The sound of footsteps made her hurriedly return the book to the drawer. Frederick stood in the doorway.

'Good afternoon, Jane.'

'Do you know, I have never been in this room before. Whenever I brought Sarah, I just went straight up to mother's rooms.' She stood beside the cutting table and fingered the material. 'So much I didn't know,' Jane said wistfully.

'I have made a list of those suppliers with whom Matilda had outstanding accounts. And there are two ladies who have been less than prompt in settling their debts,' Frederick smiled. 'Shall I pursue these matters on your behalf?'

He looked appealingly at Jane.

'I have nothing else to do.' He said simply.

They left the work room and went up to Matilda's apartment. James sat in the over stuffed chair, hunched forward, his hands fiddled with the chain of his pocket watch. Frederick Bourne walked over to stand by the window.

Emily had disappeared into Matilda's bedroom and there was the sound of cupboards and drawers opening and closing. Jane pushed open the door. Emily was at the closet pulling out dresses and capes.

'What do you think you are doing?' Jane demanded.

'Sorting out things that will be suitable for my Charlotte.'

'How dare you touch my mother's things. Get out of this room at once.'

'You can't speak to me like that. James is the eldest and he has first pick of everything.'

'Our mother died yesterday and here you are like a scavenger picking over the bones. Get out of here,' Jane screamed.

Emily rushed out in tears and threw herself on James. She beat her fists on his chest.

'You shouldn't treat Emily so, Jane. It is us who've been here regularly to mother. We've come once a month, on a Saturday, us and the children, too.'

Frederick coughed. 'May we make the funeral arrangements first of all?'

Emily raised her tear stained face. 'And, I don't think he should be here. He's not family. He has no right...'

'He has every right,' Jane interrupted.' And he will stay through every discussion we have about our late mother.'

'Believe me, I shall only do what is right for your dear departed mother.'

'Mother was well known and respected here about. We must do it right. I think there should be a carriage,' James said. 'And two, no, I think four black horses.'

'And a mourning boy,' Emily added.

'Oh, no! James. Don't you remember, when father died, mother made a particular point of saying it should be a simple arrangement. She said she wasn't going to put his hard earned money into the under-taker's pocket.'

Emily reacted at the mention of money. 'Who will pay for the funeral,' she asked.

'She would have left money for her funeral,' James said.

'But how much, James? I suppose what is left comes to us,' she looked across at Jane.

Frederick had sat quiet during the discussion but Jane could see he had been disturbed at the prospect of black horses and a mourning boy.

'I am aware of your mother's affairs. I have advised her over the past few years,' he said and Emily sniffed her disapproval. 'The rent on the premises is paid quarterly in advance and there would be no calling back of what has been settled. The wares in the shop must be sold as they cannot be deemed private property. There are a few small outstanding bills from suppliers; Matilda always paid promptly on the last day of the month. The personal items up here,' he waved his arm as he turned toward her, Jane saw his eyes were filled with tears. 'These personal things are for you to decided on their disposal.'

As Frederick uttered these words, Emily ran back to the bedroom.

'See, I told you we could have them.'

James had the decency to apprehend his wife and bring her back into the parlour.

'There is your brother, Arthur,' Frederick continued. 'An effort must be made to locate him and apprise him of his mother's death. He has a right to be included in your decisions.'

'Frederick,' Jane smiled at him as a conspirator,' I believe you said you would make enquiries at a London club. We would appreciate your efforts in this and I believe we should do nothing until we have heard from you.'

Jane led the way down, followed unwillingly by Emily and James. Frederick held the large key and turned it in the lock. He paused and lent forward and Jane felt sure she had seen him kiss the brass door plate:

MATILDA GOULT, DRESSMAKER

The chill night air crept into Jane's bones. She pulled the thin coat tightly about her throat. The rail lines hummed and she saw the welcoming glimmer of a tram.

She spoke little when she got in. George took her coat and bonnet and hung them on the door peg. He drew her close to the range and rubbed her hands. They stood silently together until the church clock struck nine.

'Time for bed,' George said.

Jane nodded and went out the scullery door to the privy at the end of the yard. As she returned, George went out back. She heard the bolt slide across the yard door and got into bed. As usual, she was on her side, legs slightly curled up. He was soon alongside her. He tentatively extended his arm across her shoulder. Jane leant back and curved into his body. He kissed her ear. She turned slightly and softly spoke his name. George relaxed beside her. There was a strong bond between them, perhaps not as passionate as their early years but a deeper, abiding love.

Frederick left the Army and Navy Club and walked along Pall Mall. In the cold January air, his breath hung in small clouds about him. The usual hubbub of London was subdued as the city prepared for the funeral of The Queen. Lamp posts were draped with purple ribbon; the Queen had said she did not want black. Frederick had moved back into his club the night Matilda died. He had been there a few years ago, before renting accommodation at the Blue Boar Inn not far from Matilda's dress shop. But now, the nearness was too painful. He was glad of the crisp morning air, it cleared his head which was stuffy from lack of sleep. At the Carton Club, the doorman saluted and ushered him in. He approached the steward's office.

'Good Morning, sir. May I be of service to you?'

'Sir Francis Wells – he is a member, isn't he?'

'Yes, Sir. Always in at lunch time before going to the House.'

Frederick spent the rest of the morning walking in the park. He knew what he was going to say. He retraced his steps to the Carlton Club and gave his card to a steward. Within minutes he was shown into the lounge. Sir Francis came forward to greet him.

'Lieutenant Colonel Bourne. Pleased to meet you.' He turned to a passing barman, 'Two whiskeys, Jones. What was your regiment, Colonel Bourne?'

'Royal Horse Guards.'

'Ah, the Blues. Fine regiment. My son's a Lieutenant in the Grenadiers. Thought they might have been required to quell the Boers. Expect he'll have his chance for honour and glory in battle some time. Did you see much action?'

'I came to ask you, Sir Francis...'

'Of course, damned rude of me. Got carried away talking about military matters. Ah, put them down, Jones. Your good health, Colonel. I've got a table for two as my son-in-law usually takes luncheon with me but I can have them lay an extra place if you'd like to join us.'

'No, really, I don't want to take up your time. But your son-in-law...'

'Here he is now.' He waved across the room and Frederick's eyes followed the direction. A tall, upright young man stood on the steps. His brown hair had tinges of chestnut, his broad face lightly tanned. He was a very handsome man. He lithely skipped down the steps; a bright smile was fixed on his face and he held out his hand. Sir Francis gripped it warmly.

'Arthur, my boy, I want you to meet Lieutenant Colonel Bourne. Colonel Bourne, my son-in-law, Arthur Grant. He's the Member for Dorset South.' He winked. 'Won't be long before he gets a post in Government, I'll be bound.'

Frederick hoped his expression did not display his feelings. No wonder they had been unable to find him. Often he and Matilda had come up West in an attempt to locate Arthur but each time she had returned home disappointed.

He shook hands. 'It is a strange coincidence but I had hoped to meet you Mr, er, Mr Grant.' Frederick kept his voice calm. 'I hadn't known of your changed name.'

Arthur's smile faded; his body stiffened.

'Lor' yes,' Sir Francis chimed in. 'Couldn't have a Member of the British Parliament with a damned foreign name like Goult, could we?'

'I came to tell you, your mother died last Wednesday. Your brother and sister wish you to join them in making the necessary arrangements.'

'What's that?' Sir Francis looked from Arthur to Fredcerick. At that moment the steward approached to invite Sir Francis to move into the dining room.

Arthur paled slightly, but he held Frederick's gaze.

'You are mistaken, Colonel. My mother died many years ago. I am virtually an orphan brought up by an aunt, now deceased. You have confused me with someone else named Goult.' He replaced his smile and turned to sir Francis. 'We really must take luncheon now, Sir. We have to get to the House.'

He took Sir Francis' elbow and began to steer him

to the dining room. Sir Francis looked puzzled. He turned back to Frederick.

'Goodbye, Colonel. I wish you luck in your pursuit but obviously you got the wrong chap. Nice to have met you.'

All the time he was speaking he was shaking Frederick's hand and staring into his face. Frederick looked back with candour which left Sir Francis with an uneasy feeling.

A light drizzle had begun as Frederick emerged from the club. His heart was heavy. How could that handsome your man, his face so reminiscent of his beloved Matilda, deny her?

Jane was splashing water onto her black dress and brushing it to freshen up the colour from its rustiness. It was one Matilda had given her many years ago; it had been made for a customer who had changed her mind. She had it over her arm as she answered the knock at the door.

'Frederick. It is good to see you. Come in. Even in the afternoon it seems like night time. Here, let me take your coat, it is quite damp.'

He had docilely followed her along the passageway and child like had allowed her to divest him of his coat. Jane pulled the rocking chair close to the range and pushed him into it. As Frederick had entered the kitchen George had stood up respectfully and waited to be addressed,

'I walked. I don't know where.' Frederick's voice was barley audible. 'I walked. Rain turned to snow. I saw a tram.'

He slumped forward, and buried his head in his hands. He began to sob.

'He denied his mother. He denied the sweetest creature this earth has known,'

Jane knelt beside him and held his hand in hers.

George moved to stand behind Jane and placed his hand on her shoulder. For a moment they were like a carved statue of manifested grief. Frederick recovered his composure.

'You and James must make the arrangements to lay your dear mother to rest without the attendance of your brother.'

One, unadorned horse, drew the carriage taking Matilda to her final resting place beside her husband in West Ham Cemetery. James and Emily and their three children led the mourners, followed by George and Jane and their children, and last came Frederick with Great Aunt Laura. At the graveside Frederick threw one red rose onto the coffin; Great Aunt sprinkled black earth brought from the Barking farmland.

The family were content for Frederick to deal with the business matters and soon Matilda's affairs were settled. The lease of the premises surrendered to the agent and personal items removed from the upper floor. Frederick asked James and Jane to meet him at the Blue Boar Inn.

'For some years now, I had been advising your mother on investing the profits from her business. Oh, not in a speculative way. They can be converted quickly into cash and divided however you decide.'

'I know mother had opened a share account with the Stratford Co-operative Society,' James said.

Jane's attention drifted away from the conversation. Her mind went back to a week ago when just she and Emily were clearing out Matilda's rooms. Emily was contrite, deferring to Jane on each item.

'What about this dress, Jane? And this cape? There are two pairs of button sided boots. Stuff the toes and Sarah could wear them. Granny Goult had such tiny feet, none of her boots would fit my Charlotte.'

The rooms were rather spartan. Matilda had

retained very little from the West Street house. Jane
was happy for Emily to have the clothes but she did
take the boots. She also chose four fine bone china tea
cups, saucers, and plates, with matching teapot. The
milk jug and sugar basin could not be found, probably
broken long ago. She had left Emily sorting through
gloves and under garments in the tall chest while she
went to the bedside cupboard. There was a flat mahogany box in the top drawer. Jane opened it and sifted
through the odd assortment of treasures. A cravat
pin – Jane remembered seeing her father wearing it;
a rose pressed between two scraps of satin – possibly
from Frederick; a piece of wood with poker etching
– what that was Jane had no idea. And at the bottom,
a small sampler, inexpertly stitched: For Mother with
Love and JG at the bottom surrounded by blue forget-
me-knots. Jane turned it over in her hand, remember she had been about seven when she had stitched
it. Matilda had ridiculed the crude effort. Jane had
thrown it down saying she would never sew anything
again. Throughout the years her mother had valued it.
Jane was surprised; she was also saddened at realis-
ing she hadn't really known her mother.

'Good Lord! As much as that! I had no idea. Had
you, Jane?' James turned to his sister.

'I do apologise, Frederick,' Jane said. 'My mind had
drifted off into the past. What did you say?'

An excited James exclaimed: 'We inherit Two
Hundred and seventy Five Pounds.'

'Matilda did not leave a will specifying beneficia-
ries,' Frederick continued, 'but I think she would like
Alice Wilkins, who has been her assistant in the shop
for over fifteen years, to have something. May I suggest
she has twenty-five pounds? The residue is an even
sum to be divided between you two. I had asked you
to come alone as I thought it best you should know of

this matter first without your wife, James, and your husband, Jane, being present. It is then up to you to divulge what you wish. You may wish to establish a trust fund for your children and if you require any advice I shall be happy to oblige.'

'What does that mean, Sir,' James asked. 'And how much would it take?'

'You determine the amount,' Frederick said. 'The money is held in a bank and earns interest throughout the years until the specific time has elapsed. Say, James you put one hundred pounds in a fund to be divided equally between James, Tobias, and Charlotte, when they reach twenty-five years of age. Then, James would get his money first, Charlotte's would stay in the fund and earn a little bit more until she was twenty-five and same for Tobias.'

'That would suit me fine. I am in regular employment and we have no need of such a sum right now. I know Emily could spend it easily enough,' he laughed. 'I will leave it to you, Colonel Bourne to arrange that for me.'

'And you, Jane. What would you wish to do?'

'Probably a dowry for the girls, a small one. May be a little bit for Georgie. But for the moment I think I should prefer to leave it in the bank, if that's all right, Frederick?'

'That will be quite in order. Shall I set aside twenty pounds each for Sarah and Laura and Fifteen for Georgie and place the remaining seventy pounds in a bank account in your name?'

Sarah was swinging her arms and marching ahead, followed by Laura who was holding Vily Walters' hand as she skipped along. Georgie, as always, dawdled far behind.

'No. You're not doing it right. See Vily. You've got to put the same foot forwards as me. Ready, now. Off we go. Left.' She set off singing: *Our Thrupenny Hop, Our Thrupenny hop.'*

They got to the gate of Number Sixteen just as Mrs Jarvis came out. 'What a to do you girls are making. Oh, it's you Stringer girls is it?' Mrs Jarvis looked at their black arm bands. 'I do think it is ever so loyal of your Ma to show her respect for the late Queen,'

'What do you mean, Mrs Jarvis,' Sarah asked.

'Why, your black arm bands, of course. Mourning for our late dear Queen.'

Laura had started to laugh but quickly swallowed it and cast down her eyes. 'It's not for the Queen, Mrs Jarvis. It's for our Granny. She died the day after the Queen,'

Georgie, who'd caught them up, wasn't going to be left out of the conversation, piped up: 'For our Granny. Did you know our Granny? We didn't know the Queen.'

Mrs Jarvis tossed her head in the air and pushed past the girls.

Laura continued to keep in step with Vily until her gate, then Sarah and Laura with arms around each other skipped along in perfect unison. Georgie clung to Laura's other hand and was swept along, his feet hardly touching the ground. Their cheeks glowed as they came into the kitchen. Laura immediately flung herself on top of her father.

'Lor, girlie, you gave me a shock. I had my eyes closed. Didn't hear you come in.'

Jane just nodded her head. It was always the same. George would eagerly wait for the girls and Georgie to come in from school. As soon as heard them come through the front door, he would ruffle his hair, slump down in his chair, close his eyes and assume deep breathing. It was a game he liked to play.

'Mrs Gowrie says I'll be going up after Easter. I don't have to wait until September. Isn't that just fine, Pa?'

NOT ALL LUCK IS BAD

'It most certainly is, girlie. Where are you going up? In a balloon?'

Laura playfully punched his chest. 'No, silly. Up into Class 5A.'

'Ma.'

Yes, Georgie.'

'Mrs Jarvis thought our ribbon was for the Queen. Wasn't that silly? I told her it's for Granny. How long do we keep the ribbon on our sleeve, Ma?'

'I suppose it must be nearly three months now.'

Suddenly Sarah screamed and pointed. They all looked at the face pressed against the window pane. One of the Oriental upstairs tenants, either going to or coming from the lavatory at the end of the yard, had been silently observing them. Jane and George rushed to the back door but being discovered, he'd evaporated into the thin light of dusk.

'For some time now, father, I've been thinking we should move further up the street.'

'No Jane. No!. No more moves. We said so, didn't we?'

'But at the top of the road, those houses have gas mantles in every room.'

'And a rent to match no doubt. Where's the money to come from?'

'Bessie says they're needing more help at the lodging house. I could work there regularly. At the top of the road it would be close to the tram stop. And, father, those houses have a water closet with a china pan outside the scullery. It would be better for the girls to be away from...' Jane swept her eyes upwards.

'If the lavatory is just outside the scullery, that will be worse won't it? And the smell. The smell will seep in.'

'No, dear. No, it won't. There's something called a cistern with a handle that flushes everything away.'

The debate was ended as the passage door opened,

admitting the lodger. Cecil Styles went straight to the table, pushed away George's paper and sat down. His hand hung vacantly above the table.

'Where's me knife and fork?'

'Supper won't be a minute, Mr Styles. Girls, George. Wash your hands, Laura put out the plates; Sarah you get the knives and forks.'

'But, Ma.' Georgie tugged at his mother's skirt. 'Ma, you never told me about the ribbon for Granny.'

'I'll take them off tomorrow, dear.'

Laura had wanted to say she wouldn't be able to wave to Vily Walters if they moved to the top of the road but to have gas light to read by tipped the scale in favour of moving. Jane served the rabbit stew and potatoes, giving the largest portion to Mr Styles. Before she had finished serving gravy and potatoes onto her plate, the lodger thrust his plate up at Jane. She smiled grimly to herself; it was as well she had removed the piece of meat from her plate and put it back in the pot. Within minutes he wiped his mouth with the back of his hand, belched before standing up and, without another word, left the kitchen.

'Well, a clean plate is a show of appreciation, I suppose,' George said, glancing at his own half eaten supper. 'But he could take it a bit slower.'

'I think he's horrible,' Sarah said.

'He smells,' Georgie added.

'Now children, manners.' Jane reprimanded them. 'Run along to bed. And before you ask, Laura, yes you can have a candle...' Jane subtly emphasised the word,' but don't strain your eyes by reading too long.

George took his boots from beside the range and pulled them back on. He didn't like Styles, either, but he did pay his rent on time and, George thought, Jane would never give HIM a second look.

'Are you going out, Pa?' Laura had paused in the doorway. She looked anxiously at her mother.

The mellow glow from the lamp gave her an angelic halo, as Jane bent to unpick the stitching holding the black ribbon onto the sleeve. She looked up at him and smiled.

George put his hand on her shoulder. 'Just for half an hour or so.'

'Have you got a few coppers, dear?'

He nodded and left.

Jane fingered the ribbon. Poor, George. Always he thought he was bing censured for not making adequate provision for the family. Yes, I know that's how you saw it, Mother, Jane mused. But George always does his best. It's just that the standards to be judged by are different. She snipped the thread and held the shiny ribbon in her fingers.

'I'm sorry if you were disappointed in me as a daughter,' she said to the empty room. 'I doubt I would have enjoyed any other way of life.'

Clear blue skies, rapidly darkened and soon the clouds released gentle April rain. Laura grabbed Georgie with one hand and scooped up her skirts with the other and ran.

'Come on Sarah,' she called back.

Vily was close behind Laura. 'She's still mooning with the Potter boy. How can she like him? He's got pimples.'

'Sarah's not mooning,' Laura declared. 'Potter likes her. Everyone likes her for she is so pretty. Sarah can't be nasty or cross with anyone.'

They were close to home as the rain eased. Laura slowed her pace and released Georgie's hand. She was a little ahead of him when she saw something in the gutter.

'Oo, look! Some lady has lost her muff.'

Laura stooped down to pick up the mud spattered object. As her hand touched the soft black fur, it moved. She jumped up in surprise. She stared at it for several seconds then bent down again and picked up the creature and cradled it in her hands. It made no sound.

'It's a kitten,' Georgie exclaimed. 'Is it dead?'

'No but it nearly drowned. Quick! We must get it home and give it some milk.'

Sarah had caught up with them and took off her bonnet for the kitten to lie in. They tumbled in through the door and rushed to the kitchen, all chattering about the kitten. George covered his ears at the din as Jane was presented with the furry bundle in the hat. It was a poor sickly little thing and George warned them the kitten may not live through the night. Laura was dispatched to the *Thatched House* with a mug.

'Knock on the side door,' Jane said. 'Ask for a penny worth of whisky.'

Milk was warmed and Jane dipped her finger in the whiskey then in the milk and forced it into the tiny mouth. Every few minutes she would repeat the process. Laura was delegated to serving out supper to the lodger and themselves. She wanted to sit beside her mother but Jane insisted she sat at table like a proper lady. Jane sat in her rocking chair and ate a little broth herself in between feeding the kitten. She sat up all night beside the range, nursing the kitten. Twice Laura had crept out to the kitchen only to be shooed away back to bed. Jane had dozed off when George came through to wash at the sink. He kissed her head and she stirred almost tipping the kitten, still in Sarah's hat, onto the floor. The movement aroused the animal and it gave a soft mew.

'There, my pretty, you've decided to stay this side of Heaven after all, have you?' Jane stroked the fine black hairs.

'You're a grand woman, and no mistake. Don't get up, mother, I can cut myself a slice of two.'

Each were allowed to stroke the kitten in turn.

'We can keep it can't we Ma?' Georgie asked.

Laura looked keenly at her mother's face. 'I found it, so it is ours, isn't it?'

'And you don't mind, do you Ma?'

'As a matter of fact, I've been thinking of getting us a cat.'

The children shrieked joyfully.

'Well, I've noticed mice droppings in the pantry cupboard, so I think our little kitten will be very useful. What shall we call him?'

'Tommy,' announced Georgie.

'Black cats are supposed to be lucky, aren't they?' Laura said. 'And this one is lucky to have been nursed all night by Ma. So I think we should call him LUCKY.'

Lucky made good progress and was soon up on his feet, although wobbly at first. He inspected every corner of the kitchen and found a niche alongside the range where he decided to make his bed. He became the most important member of the household, second only to the lodger. Jane made sure Lucky didn't go beyond the kitchen door into the passage. He had done so on one occasion and Jane was in time to see Cecil Styles put is boot under the creature and tossed it toward the kitchen. But all the back yard was his domain; he would prowl along the side fence and playfully leap at imaginary prey. He was clever enough to recognise is own family but when any of the tenants or the lodger came out to go to the privy, he would flatten himself against the fence alongside a tussock of grass.

He was also the subject of Laura's first essay for Mrs Gowrie.

'And, Pa. What do you think? Mrs Gowrie read it aloud to the class. She said it was well thought out.'

'I always knew I had a clever daughter. Now your

mother has been calling you several times, so go and help her with the washing.

Laura skipped out into the garden.

'Help me throw it over the line, Laura. But for goodness sake don't let it drop. The mangle is stuck and I couldn't wring it.'

Eight year old Laura was half Jane's height so the weight was uneven. But her arms were strong and she held onto the end of the sheet while Jane pulled one half over. Wet washing weighed heavy on the line.

'If you held one end, Ma, and I held the other and we twisted it, we'd get some of the water out.'

Each item in turn was wrung out and replaced on the line which didn't sag quite so badly now the weight was reduced.

'I think, George, I'll have a word with Bessie about working at the boarding house. If the mangle doesn't work, I can't do washing at home any more.'

They were still looking at the mangle when the lodger came home. Cecil Styles poked his head round the corner of the scullery.

'Come off its cogs,' he announced. He pushed Jane out of the scullery, shoved George to the left side, he stood on the right. Styles' small stature was deceiving, he was very powerful. He pulled out the handle.

'Lift!' He commanded and George obeyed. Deftly the connecting cogs slid back into place. Styles shoved the iron handle back in position then walked back into the kitchen and sat in readiness at the table.

Chapter 7

Sarah couldn't stop her teeth from chattering. The girls stood in the school yard, billowing gowns in varying degrees of white, transformed the down-to-earth drab paved area into insubstantial floating vapour.

Sarah had grown a couple of inches in the last year and very few of her clothes fitted. Jane had managed to find a far too long almost-white organdie dress with large puff sleeves the hem of which she cobbled in her usual way. Laura of course had Sarah's cambric dress of last year.

'Why have we g-g-got to stand here?'

'We're waiting for the Head Mistress'

'Why c-c-couldn't we wait in the assembly hall? Empire Day would be the same inside as out here,' Sarah moaned.

'I don't know why we have Empire Day,' Vily muttered.

'May 24th was set aside to celebrate Queen Victoria's birthday,' Laura whispered.

'I know that,' Vily responded, 'but she's dead and we have a King now.'

'Be quiet you girls in the second row.'

At last the head Mistress appeared and addressed the girls, reminding them of loyalty to their Sovereign and the greatness of the Empire acquired during Queen Victoria's reign. Their white dresses were a symbol of the purity of thought and resolution that had made the country great. They were urged to go forward with honour.

No doubt the boys fared the same.

Like large flapping white birds, the girls marched into the school building and as the last girl entered, the overcast sky cleared and the yard was bathed in warm spring sunshine.

'I've got a new spinning top,' Vily told Laura. 'Will you come out to play later?'

'Yes, if you give me a go with your top.'

Laura ran ahead and opened the front door. She crept along the passage, determined to catch out her father before be could pretend to be asleep. She eased open the kitchen door and Lucky rubbed against her ankles. George sat at the table as usual but he still wore his coat. She reached up on tiptoe and put her hands over his eyes.

He turned round, holding a paper. 'It's you, girlie. You're home. I thought it was your Ma.'

The sadness in his eyes frightened her, she was about to cry out when Sarah tumbled into the kitchen.

'I'm thirsty,' she declared.

'Me, too,' Georgie said following her.

Jane always waited until the children were home from school before going out to collect or deliver washing, or to go shopping. It was strange not to see her standing by the range as usual. Especially on a Friday: Jane would get everything ready for supper, before she and Laura would go to Crownfield Road stalls for bargains.

Sensing the tension, the children sat silently at the table, waiting.

'I think I'd best get some potatoes going,' Laura said,

anxious to be doing something. As she got up George waved her to sit down.

The half sheet of paper was gripped in his hands. George had read it a hundred times. It didn't make any sense.

My beloved husband. Remember always, I love you.

I have something to do which may take a little while.

I'll be back, I promise. I love you

'Ma's gone away for a while. I thought she meant the afternoon.' There was a catch in his voice. Instantly Laura was beside him, her arms flung around his neck.

'I don't understand.' He said giving the paper to Laura.

Sarah leant over her shoulder to read it, too. 'I expect Ma will be home soon, don't you Laura?'

'Pa' Laura stood close beside her father. 'Has something dreadful happened, like...like. What do you think, Pa?' she asked hesitantly.

'I don't know, girlie.' George dare not tell the children of his fears. When he was ready to go off to work that morning, Jane had kissed him. Not the usual glancing kiss, but a tender, loving kiss. It had taken him by surprise, so much so he was at the front door before he realised he'd left his bread and jam on the table. And she had looked at him, staring like, then shutting her eyes as if trying to remember. The strange look had haunted him all day. He'd bend to lift a box of apples and on rising Jane's face was before him; as the ganger talked to him, that face devolved into Jane's. He knew he should have said something before he left the house, asked her what was up, what she meant by that kiss, but he hadn't. And now, she was gone.

'Do you think she's ever so sick?' Laura whispered.

'No, girlie. I'd've known.'

'Perhaps Ma is playing a trick,' Sarah chipped in.

Laura brightened. 'She says she'll be back so we best get supper.'

She sliced some cooked mutton she'd fund in the pantry cupboard; the potatoes were boiling on the hob. This would have to do for tonight although she knew Mr Styles wouldn't be pleased.

He marched in as usual. Laura served the lodger first, as her mother always did. Her hand trembled slightly; Styles looked up, glanced round the room and frowned but said nothing. She tried to serve her father but George shook his head. Styles wolfed down his supper and went back to his room leaving the family alone.

Time dragged on. Laura tucked Georgie into his bed and joined Sarah in the scullery. Together they tidied up and put away the pans.

George still sat at the table.

'Should we go and look for her, Pa? She might have fallen over or been knocked down by a carriage. I can run to the corner. Perhaps Mrs Jarvis or Mrs Walters might know where she is. Shall I go and ask?'

'No. Sarah's right. I expect Mother will be home soon. Go to bed, girls. I'll wait up for a while.'

Laura clapped her hands. 'I know. I expect Ma has gone to that boarding house to see Bessie.'

George smiled in response. 'Of course. That's it.'

Laura tossed and turned in the narrow bed until Sarah held her still.

'There's scant enough room in the bed as it is without you rummaging around in it, sister.'

'Pa looks so sad. What do you think has happened?'

'Run off with the milk carrier as like as not.'

Laura sat up with a start. 'Sarah! How can you say such a thing? That's wicked.'

'I didn't mean it, soppy.'

Sarah pulled Laura back under the covers and they cuddled together.

'Shall I tell you something?' Sarah whispered in a knowing way, for once exerting her superiority as the eldest. 'Ma never wore her petticoat.'

'Ma would never go out without a petticoat, you daft thing.'

'Well, I expect she wore A petticoat but not the one she ties her money in.'

'How do you know?'

'It's still on the chest there under a piece of brown paper.'

The significance of the statement dawned on Laura. She scrambled out of bed and tiptoed to her parents bed and the chest on the far side. Jane's petticoat was indeed there. And the allotted coins for rent and food and school and doctor were still neatly tied into knots at the hem. She folded the garment into the paper and pushed it into the back of a drawer. Slowly she climbed back into bed and hugged Sarah.

'Why do you think she did that, Sarah? Does it mean Ma won't be coming back? Do you think that, Sary?'

'I'm no good at thinking, you know that. Let's try to sleep and see what tomorrow brings.'

Laura heard the church clock chime three. She crept out of bed. She stopped by her parents bed but it was empty. She cautiously opened the kitchen door. George was bent over the table, his head resting on his arms. Stealthily Laura filled a pan with water and placed it on the hob; she gently raked the embers.

George stirred. 'What is it, girlie?'

'Time for you to get ready to go to market, Pa. I'm just heating some water for your shave.'

'I can't work today. My heart's too heavy.'

'There's your wages, Pa. You'll have to go to get your wages. And you stop at twelve on a Saturday.'

George put up no resistance to his daughter's persuasion. He washed and shaved without protest. It was good not to think.

He worked like an automaton: lifting, carrying, stacking, lifting, carrying, stacking. Keep working, keep busy, no time to think. He didn't even take time to eat his jam and bread, it was still in his pocket when he lined up at the foreman's office to collect his wages. Most casuals were paid daily but once you got on to a regular gang, your time was added up each day and you got paid at the end of the week. Saturdays the market closed at midday instead of two o'clock.

George got the train back to Stratford. Instead of taking the tram for home, he walked to The Broadway and turned into Great Eastern Road. He looked at each building as he walked along. Then he saw the sign. Golden scrolls surrounded the words: GAIETY LODGINGS. He walked past it; then back again and past it up to The Broadway again. He turned back and resolutely strode up the short flight of stone steps to the double doors. There was no knocker, no bell cord to pull, so he pushed open one half of the doors and stood on the mat in the lobby. A variety of sounds came from all parts of the house: a fiddle playing a jig, a soprano just missing the high notes, a dog barked somewhere, and voices laughing. He strained his ears but he couldn't identify Jane's voice.

'What, Ho! dearie. Now, let me guess. You'd be conjuror. No. Not a singer, you don't look a singer. What about a strong man? You look as if you've got some good muscles. I'm, Mrs Shipton, dearie. And who am I addressing?'

'My name's Stringer.' He paused and looked at Mrs Shipton but the name didn't register with her, he was sure. 'I wondered, Madam, if I could have a word with

Bessie. I believe she works here. I don't know her other
name. she's a friend of Mrs Stringer,' he added quickly
as Mrs Shipton had nodded slyly.

'Of course. Come into the parlour and sit down. I'm
not sure where Bess is at the moment.'

Bessie hurried into the parlour. 'Pleased to meet
you, I'm sure, Mr Stringer. We haven't spoken before
but I did see you last year, wasn't it, at the bonfire welcoming the century.' She held out her hand.

This wasn't what he was expecting. He stared
wretchedly at her.

'What is it, Mr Stringer? Jane's all right isn't she?
Nothing's happened to her?' Bessie covered her face.
'Don't tell me bad news.'

'I came to you in the hope you could tell me, Bessie.
She's gone. I don't know where she is. I'd hoped she
was here with you. Didn't mean to trouble you.'

He rushed out before Bessie could see his tears.

Laura ran to meet him. 'Pa, you're late. I thought
you'd...' She went ahead of him and stood, as Jane
always stood on pay days, just inside the door. 'Did
you get your wages?' Just as Jane always asked.

George took the money from his pocket and laid it in
a row on the table as usual. Laura tried to remember
how much her mother took and how much she left for
George. Her hand tentatively took a couple of florins
and half crown; that would do for the rent. Then she
realised she had to buy food, so quickly took another
florin and half crown.

'We'll leave you for your doze as usual, Pa' Laura
said picking up the basket. 'Come on Georgie, you can
help me. We won't be long Pa.'

'You wanted to try out my new top yesterday.' Vily
was jumping up and down from the kerb.

Several of the neighbours were gossiping nearby as
Laura came out onto the pavement.

'Shame your Ma gave up the washing. Can't get my old man's shirts clean like she could. What she put in the water?'

'Why didn't you come out to play yesterday, Laura?'

Her cheeks were on fire. She couldn't speak. Somehow she felt they all knew her mother had left them.

* * * * *

A hushed cathedral reverence pervaded the lobby. Messenger boys scampered about on tip toe; the reception clerk spoke in a whisper. Even the trio in the tea salon played a muted tune; perhaps because there was no audience today so they did not have to compete with the chattering ladies. Today, the ladies with their unmarried daughters on view took tea on the front terrace. Large hats protected fragile skin from the golden rays of sun shafting between the dappled shadows of two large oaks at each side of the stepped entrance. A fishy seaweed smell wafting in on a light breeze wrinkled one or two noses but most chose to ignore it.

Clip clopping horses drew open carriages up and down the esplanade and the ladies took especial interest in those which contained only male occupants. Except when a landau stopped at the hotel entrance and a liveried footman lowered the step and assisted the elegant lady to descend. Her pink velvet jacket, with dark blue braiding, nipped acutely in at the waist, showed off her bust to perfection. Dark blue voile ruching edged the plunging neckline to contrast fine white skin. A narrow pink velvet hat perched jauntily on her pale golden curls. The pink velvet skirt swirled about her ankles as her heeled shoes beat a tattoo on the pavement.

'Have you found out who she is?' one lady asked.

'Her name is Mrs Ellen Stapleton-Clarke. But that is all the information I have been able to obtain. However, I have left my card at her rooms.'

The previous day, after taking possession of her suite, Jane had opened her trunk. Her hired maid wouldn't arrive until noon. She spread the items over the bed and chairs and surveyed her purchases. The wine red serge costume she'd travelled in had cost thirty shillings: the pink velveteen suit, two pounds ten shillings. A yellow nankeen cloth dress had been at the sale price of ten and sixpence. Unlike her mother's designs for personal customers, all of these were ready made bought in department stores. Except one. That was still in its covering.

There were chemises, nightdresses, camisoles, vests, cotton hose, petticoats, drawers, corsets. Such an army of wearing apparel Jane hadn't seen the like of. But it was necessary to keep up the appearance of elegance. She fingered the soft silk sleeved bodice and glowed at the imagined feel of it against her skin. She'd felt quite brazen walking into the bank where Frederick had deposited her inheritance and announced she wished to make a withdrawal from her account. But she had been greeted most courteously and shown into a small office to be seated at a table.

'Yes, Madam,' the man had said. 'How much would Madam like? And what denomination notes would Madam like?' His smile hadn't faltered as she'd said 'Fifty pounds'.

It had been a comfortable journey; the London, Brighton and South Coast Railway was fast and efficient and travelling in the Pullman Car was most pleasant. Brighton Station was a magnificent structure built on a rounded bend tucked into the hillside, just ten minutes walk from the sea front. Not that Jane walked!

Her maid greeted her. 'Oo, ma'am, Lady Betterton has left her card and Mrs the Honorable Pitcher-fford. Two small f's. Isn't that funny?'

Jane collapsed on the chaise-longe and kicked off her shoes.

The maid eyed the reclining figure. 'The ladies are taking tea on the terrace.'

'Yes, I know. I saw them.'

'Well, might I suggest ma'am you put your shoes back on and go down to them?'

Jane obediently put on her shoes, smoothed her skirt and made her way to the lift. The attendant smiled when he saw his passenger and opened the latticed gate.

'Afternoon, ma'am, lovely weather it is today don't you think.'

'Yes, truly delightful. Oh, may we go back up I have forgotten something.'

In the room, she quickly retrieved her gloves and pulled them on. She'd spent a week rubbing cut raw potato followed by half a lemon over her palms, between her fingers and over the backs. Next came goose grease before covering them with strips of linen and sitting idle for an hour before starting all over again to produce a lady's hands suitable to greet the fashionable visitors to Brighton. But she knew it hadn't been long enough to remove all the work worn creases.

The attendant had held the lift for her. Several tables were occupied on the terrace. A large circular one was presided over by Lady Betterton who was holding forth on some particular subject. Her associates avidly listened to every word and nodded in agreement. A smaller table beyond was occupied by four ladies and two young girls. They were much amused by the antics of those at the larger table. As Jane stepped on to the terrace, one of the ladies stood up and inclined her head. Jane threaded her way between the tables and was about to pass behind the speaker at the large table. All the listeners immediately switched their attention. The voice continued for a few more seconds. Without turning, Lady Betterton thrust out her ivory handled parasol effectively blocking Jane's passage.

'Ah, Mrs Stapleton-Clarke. How very kind of you to respond so promptly. A virtue sometimes ignored in today's society. Bring another chair,' she signalled a hovering waiter. 'You will take tea, won't you?'

Jane glanced across to the other table. The lady, and Jane presumed she must be Mrs the Honourable Pitcher-fford with two small f's, was still standing beside her chair. The look of fury was quickly replaced by guile.

'Lady Betterton, I do believe Mrs Stapleton-Clarke was approaching my table. However, so we may all officially meet Mrs Stapleton-Clarke, shall we ask the staff to put our two tables together? Excellent.'

With much shuffling, the tables were pushed against each other and the chairs spread out in two long lines on either side. In the relocation Jane found she had been conveniently sandwiched between the two battle-axes. The whole situation was so amusing, she had to hold herself in check or she would burst out laughing.

'I believe the Stapleton-Clarkes are Sussex family,' Countered Mrs the Honourable Pitcher-fford.

Jane waited but no-one else volunteered other alternatives. 'My grandmother told me the Stapletons came from Suffolk but no doubt the family spread around a bit.' She quickly changed the subject. 'Isn't the weather delightful today. It was so exhilarating driving along the sea front.'

'It has certainly enhanced your delightful complexion. You are really quite a beauty. And to be widowed so young.'

Jane blushed. As she was here on her own they had assumed her husband was dead.

Lady Betterton, who long ago married off her daughters, glanced mischievously at the mothers round the table. 'Mrs Stapleton-Clarke presents strong competitions do you not think?' She smiled graciously at her audience. 'I shall be pleased if you will be among my party tomorrow at the Pavilion. There is to be entertainment and dancing for the young ones. There is a rumour His Majesty King Edward may be present.'

A gasp ran round the table.

'How convenient, Lady Betterton. I, too shall be present tomorrow with my guests. As it has been such a happy gathering today, let us arrange to have combined tables tomorrow.' Mrs the Honourable Pitcherfford had the final word.

As last when her maid had gone out to purchase supper and she was alone, Jane laughed out loud. But it was a hollow laugh and the mirth turned to sadness. Unbidden, tears trickled down her cheeks.

She revelled in the luxury of lying in bed. Bright golden arrows shot across the room as the sun peeped through the partially shuttered windows. Vying with its glittering rays, her pale amber hair lay spread about the fat pillow and radiated its own warm glow. She stretched like a cat and grinned smugly at the prospect of the afternoon. She stirred from her reverie when she heard the outer door open and the next moment her maid bobbed her head round the bedroom door.

'You getting up, me lady?'

'No, Lucy. I shall have my breakfast in bed.'

'Tain't much of a breakfast. Just what you told me to buy. You should've come out with me to the pie shop.

They served a spanking plate and all for fourpence. This would hardly keep body and soul together.'

She unwrapped the slices of bead and dripping and laid it on the counterpane in front of Jane. Lucy couldn't make out her employer. All the other ladies she'd worked for never sat and had a good chin-wag like she was a friend. And she'd never heard of a LADY asking for and eating bread and dripping. Mind you, they didn't know what they were missing. Lucy liked Mrs Stapleton-Clarke. It was such a pity the employment was for one week only; she'd have liked to work for this lady forever.

Jane dressed with care: each petticoat being smoothed down by Lucy before another one was added. After the last layer, she stepped into the gown and Lucy pulled it up and buttoned the tiny glass beads at the back. Ballooning out the skirts over a stool, Jane sat at the mirror while Lucy did her hair. The fine silken strands were looped up into elegant coils on top of her head. Her complexion needed no aid of rouge or powder. The velvety skin, with its soft sprinkling of freckles across her nose and tumbling onto her cheekbones, glowed.

'Oo, me lady! You look a real treat. I bet the King himself will be dazzled by you.'

Jane laughed. But she was well pleased with her reflection. The dark green of her taffeta dress accentuated the natural paleness of her skin. The sleeves, a shortened version of leg o' mutton, tightened in mid-arm to reveal her dimpled elbows and the broad cut of the neckline extended to her shoulders but didn't plunge too deeply. Her white neck was unadorned with jewellery but nestling at her bosom was a handsome ruby and pearl brooch.

She glided along the corridor and stood near the lift entrance. As the gated contraption rose up to her level the attendant let out a gasp of admiration. He was too dumb struck to respond to her friendly greeting. She exited into the foyer and the hubbub stopped. The ladies and daughters made a path for her and she swept along, nodding graciously left and right, until she was before Lady Betterton.

Lady Betterton looked her up and down approvingly and almost miowed at the other ladies.

'How splendid you look, my dear. And that is an exquisite brooch. Come along, my carriage is at the door.'

The carriages left in convoy and followed along the seafront.

'I fear Brighton is losing some of its charm,' Lady Betterton commented.

'The railways now bring in the lower classes. I think this shall be my last season.' She languidly waved her hand in acknowledgement of the strolling gentlemen who raised their top hats as she passed but she knew their courtesy was directed at her companion.

The carriages rolled up the gravel pathway to the Pavilion, disgorging the ladies on arrival. Inside the attendance room the tables had been placed around the sides leaving a space in the centre for performers. At one side golden tasselled ropes enclosed one large and two smaller tables separating them from the rest. Lady Betterton and Jane had paused by the entrance to greet the following ladies who then moved on inside. When Jane finally entered the room most tables were occupied. She glanced round the room and her gaze came to rest on the Mrs Honourable Pitcher-fford. Her face was livid with fury as she watched Lady Betterton move across the royal enclosure. Lady Betterton flicked open her fan and inclined her head in recognition then turned back to usher Jane to her table.

It was a boring afternoon. An acrobat and a juggler did little to enliven the time. Many gentlemen came to the table to be introduced to Jane and after each one had left, Lady Betterton gave her a resume of his family background, his fortune and his attributes as a prospective husband.

'Don't give any time to him,' she'd say behind her fan, while eyes smiled above it at the poor unsuspecting suitor. 'He'll gamble away his fortune before he's thirty.'

'Nor him, he has a weak stomach. Doubt if he'd give you a child.'

'He is worthwhile, but he is already betrothed to another fortune in Ireland.'

There was a lethargy in the room. Even the flunkies serving tea did so with a wearisome manner. Everyone had been expecting the King to grace the proceedings with his company but he hadn't appeared. Someone said he'd been seen at the racecourse.

'My dear Aunt. All I heard was true. They said you had given your patronage to the most beautiful girl in Brighton. And to be sure, you have.'

Lady Betterton laughed delightedly. 'Horace! I had no idea you were in Brighton. Where are you staying? Not at the Grand for that is where we are. You are very naughty not to have made yourself known before. I have spent many a languorous afternoon until,' she paused and looked at Jane, 'until the arrival of this delightful creature.'

Under the intense scrutiny of both aunt and nephew, Jane felt a flush spreading across her cheeks.

'Mrs Stapleton-Clarke, may I present my nephew, Horace Bettereton. He is the son of my husband's brother. He has no title, nor any likelihood of acquiring one. He has a sizeable fortune in his own right and will inherit considerable wealth from his father. As you will observe, my dear Mrs Stapleton-Clarke, he is endowed with good stature and a pleasant countenance but he is a scoundrel.' Although he smiled as she made the remark, her voice held a tone of anxiety.

At the start of the introduction, Horace had bowed to Jane and as he lifted his head, his gaze rested on her face and didn't falter. He had approached their table from the rear and now he stood in front of Jane. His hand cupped under her elbow directed her upwards.

'Mrs Stapleton-Clarke, will you promenade with me?'

A group of acrobats were turning somersaults in the centre of the Assembly Room while at the perimeter couples sauntered around, occasionally greeting acquaintances.

Horace Betterton was tall, his muscular figure bulged under the close fitting frock coat. His pale complexion was heightened by a mass of fair curly hair. Brilliant blue eyes completed his handsome appearance.

'Did you believe all my aunt said?' he asked.

'Of course! Your aunt is a lady of integrity.'

Horace laughed. He paused to look directly at her. 'What a delight you are, Mrs Staple...No! I refuse to go on calling you that.' He had tucked her hand very effectively under his arm making it difficult for Jane to move without causing a commotion. 'Ellen – you see how bold I am. I insist you allow me to accompany you to the races tomorrow afternoon and permit me to call for you tomorrow night.'

'Unless you release my hand, Sir, I doubt if there will be life in the body sufficient to attend you a step further.'

With good humour he eased his grip and they continued their perambulation. Horace was an agreeable companion with diverse matters of conversation and a fund of amusing stories that Jane couldn't help but laugh. Lady Betterton had watched them from the moment they left the table and nodded. They made an elegant couple and, Lady Betterton schemed, maybe the young widow would be just the one to capture her eligible nephew.

Horace had deposited Jane back at the table after informing his aunt he would call for both ladies tomorrow as the day was his. In spite of herself, Jane had enjoyed being with him and she looked forward to tomorrow. A scraping of chairs drew Lady Bettertons attention. She hastily collected her bag from the table and tapped Jane's arm with her fan. The stood up to leave and gained the centre of the room before anyone else. Once again Lady Betterton had scored over Mrs the Honourable Pitcher-fford whose party was forestalled from leaving first.

Back at the hotel Lady Betterton affirmed it would definitely be her last season here.

'So little excitement this year,' she said. 'Thank goodness there is just one more day and then we can leave. At least Horace will enliven matters tomorrow. I shall rest until two. Please send word with your maid when you are ready,'

After she'd undressed, Jane rested on the bed. She had enjoyed the latter part of the afternoon, once Horace had arrived. He was witty and charming and very handsome. Tomorrow promised to be most interesting.

What started as a light drizzle in the morning soon developed into steady rain by midday. Lady Betterton's maid came with the news that the afternoon's excursion to the racecourse was cancelled.

Jane leant on the window sill. The view presented a dismal sight; no carriages passing by, no pedestrians on the path ways. The continuous rain had washed puddles into large pools. 'It must stop before tonight,' she muttered fiercely, 'it must.'

She took the parcel from her trunk and shook it out. The cotton dust cover was a little wrinkled as she laid it on the bed. Hesitantly she removed the dress. Her fingers caressed the crepe backed satin. Matilda's last creation.

As she and Emily had cleared Matilda's own rooms, each had taken a few items. Jane had taken the wash stand with basin and pitcher; Emily took the two basket chairs. Neither for them had use for the heavy cumbersome bed which Matilda had removed from West Street. And then Jane had descended into the work shop. Frederick had found a garment maker in Whitechapel to take all the remaining dress making paraphernalia. She had seen the sketch in the work shop propped up on an easel. It had startled her to see her own face on the model.

'Alice,' Jane called, 'will you come here please?'

'Yes Mrs Stringer.'

'This drawing.' She gave a half laugh in embarrassment. 'It looks like me, doesn't it?'

'Of course it's you, Mrs Stringer. All S.I.D's is you. *S.I.D. – Special Individual Design.* It always is, except when Missis G was making something for the older ladies or ones like a dollop of lard,' she laughed.

Alice took a pile of cardboard drawings from a cupboard.

'See. Here you are in a winter cape. Here you are in a pretty summer dress and here you are in an elegant ball gown. Always it was you, Mrs Stringer. Mrs Goult used to say if she couldn't see you in it in her mind's eye she wouldn't make the outfit.'

'This one,' Jane said, her voice breaking with emotion, 'do you know if it was commissioned?'

'Oh, no Mrs Goult liked to try her hand at sketching even if it wasn't ordered.'

'So it was never made up then?'

'It was. I modelled it. But I wasn't the right shape

for it.' She glanced down at her rather flat chest. 'It's not quite finished.'

From a hook behind the door, Alice lifted down a cotton sack and undid a string. As it fell away, a shimmering pearl grey straight dress was revealed.

'It will never be finished now,' Alice sobbed.

'Alice. Finish it for me, please.'

Clothed in just a chemise and drawers, Jane held the dress in front of her. There were no petticoats or underskirts to put on, just an under dress of grey silk that fell straight down from thin shoulder straps. She slipped the dress over her head. The soft texture of the material clung to the contours of her body. Tiny pleats fell diagonally across the chest from a pearl cluster at the shoulder and were caught high under the bosom by another pearl cluster. Strands of grey silk, of the under dress material, trailed from the shoulders to serve as sleeves. A sash tied the dress at the back accentuating the long drop of the front. Style and design were totally new, unlike anything currently worn. 'Oh, Madam,' Lucy exclaimed, 'I've never seen anything so lovely as that dress nor anyone as beautiful as you wearing it.'

Jane turned and hugged her. 'Thank you. At least you weren't shocked.'

'No but I reckon some of them old biddies will be when you turn up at the ball. Mr Horace will be over the moon but he'll have to fight off all the other blokes,' Lucy laughed.

With tender care, Lucy brushed Jane's hair. The soft amber gold strands were loosely plaited and coiled into a long loop before being pinned in place on top of her head. At the side small ringlets cascaded above her ears.

No jewellery, not even the pearl and ruby brooch,

were needed. Jane's natural beauty presented a stunning picture.

There was a tap at the door and Lucy opened it. 'Will you tell your mistress the coach awaits her below.'

With a light woollen shawl about her shoulders, Jane made her way to the lift. The attendant bowed her in. His mouth dropped open and his eyes nearly popped out as he stared at her from head to toe.

In the lobby, Horace waited opposite the lift exit. As it arrived and the gates opened, his good manners prevented a similar performance to that of the attendant.

Chapter 8

For a moment Jane thought he would refuse to escort her. But as his eyes travelled up to her face she saw approval there. He grinned broadly at her and extended his arm.

'I am proud and honoured that you, Ellen, should have permitted me to accompany you tonight.'

Horace led her to the waiting coach with its hood down. The dense rain clouds had disappeared and the sky was forget-me-knot blue. Daylight still lingered about the horizon. They turned away from the sea shore, up past the Royal Pavilion into the open countryside. The moist grass gave a fresh clean smell to the air and warm currents drifted about them as the coach moved forward at a steady pace. Horace still had his arm linked with hers, as his hand came to rest on her bare skin Jane felt a tingle run through her. She was aware Horace was studying her and she dared not turn to look at him. With relief, she saw lights ahead and then the coach turned into the driveway of Pendlegate Hall.

They hadn't spoken since their first greeting. They were silent still as they walked up the marble steps to the terrace and across to the brightly lit entrance hall. Jane was in a trance. For the first time since her expedition had begun, she felt she was losing control of the situation. Everything had been so clear at the start. There had been a purpose and a goal. Tonight was the end; tomorrow Ellen Stapleton-Clarke would be no more. She held her head up and fixed a smile on her face: she must play her part.

Horace led her forward. The footman took his hat and gloves and Jane's shawl. He released her hand and stepped ahead. He bowed.

'Good evening, Lord Grissom: Lady Grissom. May I present Mrs Ellen Stapleton-Clarke?'

Jane moved forward beside Horace and dipped a curtsy. As she came up her eyes met Lady Grissoms's.

'My dear, I am pleased to meet you. May I say you look exquisite. Your style of dress is most unusual. But far more comfortable, I am sure, that these cumbersome garments. You must give me the name of your dressmaker.'

'I should be honoured, Lady Grissom, if that were possible. Sadly, she has passed away.'

'No matter, my dear. I doubt if my generous proportions would be enhanced by such clothing.'

Jane smiled graciously. She had got over the threshold; her hostess had not spurned her. Her arrival in the ballroom created a sensation. Horace deliberately paused at the entrance to make sure all the guests looked at his partner. Several ladies gasped in disapproval and lifted their fans to blot out the vision. The pearl grey dress outlined the perfect contour of Jane's ample bosom and long legs. They manoeuvred around the dancers, to reach Lady Betterton's table but Horace barely paused in greeting before he swept Jane into his arms and whirled her across the floor. As they glided past his friends, Horace was badgered for an introduction. He laughed in delight that he had the belle of the ball. There were many demands on her for dances and she was always the centre of a cluster of young ardent men but Horace was always by her side.

'No, the next dance is mine,' Horace insisted.

He took her gently in his arms. Gradually, he held her closer. His lingering look of tenderness made her blush; he drew her still closer until their bodies touched. Her breasts tautened as they pressed against his chest and, under the thin clinging material of her dress, she had no doubt Horace was aware, too. His hand slid down her back to press her against his thighs when his legs moved forward in the dance. Jane twisted about and pulled away from him.

With his head bent, he murmured an apology. 'I beg you to forgive me, Ellen. Emotion runs riot within me. I don't wish to offend you.'

She was startled by his contrition. She had expected arrogance from him or boldness implying the blame was hers for dressing as a brazen hussy. They stood in silence: Horace's shoulders drooped in abject wretchedness; Jane, paralysed at the revelation. A dancing pair almost collided with them drawing them back to reality. She placed her hand on his shoulder and extended her arm. They danced in silence until the music stopped. Horace led her back to Lady Betterton's table and excused himself. There was a babble of voices about her but Jane heard nothing. Her mind was in a turmoil. She was bemused; for one delirious moment he had evoked a response within her – but only for a moment. Jane felt a deep compassion for Horace. She hadn't expected him to fall in love with her. When his aunt had described him as a scoundrel, Jane had thought him to be the ideal companion for her last days in Brighton. He would treat her as a passing fancy and she could easily cope with such advances. Now she was not so sure.

The rest of the evening passed agreeably. Horace

had recovered his composure and was in high spirits relating witty stories to Jane and their companions. A gradual dwindling of number showed it was time to go. They bid their hosts farewell and climbed into the carriage. At the hotel he led her into the foyer toward the lift. Jane held out her hand.

'Horace, I want to thank you for a most delightful evening.' Her voice was brightly casual.

Bent over her hand, he straightened abruptly at her tone. His eyes searched her face trying to define her meaning. The sadness in his eyes bore into her heart. She could face him no longer, withdrawing her hand from his she stepped into the lift.

'Indeed a delight, Ellen,' he said brusquely; bowed and walked away.

* * * * *

He didn't want to be late in. He'd promised Laura: only a half pint after work. But today, Ginger Baker was celebrating having a son after six girls, well George couldn't refuse to join in wetting the baby's head. After several pints of ale, and hurrying to get indoors, he was sweating profusely. In the coolness of the hallway, he mopped his brow with his neckerchief. As his hand came away from his eyes he saw a movement at the end of the passage. The kitchen door was ajar.

'How are you, my dear?' she asked.

'Chipper. And yourself?'

'Well.'

It was a stupid conversation for husband and wife. Jane reached for a pot.

'I'll start getting supper, shall I? I see Laura has done shopping.' She paused with the pot suspended in mid air. 'Or would you like us to talk?'

George scuffed his boots nervously as he stood

framed in the doorway. He'd never been good at talking.

'Are you staying?'

'Yes, George.'

'No need for talking then.'

The love within her was almost stifling. She smiled contentedly to herself. For a fleeting moment she had been aroused by Horace, had been eager to answer his kiss but it was soon over. Only one man could cause an aching response to his caress and now she gazed on that dear face.

George sat in his chair at the table and produced his crumpled newspaper.

The laundry room was in the basement but it wasn't a gloomy place even in late November. Windows on two sides filled it with light. One looked out onto Great Eastern Road across the stair well and the other onto the steps from the side alley. Mrs Skipton employed two young girls as well as Jane. Although they giggled a lot, Jane found they were good workers. They arrived before her and filled the large coppers with water ready for Jane to light the gas jets underneath them, a task that filled her with dread. At Maryland laundry, metal braziers stuffed with coals and wood under the tubs heated the water. She'd get the longest possible taper, stretch her arm to its limit, close her eyes and poke the light in what she hoped was the direction of the hissing gas: it always gave a mighty bang. And sent the girls into great gusts of laughter.

Maggie Short, the older of the pair, wiped her eyes. 'You look a right caution, you do, Mrs Stringer.'

'Right caution,' echoed Sally Weeks,

'You should be along of them upstairs on the boards, doing a turn.'

'Doing a turn,' repeated Sally.

The girls sat at the bench and sorted through the

washing separating the lodging house laundry from guests personal washing, while Jane grated the soap. Bed linens and table clothes were paddled in the two largest tubs and allowed to boil; personal clothing was immersed in the smaller wooden vessel then quickly rinsed. Even in winter, it was very hot in the basement room when it was filled with steam. Underneath the front window they could watch the feet of those passing along Great Eastern Road.

'There goes Mr Brown Boots.'

'Church clock will chime eight,' Sally added. 'Hark, there it goes!' she squealed delightedly. 'Dunno what would happen if he was late.'

It was a pleasant place to be and Jane enjoyed the three days she spent at *Gaiety Lodgings*. Mrs Shipton was a good employer and the regular money it brought in was a Godsend. She still did washing at home for her own customers but sometimes they didn't pay up at the end of the week. At midday, they had a break for something to eat and while the girls stayed in the laundry room, Jane went upstairs to the scullery to sit with Bessie. It was good to have a companion to talk to. Bessie hadn't questioned her when she had arrived at the kitchen door and asked for a job. She had welcomed her in and merely asked if she had lodgings. She showed no surprise at her answer. Telling Bessie made it easier afterwards to tell George.

'I know it hurt him, Bessie, going off like I did.'

'He thought you'd run off with your first lodger bloke, Reg Packard. He came here asking if I knew where you were. I had to say in all truth I didn't.'

'I'm sorry I caused him so much pain. But I couldn't explain it beforehand and I'm not sure it makes much sense now. It was while I was going through Mother's things after she died. There was so much about her I didn't know. Well, like Frederick Bourne. I never guessed there was a man friend. She was like a stranger. And it was my fault. I never understood what I meant to my mother. Oh, I know she'd always wanted me to marry some fine gentleman and she was greatly disappointed I settled on George. I thought she'd cast me out of her life after that but all the while she was sort of daydreaming of me as a lady. So as a homage to Matilda I want off and lived the life she had wished for me.' Jane laughed self-consciously but tears glistened in her eyes. 'I wish I'd known her better.'

Bessie patted her arm. 'I think it was a nice thing you did for your Ma and no mistake.'

When they were in bed, Jane calmly told George everything. Even about Horace. For a moment he had lain quite still, then he turned onto his side, slid his leg over hers and put his arm across her waist: his usual position, and nodded off to sleep.

Ropes were strung across the room to take the lines after they'd gone through the mangle. Jane wrung out the more delicate fabrics and put them on the wooden clothes horse in the corner.

'Time for a break, girls. Take the weight off your feet for a bit.'

As she mounted the stairs, Jane was bombarded with oranges. The dwarf scampered down to retrieve the fruit.

'Ever so sorry, Mrs String. I was practising a bit of juggling. I was in the way in the parlour, Mrs Ship said. I was in the way in the kitchen Bess says, so I thought I'd try it on the steps. Were you hurt at all?'

'I'm all right, Tinker. But don't you think it would be easier to start with just three oranges?'

'No point in trying something that's easy, now is there?'

Jane left him collecting up the scattered oranges

and went to the scullery. Bessie had put out two mugs of ale and was cutting slices of bread.

'We got a nice bit of dripping from the joint Missus had yesterday for Sunday dinner. Sit yourself down, Jane. How are things going, dearie? Girls all right?

Jane grinned to herself. Bessie was such a considerate person. Always on a Monday she would ask how she had fared since seeing her last Wednesday night, as if it had been a month or more.

'Laura has her head stuck in a book and Sarah's head is stuck in the clouds. Nothing's changed, Bessie,' she laughed.

'And George?'

A soft smile spread over her face. 'As loving and loveable as always. You should find a nice young man. Settle down and have a family of your own.'

'I'm content for each day. I want nothing more than a bed and some grub. And here I've got everything I want.'

Yes, it was important to have a full belly. Bessie knew that only too well. When Jane left the Workhouse for the laundry, Bessie, then a scraggy, tousled haired girl of sixteen, had taken care of her and baby Georgie. She'd been at the laundry for five years: Heaven after scavenging as a street urchin for as long as she could remember. Those years of living on her wits had aged and matured Bessie beyond her twenty years.

'Do you know, Bessie, I felt sorry for those high born ladies I met in Brighton.'

'Sorry for them! Well, that's a rum to-do.'

'Their only concern is for money and position. Their parents selected a husband who had money and position for them to marry and produce an heir who'd add to their standing. And they do the same for their daughters. The way they were assessing potential husbands was no better than the way a cattle breeder selects a prize stud. Without feeling.' Jane's gaze hovered in the distance. 'But, to lie with a man you love: to feel that fierce ache of longing in the pit of your stomach that will only be satisfied by him: to join him in surging passion – not merely submit to provide an heir.'

Bessie's face had gone scarlet. 'You still feel that for George, do you?' she asked in awe.

'More than ever,' Jane said but she was struck by Bessie's tone. 'I'm sorry to have embarrassed you. Shouldn't have spoken my thoughts, Bessie, you being a single girl.'

'Weather's taken a turn for the worse,' Mrs Shipton said, coming into the kitchen. 'Fog. Best be off home, Mrs Stringer. It looks like it'll be a thick pea souper. If it's still bad in the morning, don't come in. Leave it to later in the week.'

'Trams will run and that's a cert. So I'll be here at seven thirty as usual, Mrs Shipton. But, thank you, I'll get off now and meet the children from school.'

'I'll tell the girls to finish up on their own,' Bessie said.

Gaiety Lodgings was only a short distance down Great Eastern Road but once outside the comforting glow of its lights the street was an opaque vacuum. Jane held her hand out to the railings to guide her along but at the corner she had to cross over to the right side. Placing one foot in front of the other she slowly arrived on the far side and gratefully grasped the railings before turning into The Broadway and The Grove. The tram for home started at Maryland Point Station; she could usually walk the quarter of a mile distance in as many minutes each morning and evening. Not tonight. The straight road developed corners she'd never known before. People cannoned into each other and got spun around; they had to ask which way they were heading. Clanking wheels announced tramcars were operating: good old LCC. Jane gratefully got aboard. Shops and buildings along Leytonstone Road were invisible beyond the tram windows.

'Are we at Crownfield Road, yet?' she asked the driver.

'Not yet, missus. I'll call out when we get there.'

'How will you know?' an old gent growled.

'Vibrations, that's how I'll know. My hands on the steering wheel will feel when we cross over east track. Course, it'd a piece of cake if I still had horses. They know every inch of road. There!' He grinned over his shoulder. 'Knew I'd feel it. *Thatched House* next stop, missus.'

As the fog thickened it gathered up all the smoke and fumes and stirred it around in an aerial cauldrom. It was compressed from above down to street level. There was no brisk breeze to swirl it away.

'Sorry,' Jane called as she bumped into someone.

'Is that you Mrs Stringer?'

'Yes, who...Ah! Mrs Walters.'

'I've collected the children. Your three are home.'

For three days the fog brought chaos to London streets causing untold accidents. A child was trampled underfoot when a horse shied up in fright and stampeded into a nearby group of women; the child's hand was wrenched from the mother's grasp.

George got up each morning as usual. Trams and trains were operating but at haphazard times. Even when he arrived at Spittalfields, there was no work as delivery carts were unable to get into the city. Jane took Mrs Shipton at her word and remained at home; there were her own clients to wash for. Laura and Sarah joined their friends in the street playing *Blind Man's Bluff* without being blindfolded. Georgie was kept indoors because of his delicate chest.

As silently as it came, so it went. A light breeze in the night cleared the air. Fog gave way to frost and by Christmas the winter had set in. It was so cold in January, even though he scavenged amongst all the sweepings, her Pa could find no violets for Laura's ninth birthday.

'But you always bring me violets, Pa.'

'Indeed I do, girlie, but there were none at market today.' He moved over to Jane. 'Foreman said not to go in tomorrow. There'd be no work.'

'Ever since before Christmas, George, you've been one or two days short. And now, it's three.'

'What can I do, love. If there's no work, there's no work.'

'I'm not blaming you, dearest. It's not your fault.'

'I know we were saving up so as to move higher up the road but we'll have to give it a miss for another year.'

It had taken her months of coaxing to get George to consider a change and only then, when Jane said they'd save up the first two month's rent before the move. Now, the opportunity had slipped away before they'd had a chance. Without George's wages, their meagre savings would have to be used for day to day living. She had considered raising the lodger's rent but couldn't put it up by more than a few coppers which wouldn't go far. And she didn't fancy being on the receiving end of Cecil Styles tongue. He was such a nasty man; often she'd thought of giving him notice but she'd have to find another lodger and one who might not pay as prompt as Mr Styles.

Her plans had been made: move at the end of February. She had already approached the rent collector who told her she could move any time as Number Four downstairs was vacant. Two more weeks and they would have already been living at Number Four.

Jane undressed ready for bed. Perhaps it was just as well they'd stayed put. She rolled down her woollen stockings and for a fleeting moment her hands imagined the silk of the stockings she'd worn under the grey dress. Soft as gossamer, shimmering as liquid silver. But there was no regret at the lavish expenditure on a whim. She slipped in beside George and curled into the curve of his body. He stirred slightly then sank into a deep sleep.

With the bed under the bay window, Laura was often disturbed from sleep by rowdy passers-by. Having identified the noise, she would drift back into drowsiness. She listened but there was no sound outside. Her throat was dry and her eyes stung. It seemed the fog had come back again and filtered into the house. Laura tried to bury her face to avoid breathing the acrid air. Suddenly she leapt out of bed and ran to her mother's side.

'Ma! Ma! Wake up!'

Jane was instantly awake and cross. 'Now what is it, child, that you should disturb our rest?'

'Can't you smell it, Ma? It's far worse than the fog. It makes me feel sick.'

While Laura was speaking, Jane had risen from bed. Now she was wide awake. The smell – burning – fire – was coming from upstairs.

Jane was already rousing George. 'Quick, girl! Wake up Sarah and Georgie. Get your clothes and boots on. Go next door, tell them.'

Laura darted across the room and began dressing. She shook Sarah and Georgie and made them understand it was urgent they got dressed. George opened the door into the hallway and pungent smoke rushed into the room. The upper part of the staircase was glowing rosy red.

'You, up there!' he shouted. 'Can you get out by the window?'

George banged on Styles' door. 'Get up,' he yelled. 'Fire!'

He rushed along to the kitchen but an inner caution

stopped him from opening the door. He unbolted the side door, by which the upstairs tenants gained access to the yard, and gradually eased it open. From the side he could see their kitchen was alight. A large hole in the ceiling had allowed burning material to fall into the room. Thick black smoke whirled about. At the end of the yard he looked to the upper windows. Nothing was visible. Suddenly the window blew out and great tongues of flame swathed the space.

George dashed back indoors. Styles stood in his combs. At the door.

'What's all the hullabaloo?'

'Get dressed and get out man. There's fire above.'

Styles stared at him stupidly until George shoved him out of his way.

'Gather what you can Jane.'

She started for the passage but George grabbed her shoulder.

'No, Jane. There's no hope of getting to the kitchen. Just what is in here.'

They dragged the bedding to the front door and neighbours took it and passed it on. There was a human chain passing beds and chairs: bundles of clothes; chamber pots.

'I hope they're empty, mate!'

And the laughter relieved the tension.

Laura ducked underneath the straddled legs and made for the front door. Suddenly she was scooped up and her legs were flailing the air.

'No! Missy.'

'But I must find Lucky. Our cat. He sleeps in the scullery,' she gasped out.

'He's a gonner by now.'

'No! No! He mustn't be. Not our Lucky.'

The man comforted her. 'The heat was so fierce, Missy, he wouldn't have felt pain.'

All night Laura crooned tearfully to an imagined bundle in her arms.

The fire raged for several hours. Neighbours also had to be evacuated as the intense heat made it risky to stay in the upper floors of the houses on each side of Number Twenty Six. Laura and Georgie were looked after by Vily Walter's family; Sarah went to Mrs Jarvis at Number Sixteen and Joe Grimes, the widower at Number Twenty One put up Jane and George. Their remnants of furniture were stacked in a pile by the wall.

By the grey light of morning, the charred window frames and front door looked grotesque. During the night, fire fighters had continued to dampen down the buildings on each side to contain the fire to the one house after the upper floor had collapsed. No one knew how many had died in the fire; the upstairs flat had been a regular resting place for Laskars signing off from a ship. The intensity of the heat had bonded together shapes that appeared to be bodies but the doctor couldn't be sure. One body had been pulled clear of the rubble: Cecil Styles – crushed beneath failing masonry.

George and Jane scoured the blackened embers searching for anything usable. George found their tin plates and some spoons among shards of broken china. The range had stood rock firm and, to Jane's surprise and delight, inside untouched by flames, smoke or water was the pork stew she had prepared for next day's supper. As they rummanged about, curls of dusty smoke drifted skywards. They had to be careful no to dislodge overhanging fragments of what was the upper floor. Jane paused and listened. She gripped George's arm.

'What is it, love? What's up?'

'Listen,' she whispered.

A muted scraping sound was barely audible.

'Could it be one of those Orientals is still alive?'

'Shifting debris, I shouldn't wonder,' George said. 'Best not take to long, Jane, else we might get caught...?

'Shush! It's coming from the back.'

They carefully picked their way across the kitchen area and reached the scullery,

'Look, George! The mangle! What a bit of luck – we must get that out.'

Tucked into its recess in the corner, the heavy iron mangle had escaped the fire. Wedged in front of it was a large piece of china, probably the upstairs tenants' sink. George heaved it away. From the cavity below the rollers, out stepped Lucky. His once sleek black coat covered in bits of plaster that water from the fire hoses had glued to his fur. He gave a plaintive meow and looked at them accusingly. Jane picked him up.

'Well, Laura will be pleased to see you and no mistake. She'll have something to occupy her time getting you cleaned up, my lad.'

'You're welcome to stay here as long as you like,' Joe Grimes told Jane. 'Back room is empty. Why not put your stuff in there? You can have use of the range – I don't bother much about cooking myself.'

'Very generous of you, Mr Grimes. I do appreciate your kindness. But I had a word with the rent man when he called yesterday and he is looking out a place for us.'

The rent collector had told her downstairs Number Four was still vacant. It was ironic really. They had decided... No, George had decided they couldn't afford a move to the higher rented houses at the top of the street and now they were in need of somewhere to live.

'You say the rent man has offered us another place,

then.' George was washing at the scullery sink. 'Is it far away?'

'No, not far dear. The top of the road. Number Four.'

Water dripped from his face as he turned to stare at her.

For several weeks George was silently angry. With the help of neighbours he had carried their meagre possessions up the road,

'Where do you want us to put them?' he'd asked Jane in a restrained voice.

'In the front, like always.' She'd smiled as she replied but George's tone had not escaped her notice.

Even when the weather improved and George was back in full time work, his demeanour was unchanged. At first, Jane thought he had been upset by the fire but she soon realised it was because she had gone against his wishes. A wife should not overturn a husband's decision. They had never been able to talk easily about money problems. Whatever the difficulty, George would take it personally – a reflection on his ability to support the family. Of course, that's what Matilda had thought and Jane had resented her mother's attitude. But was that so? Perhaps Matilda hadn't thought that after all.

She determined to ignore the matter. Just go on as before and wait for George to relax. The children and Lucky were happy in the new half house. Sarah liked the lavatory with pull chain which swirled water into the brown stone pan and sucked it away.

'And we haven't got those nasty foreign men peeping in at the windows.'

'You mustn't speak ill of the dead,' Jane chided her.

'It smells nicer as soon as we come in from the street,' Laura said. 'That stuff they smoked made a really horrible smell. I expect that's what started the fire.'

'That's all behind us, girls. Let's not think about it any more. We have good neighbours upstairs in the widow woman Mrs Milton and her daughter Annie. They're friendly and keep the place nice. Just look at those stairs! She must wash over the linoleum every day.'

'At school they say Annie is soft in the head,' Sarah said. 'She does really daft things. And she's twelve and still in the same class as me and I'm only ten.'

'Now, now. You must be kind to her. She doesn't have a Pa like we have. Out and play with your friends. I'm off to the union office to see about another lodger.'

In a good week, George brought home nineteen shillings and thruppence, that is if he was picked for all the five and a half days. Mrs Shipton was a good payer and Jane got one and sixpence for the three days at Gaiety Lodgings, add on the tuppence a load from her three washing customers at home and it gave them twenty-one shillings. But there were fares to pay, money for the panel doctor and schooling for the three children to come out of that sum. Then there was food to feed the family of five. To pay the six shillings each week for rent, a lodger was vital. There wasn't much in the way of furnishings for the middle room. Her mother's wash stand with basin and pitcher had perished in the fire. As it was small for the two of them now, the girl's bed could be put in and the box that had stood by Jane's bed would serve as a side chest. And, of course, it did have gas light. She could probably ask for three shillings a weeks all found, or at least two and ninepence.

'Daylight is lasting well,' Jane said. 'Don't have to light the gas mantle so early.'

George came in from market just as she was finishing off the mangling. It was good fortune they'd found the mangle. They'd brought it up the road on a hand cart.

'And, lucky for you, too, cat,' she said as it brushed against her legs. 'Laura certainly named you well. Now stop it, you'll get something to eat as soon as Laura comes in from school. Now, scoot!' She playfully raised her boot to Lucky who darted out of the way.

George stood at the sink, stripped down to his vest. Jane stood along side of him and gazed out the window.

'I'm so happy here, George. It's a nice view. We can see to all sorts of places from our window.'

George raised his hand above his eyes, like a sailor peering out to sea. 'That looks like an ordinary brick wall to me and that looks like the privy door.'

Jane burst into laughter. She couldn't stop and soon George, too, was laughing. They stood facing each other. As their amusement subsided, George drew her into his arms. His hand caressed her face; he twirled a strand of hair round his finger.

'I do love you with all my heart, my very dear George.'

His lips met hers and he kissed her fiercely until she panted for breath.

'I'll never understand you, Jane. But I'm so very happy and proud to claim you as my wife.'

He followed her out into the yard. Leaning against the wall, he watched her strong arms reach up and peg out a linen sheet on the line.

'I'll tell you one thing, George Stringer,' she called over her shoulder, 'it'll take a thunderbolt to get me to move from here.'

Chapter 9

Along the Broadway extending each side from the Town Hall, bunting was strung from the gas lamps. Boardman's, the drapers, Roberts's, the home furnishers, the newspaper offices, and especially, *the King's Head*, garlanded their windows and displayed portraits of His Majesty, King Edward the Seventh.

They had finished eating and nine year old Laura slid from her place and sidled round to her father. She was still small enough to climb up on his knee.

'Doesn't the Broadway look lovely with all the coloured streamers, Pa? Teacher told us about it today in school. The King's proper birthday is in November but he said it wasn't always nice weather in November for all the soldiers to parade for him and so he decided to have another birthday, an official one, in the summer time so everyone could enjoy it. Wasn't that nice of him?'

'Yes, my girlie,' George cuddled her close. 'The King's a very nice man to do that for us.'

'They say there may be fireworks in the park. Can we go and see it Pa? Can we?'

'If there are fireworks, yes we will go.'

'All of us, Pa. We must all go.' She looked across the

table at the slightly built man with thinning sandy coloured hair. 'You must come, too.'

He shook his head. 'Not me, lass. I don't hold with it.'

'But the King has made this a special day for everyone,' Laura persisted.

'No, lass. It doesn't help to feed the hungry nor does it put another penny in their pockets.' His voice was tinged with sadness.

'Mr Garvey. Don't spoil it for the child.' Jane said.

'I don't mean to put a damper on the child's fun, Mrs Stringer. It's just that I don't hold with royalty nor the House of Lords. I think we should be ruled by those we elect. But,' he grinned at her,' I'll try to keep my thoughts to myself when young ears are listening.'

There had been many times Jane had wished she could change her lodger. When she'd gone to the railway union offices, at first they'd said there was no-one on their waiting list. Then another man sitting in the office said,' What about Garvey? He's looking for a place. He's kipping down on the floor of the boiler room.' The union secretary had pulled a face. 'He's a bit of a hot head but very honest and clean.' He had also readily agreed to the three shillings rent. He didn't mind that the room only contained a bed, he understood about poverty and hardship. And so, David Garvey, the militant union man, had arrived at Number Four.

When he had told her his name was David he'd added: 'Always ready to take on any Goliath that comes my way,' Jane had been apprehensive. He was a quiet, kind man and always so grateful for all that Jane did for him in the way of his welfare. She felt sorry for him and in spite of herself she liked him. Except when he would go on about the conditions of the poor. Well, Jane knew all about that but there was nothing to be done about it.

'I learn all sorts of things, Mr Garvey.' Laura had slipped off George's lap and stood in front of the lodger. 'I don't just learn about kings and queens in history.'

'That's good, Miss Laura. You learn all you can because education is the key to getting away from poverty,' He blushed as he heard Jane tut-tut and quickly continued, 'tell me about what you're learning in school.'

'I learn about writing and poems,' Laura continued. 'I like Shakespeare and lots of poets. Mrs Gowrie says I can go up into the senior class in September even though shan't be ten until January. Sarah's in the class already.'

'I wonder if we'll have to parade as well,' Sarah said. 'Like on empire Day. Will we still have Empire Day now the King has a special birthday?'

'Of course, silly,' Georgie chimed in. 'They're different.' He pulled a face at his sister. 'You'll have to parade twice!'

'Well, I hope it won't be as cold as Empire Day last year. We shivered and shook having to stand about for hours. And,' she went on, 'when we came home there was no hot supper, I remember.'

It was a casual remark but it hung in the air. For a moment Jane did not connect Sarah's statement with any particular time. She was looking towards David Garvey sitting across from George. But from the corner of her eye, she saw George's shoulders straighten although he continued to look down at his paper. She sensed someone was staring at her; she turned and looked into Laura's eyes. It was a penetrating gaze, and what? A hint of accusation?

'Come and help me bring in the washing, Laura.'

Laura carried the basket into the back yard. Shirts and combinations swung jauntily from the line in the light breeze. Jane unpegged a shirt and folded the arms together, then in half and passed it to her daughter. As each item was passed to her, Laura folded it flat and pressed it into the basket.

Facing the end of the yard, Jane reached up to the line. 'It wasn't because I didn't love your Pa that I left you all last year. I had a special reason.' She folded the under garment and faced Laura. 'I love your father more than anything in this world.'

'Yes, Ma.' A small smile twisted her lips. **'I know that, Ma.'**

Laura lugged the basket towards the scullery. 'I know you love Pa,' she said to herself. 'I've seen you in the half light, when you thought everyone else was asleep. I've seen you kissing and cuddling Pa. I know you love him because you don't love Sarah or Georgie or me.' She pushed the door with her foot. 'I love Pa very much but I also love Sarah and little Georgie,' she turned to look back at Jane, 'and Ma, I love you, too,' then eased round the door.

Jane stared at the small back disappearing through the door. Sometimes Jane found it hard to explain to herself her love for George. It wasn't something that fitted easily into words. It wasn't just the exhilarating passion of his caresses. There were so many little things. Like the way he pulled at his left ear when he counted out his wages into little piles. Like the way his hair curled onto the nape of his neck. Like the way a smile crept slowly up from his lips to his eyes. And his infinite tenderness.

Sarah got her wish, there was no parade at school for the King's official birthday.

And in September, Laura got her wish and moved up to the senior class under the tuition of Mrs Gowrie.

As they'd entered the school gates, Laura had

spotted Mrs Gowrie ahead and raced forward to walk in step with her.

'Good Morning, Mrs Gowrie. I start in your class today.'

'Good Morning to you, Stringer. I am sure you will prove the Head Mistress's faith in you was not misplaced.'

Laura's heart swelled with such praise. It would mean a lot of hard work. Reading lots of books, doing a lot of writing. Not much time for playing with Sarah and Georgie and their friends in the road. But she wouldn't mind that. Books were just as good company.

Sometimes the money came in regularly; sometimes George had deductions from his wages for spoilt goods. Carrying bags of potatoes and being a bit unsteady on his pins was all right, but carrying boxes of perishables like apples or lemons and tottering meant they tipped out of the top and ended up bruised.

'If you come in the worse for drink one more time,' the ganger had said, 'I'll not be able to cover for you and you'll never get picked again. I'll have to take for spoilage, George.'

George protested to Jane, he hadn't been drunk. He had slipped on some rotten cabbage leaves, that was what made him lose his balance. He'd made a promise to Jane which he meant to keep. Jane had wanted to save enough cash to replace some of the pieces lost in the fire but there was never any to spare. A wash stand with basin and pitcher for the lodger's room would have been nice. Not that David Garvey was fussy about what was or wasn't in his room.

'He's a funny codger, Bessie.'

Jane left the two girls to eat their meal in the

laundry room and climbed the stairs to the kitchen to join Bessie.

'He's always on about workers and bosses. But there's never a question about paying his rent. And I'm glad about that. George doesn't always get picked each day. Lucky I've got this little job.'

Bessie had turned away. Jane realised she was weeping.

'Bess, girl. What's the matter? Are you ill? What is it?'

'I was going to tell you today.' Bessie reached into her apron pocket for a large piece of cotton cloth and blew her nose. 'Misses only told me yesterday. And it won't be until after Christmas. I don't know what everyone will do.'

'Sit down and tell me properly,' Jane said harshly but she had a sinking feeling in her stomach.

'Mrs Shipton is selling up and going to sea.'

'Going to see what?' Jane said in exasperation.

'No! Mrs Shipton is marrying a sea faring gent and she is going to travel with him wherever his ship goes.'

'Getting married! I thought she was set to remain a widow woman to her dying day. How did the sea faring gent get his foot in the door?'

'It was funny how it happened. You remember that terrible fog last November. Well, Amos Kerridge, that is her intended's name. Mr Kerridge was wandering along all lost. He said he could navigate on water in a fog but not on land. His ship had got some damage on his last trip and it was in the dock. He was on his way to the Mile End Seamen's Mission to tell his crew about the extra delay. He is a good man, he is. Wanted to let them know so they can sign on with another ship, if they didn't want to wait it out. Well, Tinker finds him wandering about and tells him to put his hand on the dwarf's head and he guides him to the

Gaiety. He's been staying here ever since – it's nearly a year and he and Mrs Shipton got right chummy. And now they are going to tie the knot and get wed.'

Jane slumped down on the chimney settle. It had been such a happy time, nearly eighteen months she had worked at *Gaiety Lodgings*. There were the two girls in the laundry room and always time to chat to Bessie in the kitchen. Now it was ended. Wait a minute! What were they being so gloomy for? It was only Mrs Shipton who was leaving.

'It will just mean a different employer, that's all, Bessie. They will still need laundry hands. And you'll be needed here in the kitchen or upstairs in the dining room. There'll be work for us. May be the new owners won't pay as much but we will still get wages. Come on, cheer up.' As Jane was speaking, her words lifted the gloom from her own heart.

Bessie still held the cloth to her eyes. 'No, girl. It won't be a lodging house no more. Missus sold it to an agent and he's gone and sold it to some company for offices. Offices! Why they should want offices on four floors and a basement, I can't fathom. No, Jane. Mrs Shipton is going to give you and the girls notice but she says she'll make up your wages for a full month.'

Jane's optimism had been short lived. So it was definitely the end. Well, it had been a good niche. She would have to find something else; look around at other lodging houses. There might be an opening for a laundry woman. May be she and Bessie could go as a team.

'Well, Bessie, no good crying over spilt milk. Perhaps we could find a place together – you running the kitchen and me in the laundry. Must be lots of other lodgings around.'

Bessie smiled through her tears. 'That would've

been nice. But Mrs Shipton and Amos want me to go with them. Mrs Shipton's been really good to me, treats me right friendly like. Says I'm sort of a daughter to her. And she is such a good hearted woman. I'm happy to go along. I don't know how I'll get along with all that sea around but the ship has to put into port every now and again so I can stand on firm ground. I'm not much cop at letter writing, but I'll do my best Jane and send you a line.'

It was a sad parting. The two girls and Jane received notice terminating their employment on the 28th November but Mrs Shipton kept her promise and gave the two girls an extra three weeks wages and Jane got a whole month's pay with a little bit extra as well.

Without Mrs Shipton's generosity it would have been a lean Christmas as George was laid off two days before Christmas and the ganger had said there'd be no hiring until the first week of the New Year. When market reopened, George lined up as usual. The ganger passed him by.

'Did you give me the nod, Mister?' George asked.

The ganger didn't turn round. 'Not today, Stringer,' he called over his shoulder.

For three mornings, George got the same reply.

'I got a family to feed. Can't you find me something – anything,' he pleaded.

The ganger paused. He still kept his back to George. 'Sweeper says there's a broom going spare. Shilling a day if you want it.'

Jane was at her wits' end. For three weeks George had brought home only five and sixpence from sweeping up and occasionally a few tips for running errands. Out of their meagre income she had to feed not only her family but also the lodger who was making a substantial contribution to the rent money. When supper was served, the children and herself had potatoes and gravy, George had a morsel of meat and David got the lion's share.

'Oh, Mrs Stringer,' he protested, 'you've given me far too much. Good as it's sure to be, I'll never eat all that.' And he would ladle out portions to the children and Jane. In other ways, too, David helped them out. She would find a sixpence on the mantle shelf and he would smile disarmingly and deny all knowledge of it. Or, he would give Georgie a three penny piece saying he'd found it in the kerb so take it to his Ma. David Garvey was an enigma: a gentle revolutionary.

'I come from Swindon,' he had told Jane. 'Wiltshire was farmland until cut up by the railways. Locomotive works polluted the atmosphere and destroyed our way of life. True, Great Western brought prosperity but not for the displaced farm workers only for the share holders of the railway company. Poverty is not a self inflicted wound of the poor, it is an evil imposed by those whose education should have taught them better.'

To think that she had once wished to change her lodger. How wrong she had been. Jane silently accepted David's small acts of generosity knowing he would be embarrassed if she thanked him. And she portioned out the food equally amongst them all.

She had trudged round all the addresses Mrs Shipton had kindly given her but none needed a laundry hand.

'Sorry, missus,' was the reply at the last lodging house, but then the housekeeper called her back. Jane eagerly returned.

'I did hear that the steam laundry was looking for hands. They always are, not many can take all that steamy heat. And I don't know as to how much they pay but it's worth a try, isn't it? They're in Manby Park Road, behind Maryland Point Station.'

The branch of the Parkside Steam and Sanitary

Laundry located in Manby Park Road was housed in what looked like a tunnel. Partitions were spaced at intervals to divide up the processes. Steam billowed out from huge cylinders. A wooden wheel on its side with projecting lathes, was turned by women clad in the thinnest coverings which clung to their perspiring bodies. Beyond the next partition, the tubs gave off fumes that stung the eyes, as lime was emptied into the bubbling water. In the last section, were several long tables and balanced on each was a cumbersome wooden roller that was rotated by two women on each side of the table. At the entrance to the tunnel the laundry was sorted into items for steaming and items for laundering. Those to be steamed were taken to a separate shed. Inside were rectangular containers of boiling water, lime and saltpetre; upon each lay a metal griddle to suspend dirty washing above the steam. The Parkside Steam and Sanitary Laundry had the washing contract for the Infirmary and the asylum. Both institutions sent heavily soiled flock mattresses for steam cleaning.

The woman overseer was a tyrant who took sadistic delight in seeing newcomers retch as soon as they entered the steam shed. And, new employees were always put in the steam shed first. Within minutes of being inside the place, Jane was drenched by the steamy heat. It was difficult to breath; the stench from the fouled bedding mingling with the washing aids, produced a thick pall in the air, which burnt the nostrils and stuck in the throat. How different from Maryland Laundry! But it was a job and the job paid one and sixpence a day – seven in the morning to six at night – and for six days that added nine shillings to their weekly income.

The moment Jane stepped inside the front door, she hurried straight to the scullery and closed the door.

She stripped off her clothes and sponged herself all over. For a moment she stood naked allowing her skin to dry. The alternative clothing she put on was simply yesterday's dried ones but they felt good against her body. Today's damp ones were hung out on the line.

As usual, Laura was sat at the table copying passages out of her school books. After the first day, two months ago when Laura greeted her mother on her return home from the steam laundry and had been roughly pushed aside and shut out, Laura knew not to speak until Jane reappeared in the kitchen. George would be reading his paper when Laura came in from school and she would make everything ready for their supper before she set to with her school work. Sometimes she would leave her books and join Sarah and Georgie and their friends in the street until supper time. David Garvey rarely came in before seven o'clock as, after his shift finished, he would visit sick railwaymen or widows of railwaymen.

Jane pegged her damp clothes on the line. Something stirred in her mind and she was trying to fathom it out. Suddenly she ran back into the house and quietly opened the kitchen door. Only Laura sat at the table. No newspaper. Her heart sank.

'Here, Laura.' Jane untied a knot in her petticoat. She reached up for a tin mug. 'Go to Mary's and get a pennyworth of jam.' She turned to the range and stirred the supper pot. 'And, look into the *Thatched House* and see if Pa is there.'

Laura took the coin and cup and skipped out of the front door.

George came out of Granny's Alley into Burgess Road and saw Laura glide out of the gate, holding the mug aloft, and twirl and dance across the road. She was a bonny girl, not tall but with firm arms and legs. Her hair had darkened to a tawny brown and much of the curl she'd had as a baby had been lost in the straight plait. His gaze scanned the street and he spotted little Georgie playing skittles with his friend Percy. He couldn't hear them but he saw Georgie's hand go up in the air and guessed he'd made a hit. Although he wasn't always fit and healthy, eight year old Georgie was growing tall. After his Pa, thought George. But his pale sandy hair, blue eyes, sandy eyelashes and brows were from his Ma. A group of youngsters was standing by the gas lamp. Most of them were boys and, yes, he was right, in the middle was Sarah. What a beauty she was! Her small face, pert little nose, and only a hint of freckles across the finely etched cheekbones, drew admiring glances. Soft curls escaped from ribbons looped around the golden tresses and gave her a golden halo. Looking at his children, George was filled with pride. He strode along the road.

'Hello, Georgie, old son.'

Georgie left his friend and ran across to his father. George swept him up in the air.

'Just as well you're not a heavy weight,' George laughed and lowered him to the ground.

'Pa, I won five times and Percy only won once,'

'Well, that's good son. But, it would be nice and friendly like, and as it is Percy's game, perhaps you could manage to lose next time.'

He ruffled the boy's hair and Georgie beamed a smile at his father and nodded.

As he drew level with Sarah, George called out, 'Good evening, Sarah. You'll come in promptly when Ma calls you for supper, won't you?'

Sarah smiled and waved, and he hurried into the house.

'George, where have you been? I was worried.'

Jane stood close to him but there was no smell of alcohol.

'Tomorrow, missus, you can tell that there steam laundry you won't be a drudge for them any more.'

He linked his arms about her shoulders and spun her round and round until they collapsed on the rocking chair. Jane was breathless. It was so good to see George in a buoyant mood.

'What is it, dearest? Tell me.'

'Well, I was standing in line as I always have done even when I know ganger isn't going to pick me. But I was standing in line, I must've been about fifteen or sixteenth back when the gangers come out. There was a stranger among them this morning. He steps forward and asks if there's a George Stringer out there. Well, I was shaking in me boots. I hadn't done any wrong because I'd only been doing sweeping these past weeks so I steps out of line and says, Me, Sir. I'm Stringer. He comes over and shakes my hand. What d'you think of that? Shakes my hand! Victor Grimshaw, that's the gent's name, says he's a good friend of Ernie Weston, and Mr Weston had told him to seek me out. God bless Mr Weston, I says. He says I'm to be his Number Two and help him pick out the rest of the gang. Mr Grimshaw buys for shops in Bayswater, I think he says. As his Number Two he'll pay me an extra thruppence! I'll get three and ninepence a day. What do you say to that, Mrs Stringer?'

Jane listened to his tale. He bobbed his head as he spoke, Just like a little boy who had been give a cream bun.

'That's very good, my husband. Very good indeed. No more than you deserve.'

'I wanted to wait until you had freshened yourself up so I've been walking the streets.'

She smiled and patted his arm.

Laura bounded into the kitchen. 'Here's the jam, Ma. Oh, you're home, Pa. I'm so glad. Look what Mary gave me.' She held out a tinted print torn from a magazine. It was of a lady peeping out from under an enormous hat.

'It's Marie Lloyd. Mary says she's appearing at the Stratford Empire. I would love to see her!'

'Would you, girlie? Would you really like to see her?'

Laura looked up sharply. It sounded as if father was offering to take her! No, it couldn't be. But she quickly answered.

'Yes, Pa. I would really like to see her.'

He made a bow to her. 'If you will allow me, I shall be delighted to escort you to the Stratford Empire on Friday night.'

Laura danced around her father, clung to his knees, than fell backwards on the floor.

'What's all the hulla-balloo about?' Georgie asked and seeing Laura on the floor got down beside her.

Sarah came through the kitchen door and promptly tripped over her brother and sister and settled on the floor too. George was laughing so much the tears were running down his cheeks and he squatted down in a heap as well.

Jane stared down at them. 'Get up at once! All of you! What behaviour!'

George reached forward and tried to grab Jane's ankle to pull her down but she moved back and banged the spoon she was holding on George's head.

'Sorry, Jane.' George stood up and helped the children off the floor. 'I know it was daft but it was only a bit of fun. Best fun I've had in a long time,' He put his arm about her waist. 'Don't be cross.'

Round and round the spoon went, unnecessarily stirring the stew. She should have joined in. But a part of her resented the children romping with George. As if only she should please him.

'Marie Lloyd has an unsavoury reputation, George.

Not the sort to take a young girl to. Perhaps it might be better to wait and see what's on next week.'

Always George deferred to Jane's wishes but not this time.

'I've made a promise to Laura and keep it I will. Friday night we go to the Stratford Empire.'

The Stratford Empire was on the Number One ciruit booking only the best stars of variety. George and Laura lined up at the side door. It was fourpence in the gallery for adults and tuppence for children. When the door opened, George swung Laura under his arm and ran up the three flights of stairs. He managed to get them into the front row. Laura leaned forward and was in a magic world. The pit orchestra struck up and played several jolly tunes. Then, the house lights dimmed and the gold braided curtains were looped up to the sides and the first act came on. Each performance was greeted enthusiastically but when the second half started the hall went wild with cheering and whistles. Caps were thrown into the air. As the music began, the audience quietened only to erupt again as Marie Lloyd stepped onto the stage. The large violet velvet hat dangling with feathers was tilted back. Her purple velvet costume, trimmed with silver, sparkled in the spotlight. She hitched up the heavy skirt, revealing her trim ankles. A backdrop was lowered picturing a steam strain and she began to sing.

'Oh, Mr Porter, what shall I do?
I wanted to go Birmingham and
They took me on to Crewe.'

All the way home, Laura chanted the chorus as she hopped along the road making sure not to step on any cracks to spoil the run of good luck. She began to relate every detail of the theatre and the audience, holding back on Marie Lloyd to keep them in suspense until Jane called a halt and packed the children off to bed.

'You may not have school tomorrow but your father and I have to go to work. So hush down and don't chitter chatter.'

Laura's dreams were filled with violet velvet hats flying through star studded skies. Coloured lights swayed and danced past disembodied heads sporting white whiskers or black moustaches. Her mind was still full of the theatre when she woke. She hurriedly cleared the breakfast dishes and Sarah washed them at the sink. They filled two large zinc buckets and set them on the range to boil. As they sorted out the laundry into hot boil and cool wash, and making sure each customer's items were identified, Laura was glad Sarah didn't want to gossip. The quiet gave Laura time to write her essay in her mind. At least this week, she really did have something to write about. Each Monday, Mrs Gowrie expected the girls to hand in an essay on something they had seen the previous week. It could be about an animal, a person, a machine or event, but it had to be fully described giving colour, shape, texture, smell. 'Use all your senses,' Mrs Gowrie had said at the start of term, 'and put it into words - make the words live.'

It wasn't until after they came back from the park on Sunday afternoon, that Laura could settle down at the table with her pencil and paper. She filled three pages with words describing the interior of the theatre, the performers and the audience. There were colours: lights, clothes. Sounds: music, clapping. Shapes: stage, seats. Smells: tobacco, pomades. On the Monday morning, Laura eagerly handed in her essay and Mrs Gowrie smiled at her as her fingers noted three pages. It would be another week before Mrs Gowrie handed them back with her markings.

'Why are you running, Laura? I can't keep up,' Georgie complained.

'Pa will be home and so will Ma.'

'If they are home, what's the rush?' Georgie gasped. 'I'll wait for Sarah. I'm all puffed out,'

Laura stopped and walked back. 'Sorry, little brother. I forget you get puffed quickly. Your legs are as long as mine, even though you're younger, so you should be able to pace me. Never mind. It's just, well, I've got something to tell Pa.'

They tumbled in through the front door. Laura pulled off her bonnet and shawl and hurried into the kitchen.

'Pa! This is what Mrs Gowrie said about my essay. A good eye for details and a sense of occasion – I'm not sure what that means but it must be all right because she gave me **NINE OUT OF TEN**. Isn't that good?'

'Well done, girlie! I say! Nine out of ten, yes, well done.'

When Jane came in from the back yard, Laura related it all again and when David Garvey came in for supper he, too, was regaled with Mrs Gowrie's comments.

'I forgot to tell you, Pa. Mrs Gowrie also said I was county school material. That's good, too, isn't it?'

David Garvey jumped up and grasped Laura's hand. 'That's really good, young miss. Always said, education was the answer to poverty. Opens up avenues you'd never expect.'

'The way you talk Mr Garvey, you'd think education was a stairway to paradise. It's not. I had what you'd call a good education but it didn't teach me how to be a good wife and mother. It didn't teach me about life. You have to live it! No, Mr Garvey, education is probably fine for a boy as long as it doesn't give him ideas above his station...' And Arthur's face came into her mental vision... 'if it teaches him a good trade.'

'I happen to believe that one's station in life as you put it should be set by one's ability not by where one was born or who your parents are.' David Garvey walked through to the scullery and closed the door.

Laura had stood silent during the exchange between her mother and the lodger. She hadn't meant to show off about her essay, she was just pleased with her high mark.

'Call your sister in for supper, Laura,' Jane said.

George, too, had been hurt by Jane's tone. 'Couldn't you have given her a bit of praise. It was good to get nine out of ten.'

'What's all the fuss about? Surely she's had praise enough from everyone else.'

Only Sarah chatted and laughed as they sat at supper. Under the table, Laura felt Georgie's finger's tighten about hers. She looked up into his small serious face and gave him a cheeky grin to which he responded with a gurgling laugh.'

'I was in Mary's corner shop this morning and she told me how pleased she was with the hat you trimmed, Laura.' Jane reached across to collect the plates. 'Said you'd copied it from what you saw at the variety theatre. Is that right? She showed it to her customers. No doubt you'll be getting orders from other ladies here about. You've got Granny Goult's sewing gifts, it seems.'

This was praise indeed, from her mother.

Chapter 10

It had been a mellow autumn. Gold and bronze covered the trees giving the days a glowing aura. Now, in November a spiteful wind tugged at the branches, showering passers-by with leaf shards then puffing then into heaps to catch unwary walkers. Blowing up for rain, too, Jane thought as she pulled her cloak tight about her throat. The sort of day to stoke up the range and get a poker nice and hot to plunge into a mug of ale for George and her. Just the two of them.

She pictured George sitting at home on his own and the vision spurred her on. Time to be with George before the children came home. Oh, how she longed to lie beside him and feel his body close. To experience the pleasure of his caresses – the imagined ecstasy left her breathless. But the children were growing up, especially the girls, it was impossible to make much sound or movement without disturbing them. The only time she was alone with George was when he came home from market about three o'clock but it was sinful to go to bed in the afternoon. She would have to be content just to sit with him.

'Any good stories in the *Mail* today, George?'

'Hello, love. Let me help you with your bag. My! It's heavy. What you got in it? Half the high street?'

'Not quite. But now winter's almost here, I thought I'd best get two bags of coal, than I needed half a stone of potatoes and, Oh! I don't know, George, just our usual purchases. Don't worry, the girls can help stack them away when they get home.'

'There's a piece in the paper about a Member of Parliament who kept three establishments and each lady thought she was the one and only. Fancy that!' George laughed.

Jane reached across and pushed the paper down from his hand. 'Don't think you can try that with me, Mr Stringer.'

He took her hand and pressed it to his cheek. 'There can only be one Mrs Stringer in my life.'

Their intimacy was broken by a knock at the front door. Just one rap,

'Who can that be? Jane asked.

'Perhaps it's not for us,' George said.

'If it was for Mrs Milton it would have been two knocks.'

Jane opened the door. Standing on the path was a middle aged lady. Iron gray wavy hair framed a shiny round face. Her dark blue coat was faded but not shabby and the black skirt below was shiny from much wear. It was the hat! Bright scarlet with one purple feather stuck in like an arrow. On a raven haired coquette it would have been fetching. The shape of the visitor's head dictated the creation was worn across from ear to ear instead of tilting over one eyebrow. It was in danger of being dislodged from the grey hair as its owner nodded and bobbed her head as she spoke.

'Am I addressing Cousin Jane?' she asked.

Jane frowned.

'Are you Mrs,' the caller looked down at a paper she held in her gloved hand, Mrs Jane Stringer who was Jane Goult. I hope so. And if you are, I am Martha Theburton, who was Martha Clarke. My father,

Thomas Clarke was brother to your mother who was Matilda Clarke. My goodness!' she laughed, 'what a lot of words to introduce ourselves. I've come here on behalf of Aunt Laura. She's the only one left. Of the Clarke's, I mean.'

Jane gazed at the caller. A warm smile had accompanied her speech dispelling the foolish first impression. The plump round face had skin like a polished rosy apple.

'What must you think of me, leaving you standing outside all this time. Come in Cousin, um, Martha I think you said.'

As soon as she stepped inside, Martha flung her arms about Jane and kissed her on both cheeks. A startled Jane extricated herself and walked ahead to the kitchen.

'George, we have a visitor.'

Jane introduced her husband and Martha promptly repeated all the stages of relations punctuated by her high pitched laugh. After this she detailed her own family. Her husband, Matthew, was a carpenter. They had three boys – just like their father and two girls –real treasures. They lived in Mayesbrook not to far from Clarke's farm.

'I should have got here by midday. I changed trains in London all right and got off at Stratford but then got all mixed and muddled and couldn't find Burgess Road.'

Her story was interrupted by the arrival of Sarah, Laura and Georgie who had to be introduced and prompted Martha to tell them about her family, eldest son now twenty three and youngest daughter thirteen.

'That's not what I've come about. It's aunt Laura – your namesake little Miss Laura. Me and my bubby try to visit her regular like, we go to the farm about once a month. You know, of course, she reared me after my own mother died. Very good she was. I was a handful and no mistake. Even though I was twenty and Aunt Laura little more than an older sister. A real good sort. Aunt Laura says the homestead will be mine when she's gone.' She looked quickly at Jane. 'Because I was first born to the first born, you see. Well, she's been given an eviction notice to get out, leave the farm. Not that it's much of a farm these days. But it's where she lives. And she makes enough at market for herself and that there young lad she's looked after all these years. Do you know, some evil minded creature even suggested it was Aunt Laura's bast... I mean, you know, wrong side of the blanket as they say. But Danny isn't her real son. We all know who his mother is. But if Aunt Laura is evicted then Danny has to go too. And the homestead won't come to me. That's bye the bye. It's the eviction. This is why I've come to you because Aunt Laura Clarke says she owns the farm house. Says it was given to her father and some land and that there was a piece of paper. The four fields she rents but the house and garden is hers. She says Thomas – that would be my father – as being the eldest and inheriting the farm would have had the paper. And when Thomas, my father, died as Matilda was next eldest, seeing as both Arthur and Ellen Clarke had gone, she'd have had the paper. Did she? Matthew and me couldn't get to Aunt Matilda's funeral. Sophie, our youngest went and got appendicitis and we were at the hospital.'

A further break was caused by David Garvey coming into the kitchen.

'Beg pardon, Mrs Stringer, I didn't see you had a guest.'

'Come in, Mr Garvey,' George said. 'We'll be getting supper soon.'

Jane scrambled up. 'Whatever must you think of

us, Cousin Martha, not offering you something to eat and drink and after having such a tiresome journey.'

'Please don't put yourself out. I shall have to be getting back home. It was last Sunday when we was with Aunt Laura, I promised I would come and ask about the paper.'

Jane looked puzzled.

'Matilda was next in line,' Martha repeated.

'I wish I could help you, Martha, but I have none of mother's papers. I sorted through everything with James and I'm sure we would have noticed something like a property deed.'

'It's a shame. Poor Aunt Laura. She's sixty now and where can she go? Nowhere except the Workhouse.'

The words struck terror into Jane's heart.

Martha stood up and put on her coat. The hat had remained perched on her head.

'Knew it would be a wild goose chase,' she said rather crossly. 'Told Aunt so.'

'I wish I could have been of help,' Jane replied.

Martha regained her composure and smiled. 'I must be going. I've got to find my way back to the station.'

'I'll be happy to show you the way,' David Garvey offered.

'Most kind I'm sure.' And Martha deposited kisses on each in turn.

'Just a minute,' Jane exclaimed. 'I wonder if Colonel Bourne has any of mother's papers. I can certainly ask him. Tell Aunt Laura we'll do our best.'

'Your cousin was telling me about the eviction notice your aunt has received,' David said when he returned. 'It's possible she may not need to show deed of ownership if she has rent books for the land. I was involved with the Swindon farmers when their land was taken by the railways and I learnt quite a bit about the law. I'd be happy to help in any way I can, Mrs Stringer.'

As they got off the tram in Piccadilly and walked along St. James's street to Pall Mall, what had been a drizzle at Stratford turned into steady rain. Jane walked ahead of David Garvey into the Army and Navy Club.

'Kindly wipe your feet. Tradesmen at the rear,' the Steward hissed.

Jane hastily retraced her steps and rubbed her shoes violently on the bristle mat. She approached the reception desk and turned on her best smile.

'May I ask if Lieutenant Colonel Frederick Bourne is in the Club today? If so, will you kindly tell him Matilda's daughter would be grateful for a word with him?'

The Steward eyed her cautiously. Her speech was genteel even if her garb was not. But, the creature with her, in his rough woollen coat and trousers and a vile cap on his head, well! His nose turned up in an expression of disgust. However, he wrote a message on a card and rang the bell for a runner.

'Take this to Colonel Bourne in the library.'

A few minutes later a slightly stooped figure holding a cane appeared in the vestibule. The runner by his side assisted Frederick Bourne down the three steps. Jane was shocked to see the relic of such a fine man. How old and frail he had grown in the two years since she had last seen him. She was trying to calculate his age. Seventy-one or two?

He came slowly toward her. 'Jane, my dear, how nice it is to see you again.'

Even his voice was feeble.

'Colonel Bourne, Frederick, it is good to see you, too.' Jane bent forward and kissed him on the cheek.

'Let us sit comfortably. Steward! Is the Day Room free?'

The Steward looked as if he would prefer to throw them out of the Club, but in deference to the Colonel, escorted them into a side room furnished with stuffed chairs and low side tables.

'If you require anything,' he emphasised the word again, '**anything,** Colonel Bourne just ring,' With a glowering look at the two visitors he closed the door behind him.

'This is a friend, David Garvey, who is helping me.'

Colonel Bourne didn't bother to look in David's direction.

Jane went on, I've come to ask if you've kept any of mother's papers. Do you remember Aunt Laura, mother's sister? She lives on a farm in Essex, it was the Clarke family home. She has received notice to quit although she says the farmhouse and surrounding land was given to her grandfather. There was a paper to that effect. Aunt Laura says she saw the paper as a young girl. After her father's death the farm passed to Thomas the eldest son, and after his death, Aunt Laura thought the paper might have been passed to Matilda.'

Frederick had his eyes closed and Jane wondered if he'd dozed off but he flicked open his eyes and she saw they were filled with tears. He unashamedly brushed them away.

'A day hasn't passed when Matilda wasn't in my thoughts but hearing her name spoken aloud...' he shrugged. 'I'm afraid I cannot help you. All relevant financial papers were handed over to the solicitor dealing with the estate. But, Jane, we cleared the shop and lodgings together with James, there was nothing of the sort, I'm certain of it. There was the lease for the shop, her operating accounts books but nothing more.'

'I told Mrs Stringer her aunt may be able to establish ownership without the benefit of the deed.'

'Mr Garvey works for the railways but comes from

Wiltshire and helped those farmers. He is familiar with the law.'

'No doubt!' Frederick snapped in a strong commanding voice reminiscent of his old self.

David noted the sarcasm but smiled tolerantly at the old man.

'What Mrs Stringer means is that I have represented local farmers in their negotiations with the railway company to ensure adequate compensation. That's what I want to do for Mrs Stringer's relative.'

Jane said goodbye to Frederick Bourne, knowing she would never see him again. Not for the first time, she wished she had known him while her mother was alive. The rain had reverted to a drizzle as they left the Club and made their way to the tram stop.

'I'll have to pay a visit to Aunt Laura,' Jane told George.

'Oh, Ma! Let me go,' Laura pleaded. 'I want to see how much Rosie has grown. Please Ma! Let me go too.'

'And me, too,' Georgie chimed in.

'Stop it, both of you. We can't afford tram fares for you all.'

Laura was about to blurt out she could pay her own fare. In her own mind she saw the knots in her petticoat, nine of them. Just like her Ma. Of course, she had only farthings in her knots but they were just as precious. They were to be used to buy bits of lace, or ribbons or scraps of material from the rummage bin of Mrs Pickles's stall in the market whenever she got a request from a neighbour to smarten up a well worn hat. And when she was paid for her work, the coppers were tied in her cotton bank. But it was ages since she'd seen Rosie. And Great Aunt Laura, too. If the fare wasn't too much she might use some of her money to buy tickets for Sarah and Georgie as well.

'Would it cost a lot, Ma?' she asked.

'If you'd allow me, Mrs Stringer, I should like to speak to your aunt about how she pays for the land she rents outside of the farmhouse. It may be she could prove that the two are separate.'

'Yes, I think that would be best, Mr Garvey. You go and speak to Aunt Laura for you know what you're talking about better than me.'

'I've got some sick visiting to do this Sunday,' David said, 'the wheel greaser bloke who lost his arm. Trying to get him compensation. But, the following Sunday I'll be free to go.' He winked at Laura. 'And I'd be happy to take the three young'uns along, my treat like, for to show me the way.'

Laura whooped with delight and Sarah danced round with Georgie. Jane saw it was useless to argue against the trip. Each day, Georgie counted how many more days before the Sunday outing. Laura was getting a collection of carrots and apples. There was an excitement about the house and Jane found herself drawn into it.

'It'll be strange with the children away tomorrow,' George said. 'Just the two of us in all this space.' He laughed. 'We'll be rattling around like stones in a quarry pot.'

'What's a quarry pot?' Jane asked.

'Dunno. It was what my father used to say when the fairground caravans moved out.'

Just the two of them. Suddenly, she saw what a glorious opportunity it was. She and George – just the two of them. A whole day! Her mind buzzed. It would be like when they were first married, just George and her. No-one else to think about. She could be utterly selfish. It would be wonderful to lie beside him, feel his caress and eagerly respond without waking the children. They needn't stir all day. She smiled at George and his eyes twinkled – had he read her thoughts?

The children needed no urging to get up; Laura had stirred as soon as she'd heard David Garvey's door click. It was something he had got in the habit of doing on a Sunday: getting up first and stirring the embers of the range fire and filing the iron kettle to set it to boil. When Jane had protested the first time, he'd said she did it six days a week and he was only doing it once. She didn't pursue the argument.

In the early morning gloom, with great amusement Jane watched the children's antics as Laura tried to keep Georgie quiet. In between his flailing arms reaching into a warm jersey, he kept asking questions in a loud whisper until Sarah clamped her hand over his mouth. The two sisters managed to get his second arm into the second sleeve. Laura scooped up their top coats and Sarah grabbed hats and mufflers and they crept out of the bedroom.

David had cut several slices of bread and spread them wit jam.

'For the journey,' he said. 'Or, could be for our dinner if Great Aunt Laura isn't at home.'

Laura was crestfallen. 'I didn't think about that. She doesn't know we're coming. And if she has gone out, Rosie will be harnessed to the trap.'

'Well, the sooner we're on our way, the sooner we'll find out. Come along.'

Jane heard the front door close and rested back on the mattress. The church clock chimed the half hour, half past seven, and the house settled back into silence. No street lighting reached into their corner so Jane couldn't clearly see George's face. His head was slightly on one side and his chest rose and fell with even breathing. With her forefinger, she lightly traced the shape of his forehead and his nose. There were wrinkles on his brow now; lines around his eyes. He had aged from the young man she had married twelve years ago. But he was still the man she loved. She kissed his cheek and he opened his eyes.

'I'll get some breakfast, my dear husband.'

Later, while they were eating. George said, 'It's a right morning, Jane, even if there is a nip in the air. How about coming for a stroll in the park?'

Along the narrow streets, she walked with her arm linked through his. A few passers-by greeted them and they nodded in acknowledgement. One side of the park as yet untouched by the rays of the sun, was sprinkled with hoar-frost and crunched under foot. Neither had spoken since leaving the house. He released her arm, and softly clasped her hand. Jane felt a unexpected exhilaration; their affinity was almost tangible. She had thought only the physical act of love could generate such emotion but the heady pleasure she experienced almost engulfed her. It was difficult to breath and she swayed forward. She quickly steadied herself before George noticed. Nothing must disturb this precious moment.

'We've been walking a long time,' Georgie complained, 'do you know where we are, Laura?'

'Of course I do, I'm not barmy.'

Well she was almost sure. The trouble was she had never walked along the lane. Each time she had been they had travelled by cart.

'How abut playing a guessing game, eh, Georgie?' David asked.

'I think, Mr Garvey, I'm a little lost,' Laura concede. 'It's some time since I was here and things look so different.'

'You're doing fine, lass. But I think if we retrace our steps to the fork, and take the left track, I reckon that'd do it.'

At the fork in the road, David had noticed a broken piece of wood branded with an arrow and CLAR – and guessed it to be a sign for Clarke's farm but he hadn't wanted to spoil Laura's obvious delight at being their leader. He wouldn't have let them go too far down the wrong road. They happily skipped back to the junction and Laura sped off down the lane, the ends of her muffler flying out behind her like a pair of wings.

'Well, what a lovely surprise, my dears,' Great Aunt greeted them warmly.

'This is Mr David Garvey, Great Aunt. He's come to help you about your land. He's very good at sorting out problems like that, aren't you, Mr Garvey?'

'I'll do my best, Miss Clarke.'

Great Aunt Laura guffawed loudly. 'Good gracious, man! No-one has called me that for donkey's years. Even the agent calls me Great Aunt and you will too. And I'll call you David and there's an end on it. Children, come and have some milk, and then go and find Rosie – I know she's the only reason you came. Nothing to do with visiting your poor old relative.'

From a cupboard under the settle, snugly fitted into the huge brick chimney, Great Aunt produced a small tin trunk its hinged lid fitted with a hasp and a peg. She dragged it across the stone floor to the centre of the kitchen beside the long table. David was tempted to go to her assistance but stopped when he saw the grim determination on the old lady's face. No doubt she had to shift the box herself many a time.

'All the papers are in here,' she said. 'I just add the new ones I get from the agent.'

'How long has the family been here?'

'I can't really remember. The old memory plays tricks now and again. Something I think was last year, turns out to have been yesterday and what I thought was yesterday was years ago. But it must be nearly two hundred years I think. All the land around here was owned by the Earls of Oxford – the deVeres you know. Then there was some scandal, but it was never told outside the family what it was. It involved loss of a great deal of money. The old earl wasn't a bad sort of fellow because he deeded the homesteads to the tenants. That is the land where their cottages were built and three roods about them. He kept all the estates near the manor house and sold the rest. The land about here was sold to Lord Barstead. Jeremiah Clarke was deeded this farm in 1792. I know the date is right!'

David whistled in surprise.

'I'm certain the date is right. Each child was taught the history of the farm by grandfather or father. That's why I can say it off to you now. Grandfather would suddenly shout, *What year did Jeremiah Clarke get the farm?* And if you didn't answer immediately you got your ears boxed.'

'I wasn't disputing what you said, Great Aunt. I was surprised. So much of the land has gone from farming to accommodating more and more towns and industry.'

'That's the truth, David. Come over here.' She went to the stone sink and pointed out of the window. 'On the hill over there, d'you see those buildings? Once it was farmland as far as the eye could see. Not any more.'

She linked her arm through David's and they moved out into the cobbled yard. Children and dogs and the donkey were racing round in a circle; shrieks and barks pierced the quiet. In the barn doorway, Daniel Binder stood and gazed in puzzlement.

'Join in the circle, Danny,' Great Aunt called. 'Of course, he can't hear. Laura! Go and fetch Daniel into your game.'

Obediently, Laura skipped across, clasped both his hands and swung him form side to side as in a dance.

'Sid Kettle's land was first to go. Years ago, in my twenties I was.' Great aunt's hand pointed across the horizon. 'That was to the east, then Frank Glossop's holding went next. He was to the south of us. Harry Rawdon adjoining the Glossop's place will be gone by Easter. That leaves me and Gideon Weech. I'm sixty years of age and Gideon is a mite older. There's no living to be had from the land now. Land is no good without manure and we can't afford to keep the cattle that'd give us a good mulching. Earth's dry as dust. I haven't planted the top two fields this year even though I paid good rent for'em. Gideon alongside of me done the same. Daft thing is, they always said land was too marshy for house building. But they do summat with it and in the wink of an eye up goes all the houses and farm land dries up making it only fit for building. So we're giving up.'

Rosie trotted up and nudged Great Aunt.

'You may be sweating, old girl, but you'll get no carrot from me. It's not from me working you that you're plumb tired out. It's your own fault.'

As another butt didn't bring forth a juicy titbit, Rosie trotted back to play.

'No, David, the land's been worked out. When I was a girl, my brother Arthur – he died far away, you know, Crimea. Well, the barges would come down the River Roding and he'd meet them at the Creek, along with the other farmers. They'd offload all the London muck onto horse carts and bring it home. We'd all help spread it for ploughing in. Night soil they called it. Then the village folk complained about the smell. Well, all droppings smell, don't they, and humans is no different to animals. And some hoity-toity bloke says it's unhealthy to have it exposed.'

She stared off into the distant past. In her mind she saw herself as a young girl, tall and slender, leaping across deep furrows, chasing after Richard.

Her brother was two years older but he was no match for his long legged sister. As the two youngest children they were always together. If one got ears boxed so did the other. Her ears stung at the remembrance still. She could hear her father's voice summoning them to table. They would stand in line and move forward in correct age pattern: Thomas, Arthur, Ellen, Matilda, Richard and she came last. Only Thomas and Matilda had married and had families of their own. Matilda had three children and Thomas just one, Martha. Laura Clarke had run the farm for forty years. In the beginning there were lots of hired hands at harvest time. Gradually, the numbers got less and less. She was tired. There was no-one to take over the running of the farm, even if it was still a going concern. So why not give it up?

'But I don't just want to give it over to the agents, David.'

'Beg pardon, Great Aunt?'

'I'm tired, David. There's no real farming here now. But I'd like to end my days here,' she waved back at the rambling house. Some parts shored up, some parts allowed to fall down. 'I believe the house and land is mine. Gideon says we should fight for the roof over our heads. It's ours! He says if they want **ALL** the land then they must buy from us that bit where our farm house sits. Gideon has got five sons but none of 'em stayed to be farmers. They're all townsfolk now. But he'd like to be able to leave something behind him. Me, I haven't got anybody of my own but I've looked after Danny since he was a tot. He's got nobody. I want to leave something to Martha, for she's promised to take care of Daniel. When I am gone, she can get the best price she can. Martha's a good girl.'

Her eyes misted over. 'Danny is twenty-eight years old yet he is still a child. See how he plays with the children.'

David patted her arm. 'I'll go through the papers right now and see what I can find. When the other farmers left did they get money for their properties?'

'Sid Kettle got some money but he went while Lord Barstead was still owner.'

'Oh, so when did Barstead go and who is the new landlord?'

'I don't remember when it changed but it's not a person any more. It's *Grange Featherstone Properties Limited* whatever they might be. About three, or mebbe four years their agent's been collecting rent.' She broke off as the dogs raced up the lane. 'Well, here comes Martha with her hubby and one of her girls. What a gathering we'll have today.' A broad grin spread across her face.

Great Aunt sat proudly at the top of the table, just as he father had done. Daniel Binder sat on her left, followed by Martha, Matthew and Esther. Filling the spaces opposite them was David and Jane's children.

They tucked into the hand and spring of pork that Martha had brought and did justice to the large apple pie Great Aunt had made.

The children had been excused. Georgie rushed out to play with the dogs, Rosie and Daniel, and Sarah found a new friend in Esther. Laura stayed at the table with the grown ups.

'So, you think you might've found some proof then?' Matthew leant across to David. 'Something that'll make it right for Great Aunt to stay here.'

'Well, the old rent receipts in the days up to Lord Barstead show numbered fields by size and a fixed sum of each field. It would seem from these that no rent was paid for the house and the land around it. Unfortunately, I couldn't find any really old receipts from the Earl of Oxford's time which **included** the house in the rents. I've told Great Aunt what to say in her letter to the agent...'

'I wrote it out,' Laura interrupted.

'Yes, Laura's got a nice clear hand writing. As a start it challenges his authority about eviction. But I really think, Great Aunt, you should go to a Commissioner for Oaths and make a sworn statement.'

'First, I'll wait and see what the agent says when he gets this letter.'

'We'll let you know, David, what happens. And we're ever so grateful to you,' Martha said. Martha had sat with David as he had gone through the papers. He'd shown her where he thought the changes were and she had followed all he'd told her. 'And we certainly won't let those papers out of this house, David.'

'I should like to have a word with your neighbours, Great Aunt. The two you mentioned, Harry Rawdon and Gideon Weech. They may have similar papers to these.' David held the significant ones in his hand.

'I doubt Harry Rawdon has any. He cant't read and what he don't know he don't keep. Probably Gideon Weech has got his rent papers going back nearly as long as me.'

'If it's all right with you, I'd like to come again next Sunday and may be you could let Gideon Weech know.'

No amount of wheedling and pleading on Laura's part influenced Jane to allow the children to go to Great Aunt's a second time.

'Mr Garvey has business to do and he'll do it a whole lot quicker if you're not in tow.' She looked sternly at Laura. 'And don't go behind my back and try to get David to take you. I've got six extra loads this week and I'll need both you girls to help seeing as weather won't be favourable.'

David made an early start again. Rain lashed down and the walk up the lane was very slippery over the cart ruts. When he arrived at Clarke's Farm, Great Aunt was sitting in the kitchen.

A shawl was wound round her head and shoulders and over the top was a linen sheet. Her skirts were hitched up between her legs and her feet were encased in high leather men's boots.

'I'm ready, David.'

She gripped a stout wooden stick and marched ahead of him as they left the farmhouse and headed across the vegetable fields toward the high meadow. The ground was sodden but Great Aunt's step never faltered although David slithered continually. Keeping to the hedge boundary gave some protection from the driving rain. Emerging into the open fields again, David saw, with relief, the house and the welcoming plume of smoke curling from the chimney.

Red sparks flew up the great chimney as more logs were thrust into the blaze. Their damp clothes were spread on the stone floor in front of the grate and after a warming brew David set about examining the papers Gideon gave him.

'Like I said, David, Harry Rawdon has no papers at all. Even his rent book is kept by the agent and he just takes in what's due each quarter day. He can add up rightly enough, he knows how much he has to pay and he counts it out to the last farthing. But, knowing his letters is beyond him.'

Great Aunt and Gideon sat in silence as David turned over paper after paper and made notes in his pad. Now and then he would nod, and Great Aunt would nudge Gideon and smile.

He eased back in his chair and stretched his shoulders. 'Well, I'm pleased to see your rent is shown in the same way as Great Aunt's. Fields are listed by size and number but no reference to the house until we come to the last year's assessment by the present owners. Funny, they didn't start off that way three years ago. They obviously copied Lord Barstead's register but have since changed their minds.'

Suddenly, Gideon leapt up and flung his arms in the air.'

'My Bible!' he shouted and ran out of the room as fast as his spindly legs could carry him. He returned struggling to carry an enormous black Bible.

'Here, let me help you,' David grasped the tome and laid it on the table.

Panting for breath, Gideon unlocked the clasp and opened it. The scrolled front parchment where all the births, marriages and deaths had been recorded was blotched with age. His finger slid along the edge exposing a second page and between them were two flimsy sheets of paper.

'The Here Two Four,' he said extracting them.

'Beg Pardon? What's that?' David asked.

A sly grin spread over the old man's face. 'I'll show you. What do you see on this one?'

It contained a list of names in alphabetical order written in beautiful old English with flowing 's' that looked liked 'f'. Jeremiah Clarke's name was at the top of the list and Zachary Weech's at the bottom. In between were Glossops and Rawdons and several others.

The second sheet, written by the same elegant hand, began in bold capitals:

THOSENAMED HERETOFORE shall no longer be deemed tenant farmers.

They shall be shown in the register as **FREEHOLDERS** insofar as the occupation of premises and abutment lands recorded as exemptions to rented Fields specified by numbers.

David read the paper softly under his breath, not daring to believe at first what he was seeing. His hands shook as he placed it gently on the open Bible.

'That's it,' he said his voice full of emotion. 'That's it, Gideon. Any Court or Law would recognise that as ownership. You have no worries about eviction, neither of you. With that evidence, you are here for as long as you want to stay.'

Great Aunt stood up and towered over Gideon as she gave him a kiss.

'That's what I wanted. To end my days sitting in my own kitchen. What about you? Will you force them to buy your land?'

'Well, my boys will get it in the end. So, I think I'll just sit it out along o' you.'

Chapter 11

David had been gone over six months. Jane idly traced her finger over the iron grate surround. Funny how she'd changed her mind about him. Those first few weeks, when he was always going on about worker's rights, how the working class should stand up and fight. She used to think, fight, what with? They had nothing. But she'd never said a word. His rent money was important. After a while, though he'd calmed down and settled into being one of the family. Yes, Jane thought, he did become part of the family. She vigorously dusted the shelf and moved onto the walnut wash stand she'd got for the bargain price of four shillings. Well, Laura got it down to four shillings - she'd noticed a chip in the base of the pitcher and feint glazing cracks in the bowl but nobody else would have seen them. The scalloped edge of the bowl was outlined in gold and the handle of the jug was scrolled with gold. It looked very elegant recessed into the walnut cabinet. She'd decided to keep it in the back room, not that she or George used it.

They'd finished Christmas dinner, their best Christmas ever, with a plump goose which David had presented to Jane as his contribution. Mrs Milton and her daughter Annie were invited to share the feast.

There was a silver thrupenny bit for everyone in the plum pudding. Laughter filled the room. Jane had stepped into the scullery to fill the kettle.

'I'll do that for you,' David had said. 'But first I have to tell you, I shall not be here after the New Year.'

'What do you mean? Why?'

'It's the Railway Company. I'm a bit of a thorn in their sides always wanting improvement for the workers. Taking up claims for compensation,' he shrugged. 'I've won a few battles but not as many as I would've liked.'

'You mean, they've given you the sack!' Jane was aghast.

'No. Not like at Swindon when Great Western gave me the push. In a way, I wouldn't have been surprised if Great Eastern had done the same. Mind you, sometimes the managers have benefited from what the union has got for the workers. I'm still employed but not at Stratford Yards. I'm to move to Trowse, near Norwich. They say it's a step up the ladder, overseer of a workshop doing repairs to link connectors. I say it's putting me in backwater even if I do get an extra few bob.'

Jane was silent not knowing what to say.

'I've had a word with the union man to get you only the very best lodger,' David laughed. 'I told him they've got my reputation to live up to.'

It had been a sad parting. He had looked pathetic standing in the doorway clutching two paper parcels: all his possessions. Only Jane saw him off. George had left for market, as usual; Sarah, Laura and Georgie were at school. He'd shaken hands with George the night before but had asked Jane to tell the children about his departure. With one parcel under his arm, he reached out and patted the house number.

'Number Four Burgess Road - best billet I ever had the good fortune to rest my head.'

He'd strode off up the street and never looked back.

They had talked it over.

'I think we could manage alright, George. You're getting good wages now and with the regulars I wash for, I say we could do without a lodger. Just keep the place for ourselves. We could leave the girls in the front, have the back room for ourselves and only Georgie with us. What do you think?'

'I'd like that fine Jane if you're sure it'd be alright about the rent money.'

Yes it had worked out fine.

Jane drew herself back to the present and carried on dusting and tidying the room then moved to the front room. One half was cluttered with books, bits of material and fashion pictures cut from papers and magazines. The other side had hair ribbons and combs neatly placed in line on top of the chest of drawers, moved from the lodgers room, signifying the occupants were now Laura and Sarah. The girls had made the bed before going to school. She had thought about moving Georgie out of her room and in with the girls but decided against it especially as Laura had started her monthlies soon after her eleventh birthday in January. Now it seemed there was constantly a bucket of blood stained cloths soaking in salt under the sink. No sooner had her monthly cycle finished, Sarah's started, followed by Laura's and there were scant days before she started over again.

July was reaching high temperatures. Smells hung about the house. Jane wrinkled her nose as she ladled the cloths out of the bucket into the sink and walked outside to empty the soiled liquid down the lavatory. On top of the cistern was the special pan she kept for boiling the cloths. She'd brought it in and grated soap into it, put the cloths in, grated some more soap on top before filling it with water and setting it on the range.

There was an hour before George would be home, time enough to finish off the ironing. She moved the flat iron closer to the heat and put a flannel sheet on the table. Methodically she sorted through the clothing putting shirts at the top of the pile. A spit on the iron brought a satisfying hiss and she began smoothing out creases.

Two knocks. 'Caller for Mrs Milton,' she thought. Then it was followed by two more and two more. She put the iron back on the stove.

'Goodness gracious don't break the door down, I'm coming. Don't worry Mrs Milton, I'll open it.'

Two burly young men stood on the step. One elbowed the other and they both removed their cloth caps. They looked down at their boots and both decided to scrape them on the low step.

'We need to speak to Mrs Stringer, if you please, missus.'

'I'm Mrs Stringer. What do you want?' she asked sharply.

'We're from Spitalfields, missus. You know, the market.'

They paused.

The sun was full in her face but gradually a coldness possessed Jane.

'I know Spitalfields is the market.' No other words formed in her mind.

'It's about your man, missus. There's been an accident......'

'Is he dead?' The words rushed out, she didn't want to speak them, but they came unbidden.

'Oh, no! He's alive but in a bad way. He's in the hospital. A pile of crates crashed down on him, pinned him under for nearly an hour. They took him to *The London Whitechapel*. That's what we came to tell you.

Weren't his fault. A new bloke stacked too many. How he managed to do it so high we don't know. Must've stood on a crate himself.'

Jane's mind was racing through the variety of injuries. What would she find when she saw him? Oh, she sobbed silently, oh! His lovely face.

She left Mrs Milton to tell the children where she'd gone but impressed upon her that none of them was to come to the hospital. They were to wait until she came home. She'd be back as soon as she could.

'Tell them to get on and eat their supper and tell Laura there's some ironing still to do.'

She walked briskly to Crownfield Road for a tram. It rattled down into Stratford Broadway. In a trance she got off one tram and onto another. The rhythm of it rocking over the rails beat out the words: he's alive, he's alive, he's alive.

At the top of the hospital steps, Jane paused. The vast glass panelled wooden doors were intimidating, a barrier between her and George. She released the skirt of her faded blue cotton dress and smoothed it over her hips. For a moment her feet refused to move forward until she was jostled by a group of young men who dashed down the steps at an alarming rate. The spell was broken and she entered the building. Behind a window, a porter perched on a high stool and in response to her question merely pointed along the corridor. Nurses in well starched white aprons swished along on unseen feet. She was directed to a lift and transported to the upper floor. Ahead stretched a long vacant corridor with closed doors along each side. One of the doors opened and an imperious woman in a dark blue dress covered with a stiff white apron glared at her.

'What are you doing here? Who permitted you to come up to the wards? It is not visiting time.'

From somewhere in her head, Jane heard a voice saying she was Mrs Stringer, but it wasn't her voice.

'I am not interested in your name. You are not allowed up here.'

'But my husband... Jane began until her shoulders were firmly gripped by the stern woman and she found she was being propelled towards the lift.

Apprehension left her and anger took over.

'How dare you push me!' Jane twisted quickly and was out of her grasp. 'My husband has been brought to the hospital.' Her voice was getting louder. A group at the far end turned to stare back along the passage. A few doors tentatively opened. 'There was an accident at his work and my husband was injured.'

'Oh, Sir Herbert, I do apologise for this rowdy woman. I trust it has not disturbed you too greatly.'

A gentleman in a grey morning frock coat stood framed in a doorway,

'What seems to be the problem, Sister?'

Jane skipped past to stand in front of the man.

'Are you a doctor? Please help me. I received a message my husband has been injured at work and was brought here. I want to know....'the anger was giving way to apprehension again. 'I want to know how he is, please.'

He smiled at her and took her hand.'I am Sir Herbert Rumbold and what is your name, my dear?'

'I am Jane Stringer and my husband is called George.'

He escorted her to a large room near the lift. It was furnished with well worn but comfortable leather armchairs.

'I saw Mr Stringer when he was brought in. He'd been crushed under a heavy load and had cracked ribs and many fractures in his legs. We have not had to amputate. His legs have been put in splints. He will not be able to move for some time, but I do not see any cause for alarm.'

'Thank you, Sir. Thank you so much. It is a great relief. He will be able to walk again, won't he?'

'Yes, in time. Healing is a lengthy process.'

'May I see him?'

'Sister is very strict about visiting only during visiting time, which is from five thirty to six thirty. I shall be making my rounds in a moment and I shall tell him you have enquired after him and will visit him later.'

Jane had to be content with reassuring words instead of seeing him for herself. Outside his consulting room, Jane looked about to get her bearings. Sister was still on guard duty. Jane looked steadfastly ahead but as she drew level, Sister stepped into her path.

'There was drink on his breath,' she hissed and quickly moved on.

Jane thrust her knuckles in her mouth to stop the agonised cry from escaping. Sister's cruel jibe struck terror into Jane's heart even more than when she heard of the accident.

Her head was pounding as she got off the tram and made for home. As soon as she stepped inside the door, Laura raced along the passage.

'Is he badly hurt, Ma? Is Pa very bad?'

Georgie clung to Sarah's hand as they waited in the kitchen doorway.

Jane pushed past her daughter but Laura tugged at her skirts.

A deft movement landed a hand about Laura's ear and she walked demurely behind her mother into the kitchen.

'I haven't seen your father yet but I have spoken to the doctor who says he isn't badly hurt. Visiting time is half past five to half past six so I shall see for myself then.'

'I'll go too Ma,' Laura said, her face full of anxiety.

'No, you will not!' Jane said firmly. 'You will stay here.' She slumped into her chair. 'Children are not allowed on the ward.'

Once more, Jane made the leaden journey to Whitechapel. Inside the hospital she retraced her way to the lift and the upper floor. People mingled at the entrance to the wards awaiting the bell to signify visiting time had come. Swing doors were propped open and a nurse in striped uniform, with bell in one hand, eyes fixed on the large clock on the wall, waiting for the second hand to arrive at the half hour. Jane was relieved Sister wasn't on duty. The brass bell clanged vigorously and visitors, like a tidal wave, surged forward.

Walking along slowly, Jane surveyed each bed. At last she saw him and ran to him.

George managed a brave smile. 'Hello old girl, how was your journey?'

She held his face between her hands. A cut above his eyebrow was yellowed with iodine but there was no other visible injury. His right arm was in a sling. His legs were hidden beneath the covers.

'How are you my darling? How did it happen?' she paused, then in a whisper asked, 'were you steady on your feet?'

His left hand gripped hers. 'Listen to me Jane. It wasn't my fault. Everyone says so.'

'Sister said your breath smelled of drink.'

'T'ain't true! It happened before our break so I hadn't even had me usual half pint of ale with the lads. So she couldn't have smelt anything on my breath, Jane.'

A great weight lifted off her heart and she bent to kiss his lips.

'Nark it! There are people about.'

He pushed her roughly away and she saw he was looking towards the door. A tall broad shouldered man strode down the ward and stopped by George's bed.

'Mr Grimshaw, sir,' George said. 'How do, sir.'

'Stringer.' He bent forward and took George's left hand in a sort of handshake. 'Glad to see you're in good spirits.' He turned to Jane. 'Ma'am it's a most regrettable accident, and to one of my best men.'

George almost blushed and Jane beamed at the man.

'I can promise you there'll be compensation. No doubt about it. In the meantime, Stringer, I'll ensure you are paid full wages up to Saturday and then half wages until a compensation is settled, which I hope won't be long. And there will always be a job for you back at Spitalfields.'

He shook his left hand again and strode out of the ward.

'That was Mr Victor Grimshaw, Jane. He's a real gentleman. He it was who gave me the job after I'd been sweeping all those months. He knew Ernie Weston. It was Mr Weston who had recommended me like.'

Jane travelled home in a more buoyant mood and she hadn't seen the Sister. How good it was to see his beloved face wasn't scarred. She saw his face in her mind. It was nice to know how well thought of her husband was. And Mr Grimshaw had promised money as well.

After the first week Jane didn't call at the hospital every night. She had seen an improvement each time and so spread out her visits. George's fractured legs were swathed in bandages and would remain so for many weeks. His ribs and arms were healing and he could now move without pain. Mr Grimshaw was as good as his word and sent his second ganger round with full wages that first Saturday and half wages the next two Saturdays. But now it had stopped. In his letter to George he said he now awaited the decision of the workers' compensation tribunal.

She handed the envelope to him as soon as she

arrived and Jane saw his brows knit and forehead wrinkle.

'What does he say, George? Does he say why there was no money last Saturday?'

'Aye, he does. Awaiting the tribunal.'

'What tribunal?'

'About my compensation. He says he made the payments by way of friendship. Now the matter is before the court he can't send any more money 'cause it would be seen as admission of fault.'

'Well the market was at fault allowing the numbskull to stack so high. That's what those two porters told me when they first called.'

'True enough, girl. I don't know what to make of it all. But the good news is they might let me out of here next week. I'll still be splinted up so I won't be able to move about but I'll be home in my own bed along o'you, Jane.'

She pondered the news riding home on the tram. An invalid! The thought filled her with alarm. How long would he be bedridden?

'I've said how do twice, Mrs Stringer. You're miles away.'

'Eh? Oh, Mrs Walters Nice to see you.'

'Been visiting your hubby? How's he getting on?'

'Making good progress, the hospital says.'

Mrs Walters prattled on about how many people she had known who had accidents to their legs and most of them had to lose a foot, a leg below the knee, whole leg. Jane listened with half a mind. The other was wondering what George would do all day lying in bed. He had always been an active man, never had much learning although he liked to read his newspaper, and there was the money or rather the lack of it.

They had alighted from the tram and turned into Burgess Road. Jane's steps had turned into Number

Four before she realised Mrs Walters was still talking.

'...so Viley says.'

'Beg pardon, Mrs Walters, what did you say?'

'Your Laura top of the class. Teachers are so pleased, never had a girl get such high marks in exams, they say. And she'll certainly be put forward for that scholarship next year. Where does she get her brains? From you or her Pa?' Mrs Walters laughed. 'Best bits from each I don't wonder. Good night to you.'

In the kitchen Laura sat at the table, her neat writing filing pages in her work book. Reference works were littered across the table. She stopped immediately and enquired about her father. For an irrational moment Jane wanted to sweep the papers and books from the table. She walked to the scullery and drew a mug of water. The cold liquid calmed her.

'He may come home next week.' she said with false brightness.

'Yarroo!' Laura leapt up and danced around the room. 'Oh, I've missed him so, Ma.'

She pushed past her mother to go out into the yard.

'Georgie, Pa's coming home! Isn't that wonderful.'

'Yes' But he was more interested in the snail spreading its slime across the flagstones as it moved slowly toward the lavatory. 'I'm timing it by the church clock. Oh, no! Look! It's turned round and going back to where it started. I wanted it to go under the lavvy door.'

Jane had puzzled over how best to accommodate George. Only a month or so back she had changed the rooms over. The two girls together in the front and Georgie with her and George in the middle room. She tried rearranging the few pieces of furniture to get the bed nearer the window, but gave up on it because whichever way it was put made the rest of the room like an obstacle course. Georgie would have to go into the front room to share with the girls.

Just before August bank holiday Monday, the horse drawn ambulance brought George home at four in the afternoon.

For the first few weeks George enjoyed the novelty of being pampered. Laura would bring him his meals, she would place a cloth across his bed covers, next a tin tray with his spoon, knife and fork then his plate. She would wag her finger at him and tell him to eat it all up. There was little light by which he could read his paper, but Laura would sit by the window and read each item page by page. Georgie would sit on the bed and tell his Pa a rambling tale of exploits with his playmates. Sometimes Sarah joined her brother but didn't tell her Pa about the boys.

Four weeks, five, dragged by. George became irritable and frustrated at his inactivity, and Jane was short tempered.

'When are they going to give you compensation? When, George? When are we going to get some money? We can't live on fresh air. We have five mouths to feed. I can't take on any more washing customers, even if there were some to be had, there just aren't enough hours in the day to do it.'

'I know it's hard girl...'

'Hard! Of course it's hard! We need the money.'

She turned on her heel and walked out of the bedroom.

Eagerly Laura swept up the envelope that had plopped through the letterbox. Even though it was addressed to Mrs Stringer, she still thought it might be about the compensation.

'A letter, Ma, for you.'

'Open it, child. My hands are wet.'

She carefully eased up the flap and took out two sheets of paper covered in large sloping handwriting.

'Dear Jane,' she read. 'I thought you would like to know that Great Aunt is doing fine.' She paused. 'Oh, it's from Aunt Martha,' she said with a hint of regret. 'Shall I read it to you?'

Jane was pounding washing with the wooden dolly and didn't answer.

Laura raised her voice a tone '...Great Aunt is doing fine. The men who came to fence in her land took the line outside of the large oak. The one we always used to picnic under, gave such lovely shade, do you remember? I cannot recall, Jane. Were you ever with us in those days? But it's a lovely tree and they have put it into Great Aunt's garden. She chats to the Irish navvies building the road beyond her fence. They are ever so kind. And, do you know what? These men are doing bits of repairs to the old house and they never take but a mug of ale for their trouble. Your David Garvey did us a great service sorting out Great Aunt's papers. And we do thank him most cordially. your cousin, Martha.'

She laid the letter down. 'If Mr Garvey was still here, he would chivvy up the market people about Pa's compensation.'

Jane had listened to Laura reading the letter. She was glad for Great Aunt to be settled in her old age but Jane wished some of the good luck would come her way.

Jane had bathed his legs and saw the wounds were healing well.

'How soon after the splints have come off, do you think you'll be back at work, George?'

'As quick as anything, Jane. Once I've got up on my pins there'll be no stopping me.'

The hospital had told Jane to get their dotor to visit George once a week to replenish the dressings inside the splint, but after the second visit Jane said she would manage on her own and the doctor agreed. He understood, his visits cost money.

'What do you think, Jane? Shall I try and stand up?'

He was flexing his muscles and prepared to move his legs to the edge of the bed when Jane pushed him back.

'Not yet, dearest, it's much too soon.'

George slumped down. 'Whatever you say, Jane.'

She cleared away the washing materials and moved about the room. It would be three weeks owing on the rent come Friday. What else could she pawn? George's best trousers and coat and his boots had already gone. She rustled through their clothing hanging on the wall hook. At the back was the cotton bag covering the grey silk dress. Her hand tenderly passed over the package. Dreamily she went back in time. Music played and she floated across the floor in HIS arms. Twinkling chandeliers scattered stardust about them. Brightly gowned ladies promenaded with elegantly attired gentlemen. Opulence pervaded the room and equisite perfume scented the air. She shook her head to dispel the past. No! The dress was Matilda's. There was still a balance in the bank account which Frederick had opened for her, but that too was Matilda's. True, she had used some but only for Matilda's sake and when her elaborate wardrobe had served its purpose, it had been sold and the money put back into the bank account.

George's urgent call put an end to her musing.

'Get us the chamber pot, Jane I've got to do me business.'

Uncle's was the last shop before the junction. In her bag were five knives and forks- she had kept back the spoons. Perhaps she would get a shilling on them if he was feeling generous. Through the window Jane saw he already had two customers so she aimlessly walked on unaware of her surroundings. The high street was bustling with traffic, carts and carriages dashed along at speed, horses hooves clattering on the cobbles. Pedestrians jostled along the pavement and Jane was knocked into a doorway. For a moment she stared at her reflection in the glass. A gaunt and haggered face stared back at her. Was this how she really looked? But then her eyes focused on the hand printed card propped up on an easel.

BURNETT'S AGENCY
We maintain only the highest register of
Domestic staff for placement
with only the best of establishments.

It took but a minute to adjust her composure before she pushed open the door.

She retraced her steps to Uncles and was pleased with herself for she had wheedled a shilling out of him. There was something to put towards the rent when the collector came to call tomorrow. As school was restarting next week, Laura was at the table sorting out her books. Sarah was leaning over her shoulder.

'I don't know how you can like all that old stuff. Shakespeare! Ugh!'

Jane looked at her two daughters, so close in time, yet so different. It was a hard decision but there was no other way. Her voice was weary.

'Sarah.'

'Yes, Ma.'

She held a straw case in her hand for which she had paid tupence out of the precious shilling. She presented it to Sarah.

'I want you to put a few of your things in here.'

Sarah eyed her mother quizzically but said nothing.

'Today I have arranged for you to start work with a nice family in Woodford. You will be a scullery maid to begin with but, you're bright you'll quickly move up the ladder, so there will be no more school for you.' Jane forced a smile.

The meaning of her mother's words dawned on Sarah.

'Oh, Ma!' She cried, 'Don't send me away please.' She flung herself at her mother's skirt and sobbed.

There came a banging on the wall.

'What 's up out there?' shouted George. 'Who's been hurt?'

Jane sat on the bed and told George about her visit to the agency.

'She was a very nice lady. Asked me all about Sarah, and gave me a list of houses where she thought Sarah would be best suited. They all seemed very nice. It was difficult to decide which one to pick for her. It will be strange for her at first, but she's twelve and a half and will soon get into the routine of things.' Jane's voice carried a conviction she did not feel. 'Anyway, she was never too keen to go to school and after she passed the labour exam she could leave. Her wages will be paid to us. It'll be a shilling a week and she'll get all her food and a nice uniform and if she does well the wages go up to one and thruppence after three months. Wages are paid quarterly but I asked the lady if she could see her way to paying them monthly at first just to tide us over. She agreed the agency would be the go between for Sarah's wages for the first three months.'

Humiliated and ashamed at his inability to provide for his family, George turned away and buried his face in the bed coves.

Laura carefully folded two petticoats, three pairs of drawers, two bodices, three hose and one dress and placed them in the case. Sarah sat on the bed staring into space.

'I'm frightened, Laura, to be on my own. It won't be like at Granny Goult's house and I won't have you close by to tell me what to do.' Tears coursed down her face.

Laura flung her arms about her sister and hugged her tightly.

'Shush, shush,' she crooned as to a baby. Her own fear no less than Sarah's. They spent the sleepless night silently clinging to each other.

'When the rent man comes, give him this shilling.' Jane told Laura, she had managed to find the extra coppers. 'Say we'll be able to pay more next week.'

Jane took the straw case and ushered Sarah ahead of her. Laura stood in the doorway, cuddling Georgie who was trying to extricate himself from her grasp. Laura didn't wave. Sarah never looked back.

His sister's departure had little effect on Georgie. He had his own play mates in the street for skittles, or pitch and toss. And Jack Forest had a wheeled hobby horse which he let everyone have a go on. Then there was Knock Down Ginger and Georgie, being the smallest, was always elected to tie the thread through the knocker. But to Laura the loss was traumatic. There was no-one to trade confidences with. Vily Walters was her best friend but it wasn't the same. She couldn't tell her all her secrets. It was different with a sister; sitting in the darkness whispering their thoughts and ideas and longings to each other.

'I don't understand,' Sarah had said, 'how bleeding down below can make a baby.'

'Neither do I,' replied Laura, 'except one of the girls in school said you don't bleed if you are making a baby.'

'But how do you stop it?'

'Perhaps it's something you swallow.'

And they had fallen back on the bed smothering their giggles lest Georgie-or their mother--should hear the noise.

'But I shan't have a baby for years and years,' Sarah said. 'I can't take a baby onto the stage, can I?'

'Still got your heart set on being a dancer, then have you?'

For answer, Sarah stood up in the darkness and daintily held the hem of her flannel night-dress and pointed her toe. Gracefully she swayed about the room. Her thick curls of molten gold seemed luminous in the gloom as they twirled about her shoulders. She crawled back onto the bed.

'And you, Laura, do you still want to be a teacher?'

'Yes, that's what I want to be.'

'But it's such a lot of book work. Don't you tire of it?'

'I've got to be sure of getting the scholarship. Mrs Gowrie gives me extra work so I'll know what to expect in the exam next year. I do so want to go to the County School. David Garvey said learning was the only way to better ourselves. Ma and Pa work so hard, I want to be able to do something that will really help them.'

The nights were lonely now. Sometimes, Laura would creep into the kitchen and gather Lucky into her arms and tip toe back to the front room. She cuddled him and whispered into his ear all she would have told Sarah until Georgie grumbled at her to be quiet.

On Monday the third of October, Jane went to Burnett's Agency to collect Sarah's first month's wages.

'But, but...' she spluttered. 'What's this? You said a shilling a week.'

The woman sitting behind the plain oak desk, sighed as if dealing with an imbecile.

'That is correct.'

'Well' you haven't given me four shillings. Look.'

'I am well aware of the amount I have handed over. Two shillings and tuppence. The difference,' she turned back a page in her ledger, 'the difference of one shilling and ten pence is deductions for breakage's.' A simpering smile played about her lips. 'Your daughter is very clumsy.'

With a heavy heart, Jane returned home. She longed for the comfort of George's arms about her.

'It'll be good when you are free of those splint. It's not right for a piece of wood to come between husband and wife,' she murmured playfully in the darkness. But as she made an approach to him, he turned away. It was as if in some way he was blaming her for sending Sarah into domestic servitude. What else could she do? They were destitute. She had a recurring nightmare that the workhouse wasn't far away.

She was surprised, and grateful, when Joe Grimes approached her as she came out of the corner shop.

'How do, Mrs Stringer. Nice weather for the time of year don't you think. How are you and yours?'

'Fair, thank you, Mr. Grimes. And yourself?'

'Not so good. I've been meaning to ask you for some time. I know you do washing for several of the folks about here.'

'Of course, Mr. Grimes. I can certainly accommodate you.' Jane jumped at the chance of extra income.

'Well, it's not only the washing, dearie. I was wondering if you could find your way clear to do a bit of cleaning up of my place. I don't have a lot of sticks of furniture so it wouldn't be hard. And, may be, you could also leave me a pie or a pot of stew for me suppers. I'll pay whatever you think is right.

'I don't know what to say, Mr. Grimes. The women pay me one and six a load of washing. But I can't say as to how much for cleaning.'

'Would five shillings cover it do you think?'

Jane's mouth almost dropped. She quickly swallowed and took a deep breath to settle her heart beat. She could have hugged him right there in he street.

'We were so thankful when you took us in after the

fire, Mr. Grimes, so I'll be so happy to come and do for you. And five shillings will cover it nicely. When shall I start? Will tomorrow be convenient?'

Jane doubted there was any reason for Joe Grimes to have asked her to look after him. True, he was a widower, his good lady having passed away many years before and there were no children. But he was always doing jobs for other people. He was a tall, well built man who belied his sixty-nine years. He had worked for the Great Eastern Railway Company as a driver earning one pound sixteen and nine pence at the time and now got a bit of a pension.

'How is Mr. Stringer doing? It's a good job that compensation act is in, helps the likes of him.'

'Humph!' Jane snorted. 'It's not all right for him. He didn't get a penny.'

'But that shouldn't be so, Mrs Stringer. As I said this new act is different. In the old days even when entitled to compensation, men were expected to waive their rights when they signed on for work. The new law says this is forbidden and compensation is payable in all cases of accident, whoever is at fault. You must keep pressing for it, Mrs Stringer.'

Spurred on by Joe Grimes, unbeknown to George, Jane wrote to Robert Horner, the owner of Spitalfields' Market.

The extra money from Joe Grimes eased the tension following Sarah's departure. For George, it made his resolve firmer. Each week, while Jane was out of the house, he tested his legs easing himself off the bed to stand on the floor. By the beginning of November, after nearly five months of inactivity, he asked Jane to call in the doctor.

At one and thruppence, the doctor's fee was money well spent to hear him say, after he had removed the splints, the fractures had healed and he was no longer bed bound. Of course, his muscles were flabby and useless. Lots of exercise would soon strengthen them.

'Give it about a week or ten days, then you can go back to work.'

Round and round the house with two upended brooms taking some of the weight, he practised moving his joints. In less than a week he set off for Spitalfields.

Above the floor of the market were several rooms used by buyers and managers. It was three in the afternoon and the main hall had been swept clean. The floor was silent, no cries of porters dashing to and fro with loads of fruit and vegetables. George stood for a moment and sucked in the familiar smells. Around the sides were the banners of the main buyers. He strolled over to the south side but he couldn't see the Grimshaw flag. Mr. Grimshaw often sat upstairs and made up his orders for the next day. George thought, I'll just let him know I'm ready for work. Of course, he would stand in line along with the others tomorrow morning but it would be nice to give Mr. Grimshaw the wink. And, as he had promised Jane, he would tell Mr. Grimshaw he hadn't yet received compensation.

He knocked on the door and was told to enter.

'Excuse me, gents. I was looking for Mr. Grimshaw, Victor Grimshaw, fruit and vegetable merchant.'

'Not here' one man called over his shoulder while still turning over pages in a ledger.

'Has he left for the day, then?'

'Told you, not here.'

The other man turned round to face George.

'I know you, don't I? Porter, ain't you?'

'Yes, sir.' George touched his forehead. 'I worked for Mr. Grimshaw, sir. Was his ganger,' George said proudly.

'Well, he's not here any more. Sold out about two, no three months back. Why haven't you been around to know that? Oh, I remember you now. Bumped into a pole of crates, didn't you?'

'No, sir, I did **NOT**! They weren't stacked evenly and the stack was too high. The man who did it was new to the job but his ganger should have kept an eye on him, to see he did it right.'

'You're all the same, you lot. Always blaming someone else when things go wrong.' He turned back to his companion. 'Scoundrels, the lot of 'em.'

Crestfallen, George made his way back down the iron staircase. He intended to be first in line tomorrow morning but knew in his heart, if these were the merchants looking for a team, he would not be picked.

Chapter 12

George was wrong. He got to market at half past three and joined in the line waiting for hire. There were five ahead of him. As others came up to queue George searched to find some of his old pals but these men were all strangers. Most of them were older men. Prompt at four the doors opened and the first man through was the one who had chided George the day before. He swaggered down the line and as he drew level with him, George looked down knowing he wasn't to be chosen. The next two buyers called out names of men who had worked for them before. Despondently, George scuffed the toe of his boot. The number waiting in line dwindled. George was aware of a shadow in front of him.

'Stringer, isn't it?'

'Yes, sir,' and George saw it was the other man he had seen yesterday.

'How are the legs? All healed now?'

'Yes, sir. I'm as fit as ever, sir.'

'Who were the porters in your gang?'

'There was Bodger, and Flitton, and Cowley were the regulars, sir.'

'Any of them here now?'

'No, sir. I don't understand it. They were always early.'

'Probably gone to Covent Garden. Anyway, pick four men and come inside. My name's Cook, Augustus Cook. South Wall.'

George hesitated. 'Come inside, you say. Am I hired, sir?'

Mr. Cook smiled and tapped his arm. 'Course, you are. Get your men and get a move on. Don't want to miss the best bargains.'

George almost danced down the line, looking at the remaining men. He picked those who looked the youngest and fittest and marshalled them over to the South Wall. Mr. Cook strode round the market selecting his purchases and George followed behind tying tickets onto crates of apples, sacks of potatoes, onions, turnips. He'd race back to the gang and direct them to collect the produce for loading onto wagons in the road outside. The horses were secured to the railings and some had nose bags. in the first hour of trading, the feverish pitch was tiring. George once or twice felt his legs buckle slightly under the strain of carrying three boxes on his head. He had to pause a moment.

Mr. Cooke touched his shoulder.

'I was only taking a breather, Mr. Cook. Just to steady my legs. Been a bit out of practice like. But I'm moving on now, sir.'

'I was going to say, Stringer, don't put too much pressure on your legs. Use this.' From the side of his stall he wheeled a hand cart. 'Let the rest do it the usual way, but,' he winked, 'you're the ganger.'

Augustus Cook proved to be a good employer. He was a considerate man to all his hired help. When George approached him about not yet receiving compensation, Cook was astounded.

'I'll have a word with Mr Horner myself to find out why the Tribunal has taken so long. Do you know, he once worked here as a porter? Now he owns the market.'

Cooke was as good as his word and a week later, at the end of trading, he joined George at the tavern.

'The Board has approved settlement, Stringer, so you'll be getting payment shortly. When I spoke to Robert Horner, he said he was already looking into why your case hadn't been settled. He'd had a letter about it from someone.'

George received a first payment of three pounds and three instalments to be paid monthly of two pounds ten shillings.

Laura walked home from school on her own. Georgie didn't want to be seen walking with a girl even if she was his sister; he had his own group of friends. Vily Walters had a new best friend and the partnership excluded Laura. Not that she minded; they never talked about anything interesting like theatres and plays, novels and writers. And she had a lot to think about. Mrs Gowrie told her the examination date had been announced. It would take place on Thursday the thirteenth of July.

'Are you sure, Laura, your parents will allow you to continue your education?'

'Yes, Mrs Gowrie, I'm sure they will.'

'Perhaps they may wish you to take employment at the end of summer term. There would be no way to prevent them from taking you out of school when you have passed the Labour Board criteria. You were twelve in January and you will take that test in March.'

Although the government had raised the school leaving age to thirteen, children could leave after their twelfth birthday provided they passed a test showing they had attained basic education standards in reading, writing and arithmetic.

Laura was disconsolate. What Mrs Gowrie said was very true. Like Sarah, she may also be put to work.

They had walked in silence to the end of the corridor. Mrs Gowrie put a hand on Laura's shoulder. She bent forward to put her head near to Laura's.

'Of course,' she whispered, 'there would be no question of you leaving school before your thirteenth birthday if you failed the Labour test.'

Laura was about to protest she couldn't possibly fail such an easy test when she saw Mrs Gowrie smile and wink.

Yes there was a lot on her mind. It would have to be sums where she could make an intentional mistake, not spelling, no-one would believe her if she made a mistake in spelling. Could she really do it? Could she deliberately fail?

A group of rowdy youngsters hurtled round the corner, knocking into her, as they bowled a hoop along.

'Bet you can't bowl it fast.'

'Bet I can do it faster than you.'

'No you can't.'

The five children squabbled over the hoop.

She was older than them but Laura was caught up in their excitement. She was about the same height as the children.

'Bet I could bowl it faster than any of you,' she boasted.

A tall boy had followed in the wake of the hoop bowlers. He was amused to see the group were silenced when Laura threw down her challenge. He looked at the small oval face and saw the defiant glint in her eyes.

'Go on, then. Try!' he commanded.

Laura's hand skimmed over the shiny wooden hoop to send it hurtling along. In her agitation to keep it upright, her short legs, clad in black stockings, became a smudge as her button-sided boots barely touched the flag stones. Her russet hair flew out behind her loosening out from the confines of the plait. The sound of frightened whinnying, stilled her enthusiasm as the big hoop bounced off the stone trough where the horse of a four-wheeled growler had been watering.

'Look out, you urchin!' the cab driver shouted.

A contrite Laura looked up at him. 'I'm very sorry, sir,' and dropped a quick curtsy.

Smartly retrieving the hoop she marched back to the youth.

'There!' she surveyed the group. 'I bowled it faster than any of you.' She swished the hoop in their direction and turned her steps toward Crownfield Road. She had crossed onto the other side when she sensed someone beside her. It was the lanky youth.

'For a little one, your legs move fast. You were ever so much quicker than the others.'

'It wasn't really fair. I'm older than them. I'm twelve.'

'You won fair and square.' He stepped in front of Laura as his long bony fingers plucked off his cloth cap. 'My name's Eddie. Eddie Sawyer.'

'I'm Laura Stringer.'

They were at the corner of Burgess Road outside *Mary's*.

'Here, come into *Mary's* and I'll buy you something for winning.'

Mary's had an exciting spicy smell which always thrilled Laura on those special occasions when she was sent out get a pennyworth of jam. She would watch every movement as a wooden spoonful was extracted from a seven pound jar of plum jam and the sticky red mess ladled into the cup she held tightly between her fingers.

Eddie's arm expansively offered Laura her choice: bullseyes, pear drops, cough candy, stick jaw - each in its own wooden channel fronted by small mesh chicken wire. Laura's gaze greedily slid along each tray.

'No, I couldn't honestly!' And she turned to leave the shop.

Eddie's voice held authority: 'Two ounces of stick jaw, please Mary,' and he put a farthing on the counter.

Outside the shop, they stood under the gas lamp and shared the confection.

'I'm fourteen, well fifteen next week. I'm working, you see. At the Great Eastern. I help load the delivery carts and sometimes I ride on the tail to see none of the load shifts. When I'm eighteen I hope to go into the sheds and be a wheel greaser.'

'Oh you must be ever so careful,' Laura said with concern. 'I was told of a wheel greaser who lost his arm.'

'Course I'll be careful. I'm going to live to eighty. Gypsy told my fortune. That's a lark, ain't it? Got to get off to my tea, now. I'll meet you again tomorrow. By the horse trough. Ta-ta.'

He raced off down the road leaving Laura speechless.

Astutely, Laura decided she should not be seen with her books at the kitchen table. In her room, she quickly made notes of dates and places she wanted to memorise and then put them carefully in a box under her bed. She took her box of cloth scraps through to the kitchen and sorted out a few pretty pieces of ribbon. At the bottom of the box were her notes and occasionally she would lift the material and silently recite them.

It pleased Jane to see her daughter was doing something useful rather than having her head stuck in a book.

'I'm making this for Sarah's birthday next week, Ma. Do you think she'll like it?'

She held up a delicate piece of lace which had been

fashioned into a cap and edged with pale pink satin ribbon.

'It's very nice, Laura and I know Sarah will be delighted with it.'

'May I go and see her on her birthday, Ma? Do you think it will be all right'

'I don't think the Master and Mistress would like her to have visitors. But we'll see, child.'

Several nights Laura joined in the street games with the other children playing tag or hopscotch. When it wasn't her turn, she stood beneath a gas lamp and took out her notes to memorise.

Coming from the cat's meat shop, she passed Mary's open door.

'Dearie! Laura! Come here a minute.'

'Have you got any more pictures for me, Mary?'

'No, but I got a message from your beau!'

'Whatever do you mean?' Laura laughed.

'Young Eddie Sawyer was cut to the quick because you didn't keep your...hassignation...with him. Says you were to meet last Wednesday and you never showed.' She leaned forward. 'He's a very good lad he is,' she said earnestly. 'Says he'll be at the horse trough each night about eight. Go on, love, go and meet him.'

Laura could feel her cheeks burning hotter with every word Mary uttered. She held her parcel tight and ran out of the shop, heading for home.

Except when it was raining, or snowing, or if it was bitterly cold, all the children played together in the street. It saved on lighting indoors and kept them out of the way while the bread-winner ate his food. They were called indoors at internals of age, the elder ones staying out until nine o'clock. After a few games of Bogey Man, Laura moved off to the end of Burgess Road. She wondered why she was walking along Wingfield Road in the direction of Leytonstone Road. But that was where the horse-trough is, a voice in her head said. She saw the junction ahead. Leaning against the lamp post, seeming to be almost as tall as the glass box, was Eddie. He saw her and waved. Within seconds, his long legs covered the space between them.

'I'm glad you've come,' he said. 'I've been thinking about you all day. Somehow I knew you'd come tonight.'

He looked down at her and smiled. Laura saw he had the bluest eyes she had ever seen. They were like sparkling gem stones.

'There was a lot doing at work today. Mind you, it's always a lot of rush and hurry. Got to get a wagon unloaded and onto the carts and delivered before you can say Cock Robin. But we have a good team. If it's not heavy stuff, we make a line between the wagon and the cart and pass it to next bloke and it gets loaded in no time. Of course, we don't use horses no more. No, we've got engine carts. Don't half go at a fair lick.'

They were walking side by side and after the first few paces, when Laura was having to almost skip along to keep up with him, Eddie reduced his stride to match her step. They walked and chatted until a clock chimed nine.

'Oh, its late. I must get home.' Laura said.

'I'll walk with you, Where do you live?'

'Burgess Road.'

'Well, then, we're almost neighbours. I live in Argyle Road.'

'Argyle road!' Laura said in amazement. 'That's on the other side, across the main road.'

'I know it is,' he replied with a grin, 'but not that far we couldn't be neighbours.'

They retraced their steps toward home.

'I don't finish at the depot until seven, so I can't see you before eight o'clock. Last week when I saw you in the afternoon there'd been a fire and they closed the freight sheds. But I don't work on Sundays. When the weather perks up we can go and hear the band in the park.'

Eddie seemed to be organising her life. Somehow, Laura didn't mind.

'Here, I tell you what. Friday is my birthday, we could have some oysters from Charlie's. What do you say?'

'Friday? The twenty-fourth? That's my sister's birthday, too.'

'Oh, yes, I see. You'll be with her.'

'No she doesn't live at home, she's in service. I've made a lace cap as a present for her but I don't know when I shall give it to her. She's a long way away in Woodford.' For a moment her heart ached with sadness at the distance between her and Sarah. Then she remembered about Charlie's.

'It would be nice to have oysters.'

Laura snuggled down under her blanket. Mary was right. Eddie was nice. He was easy to talk to and fun to be with. Lucky ambled into the room and leapt onto the bed.

'Not tonight, puss. I'm a bit tired.' Laura pushed him gently to the floor and he stalked off with his tail in the air.

Laura found she could tell Eddie all about school and her hopes about the examination which would take her into the County School. He offered to help her and they would sit on the kerb under a light, Eddie holding the books testing Laura. She also confided to him the problem of the qualifying test and was surprised how strongly he supported Mrs Gowrie's proposal of deliberately failing. It was a relief to be able to share her secrets with someone.

Standing at Charlie's Eddie bought four oysters for a penny.

'Two each,' he said, handing her one.

Laura looked at the pretty pearl shell with the pale peach coloured yolk sitting in a gluey sea. What did one do with it? Under her lashes she glanced up at Eddie. The stall holder had handed him a small knife which he slipped under the yolk and then, my goodness! He tossed it straight into his mouth. Oh, she couldn't do that!

'They're fresh,' Charlie said defensively, seeing the expression on Laura's face.

'Ain't you had 'em before, Laura?' Eddie asked.

She shook her head.

He smiled kindly at her. 'Never mind. Another time you might like to try.' He deftly took her two oysters and devoured them with a gulp. 'Very tasty oysters, Charlie. Thank you. Goodnight.'

They walked along in silence. Laura felt close to tears.

'Oh, Eddie. I didn't mean to spoil your birthday treat.'

'There, girlie, don't you fret. Spoil my birthday? It's the best one I've had, with you for company. Hope your sister's had a good day too.'

Even Sarah forgot it was her birthday. The morning had started as all other mornings start: up at five o'clock, down to the kitchen to rake out the range. Into the breakfast room, clear the grate and lay a new fire. Up on the first floor, same for the morning room, the withdrawing room and the parlour. Mr Paget would inspect them and, if he'd got out of the wrong side of the bed, he would demolish them and she would have to start over again. She prayed for a long, hot summer to start at Easter so there would be no more fires to set. By the time she had made up the last grate, Mrs Bumstead, the cook, had filled the sink with dirty dishes.

It was afternoon and Mrs Whitaker was 'At Home'

with lots of comings and goings of ladies and their eldest daughters. Cook was making up the weekend order book for the errand boy.

'Mr Paget. Will you be so kind as to recite to me the date on your newspaper?'

Paget wiped his watery eyes and loudly blew his nose before answering, his thin reedy voice matching his thin reedy build.

'The date on this newspaper, which is today's says Friday, Twenty Fourth February Nineteen Hundred and Five.'

Sarah was heaving a large copper pan out of a sink full of suds.

'Oo,' she squealed. 'It's my birthday.'

Her grasp on the pan loosened and dirty, soapy water cascaded onto the black and white tiled floor. It raced like a tide towards the table and waves of scum lapped over the highly polished black leather boots of Mr Paget and the brown calf slippers of Mrs Bumstead.

In the tiny attic room, Sarah shared a truckle bed with Lizzie Hedges.

'Stop laughing, Lizzie,' Sarah nudged her companion. 'You'll have us on the floor.'

'Ah, but it was such a treat to see missus hopping about on one leg, shaking the other one and splashing old Pinch-me-Paget. Beats the best turn on the Halls.' Lizzie erupted into laughter again.

Sarah had found Midmellian House a daunting place. Dark woodwork outside and dark woodwork inside created a gloomy atmosphere. Mr Whitaker had black hair and a black beard and bushy eyebrows that went up and down like a yo-yo when he spoke. His booming voice struck terror into all the servants, including Paget. Mrs Whitaker, a thin waspish woman, had a waspish temper and was to be avoided at all costs.

She sorely missed Laura but it was with happy relief that Sarah found a companion in fifteen year old Lizzie. Sarah had been taken on as a scullery maid; Lizzie was employed as housemaid but there was little difference in their duties except Sarah did not go beyond the first floor. Lizzie prepared the fires in the family bedrooms on the second floor and in the nursery on the third floor and for the other servants.

In spite of herself, Sarah couldn't stop from laughing.

'Well, I've had a good birthday even if they do stop my wages.'

There were those who were not surprised at Laura's failure. Mrs Gowrie professed disappointment but declared even the best of students can succumb to nerves at examination time, even simple ones. Vily Walters had other ideas.

'Mooning about with the boys - well, one boy special like - that's what done for you, Laura. Your mind wasn't on the test but on him, I'm sure of it. What will you do?'

'Well, Vily, I'll have to take it again next year after my birthday.' She almost added, 'I hope it won't be necessary.' The results of the entrance examination to the County School would be known long before that.

Eddie was waiting for her as usual.

'How did it go, Laurie? Did I say that was to be my special name for you? No? Well, it is.'

When he smiled he didn't grin from ear to ear. His lips parted, showing his small white teeth, his cheeks gently rippled and crinkles spread around his eyes.

Laura gazed up into his face. She felt a glowing warmth in his presence.

'It went very well. I failed.' she laughed.

The Easter weather was not as Sarah had wished but it was sunny and there was a hint of warmth in the air. They took the tram to the terminus and changed to a horse drawn bus for Wanstead where they boarded the bus for Woodford. Trees along the edge of Epping Forest were just unveiling virgin leaves. In the soft Spring light, they glinted like pale green stars. Scattered among grassy patches, bright yellow daffodils swayed and nodded in the breeze.

'Oh, it's beautiful here,' Laura said with a sigh. 'How lovely to live among tall trees with flowers at your feet'

'Yes, it looks right enough but it's not for me. Give me the busy London streets, the shouts and cries of the vendors. That's life!'

'I'd like to have both, Eddie. A nice patch of grass and trees near to the city,' Laura laughed.

In the village they asked directions to Midmellian House. It wasn't far from the main road. They walked along the lane, past two large houses with painted name plates and the next, taller than the first ones, had an elaborate gilded sign.

'We'd best see how to get round the back,' Eddie said. But there didn't appear to be a side alley. All the houses, although set in their own grounds, were connected by a communal fence between them.

'I suppose we'll have to go through those,' Laura pointed to the tall iron gates with a scrolled initial **M** inserted in the centre.

Eddie tested the gates but they were firmly shut.

'Look, here.' Laura had moved behind the stone pillar supporting the left gate. A swing gate was set in an iron half circle which opened wide enough for one person at a time to move through.

Inside the boundary, a shingle drive led to the pillared front steps. Leading directly from the swing gate, a narrow path wound around the periphery to the back of the brick house.

Laura wondered if they had dogs like at Great Aunt's

farm. They had a ferocious bark but were as meek as lambs. No barks announced their approach. They turned the corner of the building and saw a partly opened door. Nearby was a bicycle with a large front basket and a smaller one at the rear.

Eddie knocked on the door. The chattering voices inside ceased. A chair scraped and then the door was flung wide.

Mr. Paget's watery eyes looked them up and down.

Laura stepped forward and curtsied. 'Beg pardon sir.'

She got no further. Mr Paget waved her away.

'We do not buy from gypsies.'

Before he had time to close the door, Eddie had leapt forward and neatly put his foot on the step.

'Beg pardon, sir.' he repeated and heavily emphasised **Sir**, 'but this young lady would be most obliged if she could see her sister, Sarah Stringer. She is in service here, is she not?'

Paget was surprised at the determined manner of the young man and merely nodded in response. Several people were seated around the table and, once the door had been pushed back by Eddie's foot, were following procedures with interest. A large woman stood up.

'What is it, Mr Paget?'

'They want to see the scullery maid, Mrs Bumstead.' With that he relinquished his position to Mrs Bumstead and retreated to the table.

Laura smiled sweetly and decided to curtsey again. 'How do, ma'am. I should so like to see my sister. I have come all the way from Stratford to bring her a present.'

Mrs Bumstead moved away and the errand boy came out and climbed upon his bicycle. The door was closed.

'Well! They are a rum lot,' Eddie commented. 'Why can't they offer a civil word to a creature?'

'Should we go home?'

'No. Let's give it a minute or two. Something might turn up.'

They waited by the corner. Clouds had built up shutting out the weak sun. The latch clicked as the door opened and Sarah stepped into the courtyard. Laura ran to her and flung her arms about her sister. She kissed and hugged her until they were both breathless. They both began speaking at once.

'No, you first, Sarah. How are you getting on?'

When Laura stood back to look at her sister she was distressed to see the lovely round face with the pink blushed cheeks, now thin and pale and, yes, dirty, were streaked with tears.

'Tell Ma I'm well, won't you, Laura?' Please tell her and Pa everything is all right.'

Laura reached up and pushed back the grubby mop cap from her forehead. Straggly ends of hair poked out.

'Your hair,' she almost shrieked. 'What has happened to your beautiful hair?'

'I couldn't keep it in the cap, you see. It would come out.' Sarah's eyes filled with tears. She roughly brushed them away and Laura saw her reddened, swollen hands.

'Don't tell Ma. Please Laura.'

Eddie came to stand close behind Laura. He gently put his hand on her shoulder. He understood.

Laura smiled brightly. 'Oh Sarah. You must meet this friend of mine. His name is Eddie Sawyer. And, what do you think? His birthday is the same as yours, twenty-fourth of February.'

'How do, Sarah.' Eddie shook her hand warmly. 'Heard a lot about you from Laurie. Here, Laurie. Where's your present for Sarah?'

Sarah was pleased with the gift. 'I'll wear it next Sunday. I have a new friend, too. She's called Lizzie and we share a bed and have a high old time at night Real larks we have. Better go now, got work to do.' She grasped Laura tightly. 'Ever so pleased I am that you came to see me. God Bless you.'

She slipped the lace cap into her bosom and ran back inside. Eddie and Laura walked slowly back to the swing gate, neither said a word. Their shared silence lasted until they were on the tram.

'Look at them there lights,' Eddie pointed to the shops along the Broadway. Large gas jets flared from the pathway throwing a brilliance onto the display windows. 'Country's all right in the summer time, Laurie. But, come the dreary winter days and the trees all bare, no colourful flowers and what was green fields in summer is covered white with snow, country-side ain't inviting.'

'You're right of course. I hope Sarah won't be too unhappy there.'

'She says she's got a friend. And a trouble shared is a trouble lightened. We'll visit her again, Laurie.'

She had asked her mother for her address, so Jane knew she was visiting Sarah. Although she was troubled by her sister's appearance, Laura kept her promise and didn't mention it.

'Yes, Pa she's well. She has to work quite hard but there is another girl about her age. Lizzie, I think Sarah called her. They re friends and spend time together.'

'I expect she'll be all right,' Jane said. 'I hope there haven't been more breakages.'

In her mind, Laura saw the swollen red fingers. It must be difficult to hold bowls and dishes with sore hands. She said goodnight and went to her room. Georgie was already asleep in his corner. From under the bed she pulled out her books. Not daring to use the gas mantle, Laura lit a candle. With them open on her lap, her eyes did not see the page. She thought about Sarah. 'Whatever work I have to do. I shall **NEVER** be a servant. **NEVER!**'

She heard the door close and stepped back from the sink to look along the passageway.

'What's up, love? You're home early.' For one rapid moment Jane surveyed George's figure. There were no bandages.

'No work,' was his brief reply. He dropped into his chair. 'It's been running down ever since I went back. Oh, it got a boost over the Christmas but not much'

'I expect it'll get going with the summer trade. Lots of apples and plums and suchlike and then there's all those foreign fruits. You'll be busy again soon.'

'Mr Cook is doubtful. There's only him and two other buyers that use Spitalfields. Covent Garden is to blame. They've taken the trade. They were just flowers but bit by bit they've been pinching the fruit and veg. Suppliers as well. Mr Cook has laid off his other blokes, only kept me on out of the goodness of his heart I reckon. But we had to shut up today, the owner closed the gates.'

'Well, perhaps Mr Cook will transfer to Covent Garden and you can go too. There'd be nothing in it for the journey, dearest, would there?'

'No chance of that! Mr Cook says he'll pack the whole lot in if Spitalfields closes. And Covent Garden has a different system. You can't stand in line to be hired. You have to know somebody to speak for you.'

'Don't cross your bridges until you come to them. Things will work out, I'm sure. We'll manage. I've got my regulars I wash for and there's the five shillings I get for doing for Joe Grimes. Yes, we'll manage.'

For several weeks, George worked only three days out of six, one week he only worked a day and a half. He hardly earned enough to pay his fares. Luckily, there was still some of his compensation money left.

The first payment had gone towards clearing debts, as well as the second instalment. The next payment went to the tally man but the last one went into the savings tin. After the week of only a day and a half's money, Jane dipped into the tin to give George sixpence for his Saturday night at the *Thatched House*.

He looked at the coins in his hand. 'Is it all right, Jane?'

'Of course, it is dearest. Go on, go out and have a drink with your pals. Cheer you up a bit.' She leaned forward and kissed him. There was no ardent response from George. She stood on the doorstep and watched him walk up the road. He never looked back; she waited until he had turned the corner. An anguished sigh welled up in her. Had their love really died? Had it been killed by the drudgery and grind of surviving from one day to the next? Was it something that could be chipped away leaving nothing but flakes? Her life was structured around love for George; she could endure any hardship knowing she would find peace in his arms, solace in his caress. But, if she didn't have that?

'Was you coming in or going out, Mrs Stringer?'

Jane jumped. Her fingers were stiff from gripping the door frame.

'Beg pardon, Mrs Milton. I'd just seen George off and I must have got into a day dream.'

'I'm just going round for a ha'porth of gin,' she held up he tin mug. 'I don't like sitting in the snug by myself so I bring it home. You wouldn't care to join me, would you, dearie?'

'Another time, Mrs Milton. I've got several loads of washing to finish.'

Jane had got a fat rabbit and made it into two pies, a large one for them and the small one for Joe Grimes. She had cleaned his house in the morning and brought home his washing to do with her other regulars. George had done a full day at market and while he was taking his nap she had made the pies. She was proud of her pastry. Everyone said how light it was. She left the large pie at the side of the range and covered the small one with a cloth and walked down to Number Twenty-One. She lifted the knocker.

'It's Jane Stringer, Joe.'

He's probably out in the privy, she thought. She pushed the door and stepped inside. Calling all the while, she walked through to the kitchen. Leaving the pie on the table she moved toward the scullery but the door was shut. It was hard to push open, something was blocking it from the other side. Her strong arms forced a gap and she peered round. Slumped against the door was Joe's crumpled body.

Jane didn't remember calling for help but the kitchen became crammed with people. Later, sitting in Mrs Walter's kitchen, Jane asked if the doctor had been.

'Yes, dearie. Said it was his heart.'

'But he was such a fit man. So strong. Never a hint of illness. Why should his heart give out?'

'Comes to all of us, dearie, sooner or later. Joe had had a good life. He was seventy - can't expect more than that.'

It was a simple funeral arranged by Joe's brother. He made no contact with the neighbours nor asked anyone to prepare the funeral supper. In fact, some of the neighbours missed offering their last respects as the hearse left as quickly as it arrived. The house was cleared in a couple of days the rent collector said a new tenant would be in by the weekend. Just as if Joe had never existed.

Losing such a well paid job came at the worst time. But it wasn't just the money she missed. Jane had enjoyed the time she had spent tidying up his house, dusting trinkets and pictures. There was a delicate set of cups and saucers displayed in a glass fronted cabinet as well as china animal ornaments and coloured glass plates. A welcome break from dirty laundry.

Now it was all over. By the second week of June, every last farthing in the savings tin had been spent. There were no knots in her petticoat and Jane owed three weeks' rent money.

'But, Ma,' Georgie wailed, 'it's only sixpence. That's not a lot of money, is it?' All the others are going. Freddie and Ginger and even Josh Meekers said he was going. I must go.'

'Ma would like you to go, Georgie son, but money's tight right now. Another time. You'll be able to go another time.'

'But it's **NOW** I want to go. Another time will be different. Why can't I go?'

Jane flung the savings tin across the room. 'That's why!' she shouted.

Georgie burst into tears. His mother had never shouted at him in all the ten years of his life. George stared open mouthed at his wife. Laura silently witnessed the scene, she felt the hurt of her young brother's disappointment and the humiliation of her mother's despair.

Jane turned into the scullery and slammed the door. She ran the tap and bent forward. With cupped hands she dowsed her face repeatedly until it was quite cold. She came back into the kitchen and busied herself at the range. A few bones, a few vegetable scraps. As she turned them round in the pot her mind flew to another stew pot balanced on a few sticks in a fire grate many years ago in Granny Stringer's place. And the awful smell of boiled cabbage leaves.

Eddie took Laura's hand. She was startled they had never touched each other during the many hours they were together. Sometimes talking - they always confided in each other. Sometimes just sitting together in silence.

'Here,' he said. 'Give this to young Georgie.'

Laura looked at the shiny silver sixpence nestling in the palm of her hand.

'Oh, Eddie, I couldn't take it. Really, I couldn't.'

'Why not, Laurie? It's a good coin of the realm.'

'I know, Eddie,' she managed a smile. 'But I can't take it from you.'

'Laurie. You and yours is my family.'

'I'm not sure Ma wants him to go. Last time he went, Oh, it was years ago, he was only little and I took him along. Well, he caught measles and was ever so ill.'

'I remember, you told me. And you caught it and nearly went blind. Give him the tanner. Tell your Ma I want him to have it.'

They were walking along The Broadway and drew level with The King's Head. A portrait of King Edward the Seventh was displayed with a placard saying: Birthday Greetings to His Majesty.

'If he has two birthdays, does he get twice as old?' Eddie asked with a grin.

Laura walked home deep in thought.

Chapter Thirteen

She was tired. It had been a long day. Her feet dragged her body along. If only she had longer legs she could run twice as fast. She turned the corner of the familiar street and up the short path to the front door and counted the clock chimes to eight. She had prepared in her mind what she was going to say. The kitchen door was closed but she sensed they were standing in the room.

'Hello, Pa. Ma' She reached up and kissed her father as she always did when she came home from school and he got up from his rest.

'Where have you been?' George demanded.

'Georgie said you didn't go with him this morning nor come home with him. I asked Vily Walters,' Jane added, 'and she said you were not in school today.'

'So, where have your been?' George repeated.

Twelve year old Laura was tired and weary but she knew she must have her say now.

'I've got a job,' she told them.

'A job? What do you mean a job?'

'What's this nonsense?'

'It's not nonsense, Pa. I've got a job. In a factory in London. I went up there this morning and they took me on straight away.'

She'd given much thought to the problem. The family needed money - she would have to work. Laura had seen Uncle Will pushing his vegetable cart and raced after him. He'd stopped to speak to two cronies but listened to Laura's pleas.

'No, lass. I can't pay for a helper, especially a girl. And a small girl at that.'

'You'd do better in a factory. Yardley's along the Mile End Road take girls,' one said.

'Yeah, but they pay farthings,' the other said. 'Better pay in the city and an early workman's ticket don't cost much.'

He turned away from her and shouted to a group about to enter the public house. Two men came over to him.

'Arnold. This lass wants work in a city factory. Can you help?'

'Well, that's queer! Place next door put up a notice about training for youths.'

It was just what Laura wanted. She agreed to be at the station at seven o'clock.

She had to ask Uncle Will to lend her the fare money.

Laura told Georgie she was doing something special in the morning and he'd have to go to school by himself. And, he was to say nothing to Ma. She slipped out of the house as soon as Jane had left to collect washing orders.

'This pal of Uncle Will's told me about this factory giving training to youths but when I got there they said it was for boys. But the nice old man on the gate told me a factory further along took girls. It's called Garsten's and they make leather bags and cases and I started work today.'

'A factory!' George snarled. 'No child of mine's going to work in a factory!'

'I've already started, Pa. I'm a run around girl. They

pay two shillings a week. It's tuppence a day on the train from Stratford to Aldersgate so I'll need a shilling a week for fares but the rest is yours, Ma. Except, I'll have to pay back the fourpence I borrowed from Uncle Will.'

'Borrowed from Uncle Will! Really girl.'

'I needed the money for the train fare.' Laura looked down at her boots then raised her eyes to Jane. 'And I shall need to borrow Sarah's birth certificate, Ma. Please, Ma.'

'Whatever for?' George was losing track of the conversation.

Jane had sat down in the bent wood rocking chair and was gently swaying back and forth. She stopped the chair's motion and looked intently at Laura.

'Because she is only twelve years old. A child can go into service at twelve, or as young as nine, but can't do any other sort of work unless they have the Labour Test Certificate. And Laura failed the test.'

Laura began to squirm under her mother's penetrating gaze.

'So you told them you were thirteen, did you?'

'Yes, Ma. But I didn't think it was dishonest, I just sort of had another birthday.' Laura gave a false laugh, 'I thought, if the King can have two birthdays in one year, then why can't I?'

Jane poured some broth into a bowl and cut a hunk of bread.

'Eat your supper, girl. It'll give you some nourishment. I'll look out Sarah's certificate for you.'

Laura drank the hot savoury liquid and mopped up the last dregs with the bread. With each mouthful, her head dropped lower and lower. A last crust was still between her fingers as she fell sound asleep. Jane stroked her head and looked at George. He nodded. He picked up his daughter's exhausted body and gently carried her to bed.

She was the first one standing there. Inset in the high brick wall, were two iron doors. Within minutes a small group had gathered and when a siren sounded, the doors swing inwards and they surged forward jostling Laura to the back.

She found the clerk's office; Mr A Pilgrim painted in gold letters on the glass door. A shadowy figure was behind a desk and raised an arm after she tapped at the door. Did that mean come in or stay out, she wondered? She ventured to turn the handle and went in.

'I've brought my birth certificate, sir,' she said demurely.

He looked over the top of his pince-nez, his eyebrows rising up to his hairline.

'Why aren't you at your bench? Doors open at two minutes to eight; eight o'clock work commences.' He took out a watch from his vest pocket. 'It is now two, no three minutes AFTER eight.'

'Yes, sir.' Laura ran from the office still clutching Sarah's birth certificate.

They found her an orange box to stand on as she was unable to reach the bench with ease. There were troughs of buttons, studs and buckles of different shapes and sizes. She had to make sure only one kind was in each numbered box. The work benches were numbered, too, and if there was a shout of SIX NUMBER TEN FOR TWO she had to scoop out six items from box number ten and run with it to bench number two. Sometimes if all stitching machines were operating, it was hard to hear anything at all. The overseer would bring his fist down hard onto the bench making studs and buttons whirl up in a frenzied dance.

'Twelve Seven Five,' he'd bellow in her ear.

The large floor area was divided into two. One half was the cutting room where only men were employed. Soft skins were piled around the walls and the men selected the appropriate skin for cutting. They were wheeled through on a trolley to the second half of the room where men and women worked at benches, gluing cardboard and material linings to the leather, smoothing each surface before they were passed to the machinists for sewing. Three stoves were spaced out in the room and held large tubs of glue. Bench hands used a ladle to fill their individual tin cans.

Laura nearly choked as the smell filled her nostrils and throat. 'You get used to it, love. After another few days you won't even notice it. Here, Maisie! You got any of that lavender water left. Give the youngster a sniff of it before she's sick all over the place.'

Her Pa was wrong, Laura decided. He said factory folk were a bad lot but most of the women were kind to her. Prompt at twelve o'clock, the factory shut and workers filed out into the street. Most sat on the ground leaning against the wall to eat their midday meal which consisted of bread and jam. Men sat one side of the gates and women the other, just occasionally they mingled.

Laura sat with Maisie who had given her a dab of lavender water on her dress. Jane had spread one small piece of bread with a bit of dripping and another piece with a dab of jam and wrapped them into a small kerchief. She didn't think she was hungry; the smell of the hides, glue and sweating bodies made her nauseous but outside in the dusty street she could breath again and quickly devoured her food. Sharp at one o'clock the gates reopened and the workers trooped inside.

All afternoon Laura was running from bench to bench, handing over studs, collecting segments of bags to deliver for stitching; taking stitched pieces back to benches for more studs or buckles or buttons. Just as she picked up a large pile of half finished bags, the siren sounded. Everyone put down their tools and made for the exit.

'What shall I do with these,' she asked a tall man as he passed by.

'Put 'em back where you took 'em from. Tomorrow's another day, missy.'

It took such a long time to walk to Aldersgate Street station.

'I'm sure I'll get used to it in time.' she told herself.

At five minutes to two on Saturday afternoon, Laura stood in line to receive her wages. Men were paid first then the women and after them the juveniles. There were three: thirteen year old Jack Armstrong, who stacked up the pelts in the work room from the basement store; Daisy Sudson, whose sole task was to sweep the entire floor space from one end to the other before doing it all over again in reverse order; and run around girl Laura. Daisy could neither read nor write and didn't know how old she was.

The coins were counted out on the table by Mr Pilgrim and passed to Johnson, the overseer. After Jack had taken his pay, Laura stepped forward. The coppers were lined up at the edge. She scooped up her first wages: nine pence. She would still have to borrow thruppence to cover the train fares for six days but it was a start.

She was waiting at the horse trough and saw his tall figure approaching. He broke into a run.

'Laurie, girl. I've been worried out of my mind about you. Why didn't you come on Wednesday and Friday like always? If you hadn't come tonight, I was going to pluck up courage to call round your house. What's up, Laurie?'

They walked along side by side as she told him.

'No, Laurie. No!'

She looked up into his face. His blue eyes were masked by tears; there was a break in his voice.'

'You only needed another week before the County School Examination. You shouldn't have done it, Laurie. You knew you'd get through the test to win a scholarship place. You knew it. You were going to be a teacher.'

'Eddie, don't take on so. I don't mind, really I don't. I think I knew in my heart it was just a dream. Like Sarah going to be a dancer. We used to play at being dancer and teacher. We almost believed it would be possible. Well, you have to have something to dream on.'

'It **WAS** possible. You were almost there. Look how much you've taught me. I enjoyed learning along with you because you made the book pages mean something. I enjoyed it more than I ever did when I was in the school room. That's good teaching.'

'There was no other way, Eddie. We are poor and there is still young Georgie at home. I was **NOT** going into service like Sarah.'

He strode ahead for a while then slowed his step until Laura drew level again.

'I wish you hadn't done it. But I'll say no more.'

Laura settled into the factory routine. By the end of the fourth week she had worked out a pattern of collection and delivery. She ran from one half of the room to the other and seemed to anticipate the workers' needs.

'How did you know I wanted studs?'

'When I passed a moment ago I saw your tray was nearly empty,' she replied.

She was so efficient, she found there was time to spare and spent it sorting out the leather cuttings. Suddenly her ear was being pulled off her head.

'I've been calling you, Sal, for half an hour. You deaf, or something.'

'Ouch! My ear!.'

'Give over, Kate,' Maisie called. 'She may not answer to Sal, or even Sally. Eh, Sarah?'

'So what's your name then?' Kate let go of her ear.

'My name's Laura,' she blurted out as she rubbed her sore ear.

'That's a damned fine thing. How the bleedin' Hell do you make that out of Sarah?'

Too late, Laura realised what she had done. Her cheeks reddened and she put her hands over her face.

'Look what you've done, Kate. Poor kid.'

Maisie left her bench and came over to console her. At that moment the overseer came out of the lavatory.

'Back to your benches at once! All of you. Get on with your work.'

The women hurried to their places. Laura scooped up a selection of studs, buckles and buttons, ran to Kate and deposited them on her bench.

At midday, Laura walked to the far end of the wall and squatted down away from the line of women. She didn't want to talk to them. Her mind was miles away as she unwrapped her bread and jam until she became aware of someone beside her.

'All right if I sit alonga you?' Daisy asked.

Laura forgot her own problems and smiled at the girl. As she broke the bread into pieces, she casually passed a piece to Daisy who took it as daintily as she knew how but wolfed it in one swallow.

Kate stood in front of them. She was a large girl with massive hands, looking much older than her fifteen years. 'Go and sit at the other end for a bit, Daisy. I want to have a word.' Daisy reluctantly moved away. 'I know it's none of my business, but I'm the nosey sort. When I smell a mystery I like to unravel it. So, you going to tell me why you got two names?'

Al first, Laura was indignant. It had nothing to do

with Kate, or any of them, except Mr Pilgrim, of course. Her mouth was set in grim determination. Kate had slid down onto the pavement beside her and playfully dug Laura in the ribs and laughed.

'You done a murder and you changed your name!'

In spite of herself, Laura joined in the laughter and told Kate about borrowing her older sister's birth certificate as she was only twelve.

'But please don't tell Mr Pilgrim. I need the money to help out at home and I didn't want to go into service like Sarah.'

'Is that all? Much more exciting if you'd done a murder,' Kate said with a grin. 'Your secret's safe with me and with all the rest. They don't like the bosses to know any more than they have to.'

Jane viewed the approaching winter days with less apprehension. For the past months, George had only missed a full week twice and with Laura working there'd be money for coal. Although she had lost one regular customer who had moved out of the district she had found a situation as an out servant for three days a week at a lodging house for single men in Renalagh Road. One of the days was a Saturday, which was a nuisance especially as she didn't finish until seven o'clock but the pay was half a crown.

She hurried to the corner. Maybe there were still a few bargains to be had at the meat stall and vegetable barrow near the high road. Her thoughts were on shopping. The next minute she was tumbling to the ground after colliding with a tall man. He hesitated unsure what to do.

'Help me up, if you please,' Jane's tone was brusque.

He grasped her arms then suddenly let go.

'Jane!' he exclaimed.

She adjusted her hat so as to clear her vision and saw an astonished James staring down at her.

'That's a fine thing! Being knocked about by my own brother. What are you doing in Stratford?'

She grabbed his still extended arms and hauled herself up. When she was upright and had dusted herself down, she shook his hand.

'Why, James, what ails you? You are so thin and pale.'

'I came to find a special apothecary. My Emily is dying.'

She was at a loss for words. Often, Emily would put on an act of illness.

'Come home with me, James. Just a few streets from here.'

'I must find this special medicine. This place has got to be somewhere here.'

Jane took the scrap of paper he held in his hand and read the address. She held his hand and led him along like a little boy. After several turns, they came to an end house, its window filled with coloured glass bottles.

A Chinese gentleman came from behind a beaded curtain at the back of the room. James gave up his piece of paper. Small quantities of powders and liquids were dispensed into a glass vessel and shaken vigorously before distilled into a small phial.

'Three shilling, please.'

'Three shillings,' Jane repeated in astonishment.

James reached into his pocket. Before he handed over the cash Jane restrained him.

'What is in the concoction?' she asked.

Between slit eyelids, the black eyes glinted. He showed even white teeth in an assumed smile.

'If I told you that, Missy Lady, you should have as much knowledge as I,' he said in a high pitched voice.

The exchange was made and they opened the door.

His sing song tone continued. 'It will not cure what

ails the person but it will relieve the suffering.' The impassive mask was back in place.

'I'll come home with you, James, but first I must call in on George and let him know. It'll only take a few minutes.'

'No! I must get back to Emily. I've been away too long as it is.'

'Isn't Tobias with his mother?'

'We haven't seen Toby for months,' was James's anguished reply.

'I'll come directly I've told George.'

On her way, Jane made a few hasty purchases at the stalls as she passed. She briefly told Laura and George about casually meeting her brother and of Emily's illness.

'I must go and see what I can do to help.'

After Benjamin, their youngest child had died, James and Emily moved to a new house for a new start. It was also in keeping with his promotion to foreman clerk sitting in an office instead of carrying a bag of tools. James had taken a long lease on a house facing West Ham Park. It was spacious and light and airy. Emily had over furnished it, especially the large parlour room. There were two sofas, a number of chairs, glass fronted cabinets displaying cheap trinkets, dressers over loaded with unmatched crockery and a piano with brass candle holders, although none could play.

As Jane approached the house she remembered the only previous occasion she had stepped over the threshold: Charlotte's wedding day two years ago. Emily fussed around everybody and then collapsed, fluttering, in a chair declaring she had the vapours with so much excitement. Even though it was a bright, sunny day, Emily persisted in switching on the newfangled lights from electricity just to show them off. Jane had dressed up her family as best she could which made George most uncomfortable. He kept tugging at the waxed wing collar until the stud popped out and the collar sprung backwards landing on the food table right in the middle of the bowl of jelly. George had ducked down to retrieve the stud just as the bride and groom entered. Guests pressed forward tumbling on top of George. Laura had deftly scooped the collar out of the jelly and tucked it into her bodice. Emily remained blissfully unaware of the cause of the commotion.

Jane had thought Charlotte, at seventeen, was too young to be wed especially as she was to be so far away from her family.

'Nonsense,' was Emily's reply. 'She will have an exceptional life in India as the wife of a missionary. They will have a big house and lots of black servants. She is the envy of all her friends.'

The wedding was also a farewell to young James. He had booked passage on an immigrant ship sailing for the United States of America.

'Poor Emily,' Jane thought as she walked up the three circular steps to the large front door. 'To be so ill and not to have one's family close.' She had been shocked to learn Tobias was no longer at home. Jane tried to work out his age. 'Charlotte was married at seventeen, so she would be nineteen now, young James would be twenty - no, twenty-one, so Tobias must be sixteen, a couple of years older than Sarah.'

The door was opened in response to her knock but by the time she stepped inside, she heard James' feet running back up the staircase. Jane closed the door behind her. She noticed the smell first. She reached into her bag for a piece of cloth and held it to her nose. In the darkness it was difficult to get her bearings. She walked along the passageway feeling her way along the wall until her hand touched a raised oval. Of course! Electric light! She swivelled the knob and harsh white light flooded the space. She was at he entrance to the kitchen. Soiled linen and clothing was scattered over all the floor space; every inch of surface was stacked with dirty dishes; the large butler sink was blocked with filthy water. Jane retraced her steps. Hesitantly, she opened the parlour door. Light from the hallway illuminated a squalid vista. She turned and ran up the stairs, calling softly for James.

'Here'

Jane located the voice and walked into the lighted bedroom. She had expected the same foul mess as in the downstairs rooms. There was no clutter but the stench was nauseous. James stood by the bed spooning mouthfuls of liquid between Emily's parted lips. Most of the liquid oozed down her chin onto the grubby bed clothes. Tousled hair spread across the dingy pillow; transparent skin stretched taut over thin bones. A wracking cough shook the emaciated body causing the match stick arms to flail futilely.

A great pity welled up in Jane. She had sometimes thought fate had dealt unfairly with her. But for James and Emily it was mercilessly cruel.

It was two o'clock in the morning when she finished. Luckily she had warned George she may not return that night. Clearing the blocked sink took some time but eventually the murky fluid gurgled away. Instead of covering the floor, there were now two piles: one she would try to get cleaned the other she instructed James to burn. In a dresser Jane saw two Damask table cloths. She went upstairs and began tidying the sick room. She stripped the bed. First she gently bathed Emily's frail body. On a side table she found a hairbrush and tenderly passed it through the locks to untangle them. After propping her up in a chair, Jane spread one table cloth on the mattress and covering the pillow. The only clean night attire was a flannel night-shirt which swamped Emily but it would have to do. Jane carried her back to bed.

'Dear God! You're lighter than a sack of potatoes.'

The second crisp, clean, white cloth was placed on top. Jane gave the blanket a good shake over the bannister and tucked it around Emily. Her work done, she rolled down her sleeves and sat back in the chair. She must have dozed off into a light sleep, her head jerked forward and she woke. She yawned and gave a good stretch before she became aware Emily was awake and staring at her. For a fleeting moment she remembered Granny Stringer's eyes watching her as she had cleared out mouldering rubbish. Would Emily resent her interference? The pale grey eyes flickered shedding tears, a wavering hand beckoned and Jane went to her.

'Thank you,' came an almost inaudible voice.

There was sincerity in those faded eyes and a warmth of feeling in the cold, bony hand that clutched hers that Jane felt humbled in her presence. She dabbed her brow with a little lavender water she had found in a drawer.

'Try to sleep now, my dear. James will come up to see you later.'

She walked slowly toward the door. Before closing it she glanced back at the limp bundle on the bed. She knew it wouldn't be long now. She busied herself downstairs turning out the parlour, vigorously brushing the Persian carpet, wiping shelves, dusting ledges. It was ready.

George and Laura accompanied her when she returned to the house across the park. Georgie had been left with Mrs Walters.

It was a sparse assembly in the parlour. James stood alone in his grief; no child beside him to remind him of the union. The clatter of hooves announced the arrival of the carriage. No-one moved. Emily's sister stood huddled with her husband and their son, a spindly, spotted faced youth who kept sniffing. George opened the front door and escorted the undertaker into the parlour. He doffed his high black hat, the swathe of black silk sweeping through the air. No-one moved. It was as if they were statues. The undertaker coughed discreetly. George stepped forward and took James' arm.

'It is time to go.'

He guided James through the front door and into the principal mourning coach and was about to step back when James gripped his arm and pulled him in beside him. George gave a startled glance at Jane. She nodded and smiled and felt pride in George's manner.

Throughout the service and at the graveside, James clung tightly to George. When they arrived back at the house, George led James to a seat and ushered in the other relatives followed by Jane and Laura.

Laura knew what was expected of her; Jane had shown her what to do. The kettle was already filled and sitting on one of the rings of the gas stove - another of Emily's proud possessions. She filled the pretty cups and carried the tray through to the parlour. Next she brought a plate of ham and cold mutton and wedges of bread. Laura found it strange that people could eat so heartily after such a sad event.

They walked home across the park.

'Poor James,' Jane said, 'he's a broken man. I don't know what he'll do.'

'We'll keep an eye on him, regular like,' George said.

Head down against the biting wind, they hurried home. Laura collected Georgie and thanked Mrs Walters.

'Did you see her?' Georgie asked eagerly. 'What does a dead body look like, Laura?'

'You are a gruesome child,' Laura scolded. 'No, I

didn't see Aunt Emily. She was already in the coffin.' She paused for a moment. 'I don't think I should have liked to see her. Ma said she was wasted away. So sad for Uncle James. He has no-one now.'

Each night Laura wrote to Sarah, not a letter for she never gave it to the carrier. It was more a journal, relating the day's events as she would have done when Sarah shared the room with her.

'Such an air of sadness in the house. It seemed stuck to the walls and the floors that no amount of electricity could melt it. There was a piano, Sarah. How you could have danced if it had played happy tunes. Poor uncle James. He has no-one now. He's had no word from the United State of America for nearly a year so does not know where James is. Charlotte writes regularly. He showed them to me. Such strange letters as if she had a number of copies made up and simply signs one every two months for they say the same thing. They are well. Hoped they were too. Isn't that odd. I should never want to leave Ma and Pa. I know you went away not because you wanted to but because we were so poor. Things are getting better so perhaps you'll be home soon. Pa says we will visit Uncle James each fortnight to keep him company as we are all the family he has now.'

Only George and Jane went the following Sunday but when they arrived they found the house was boarded up.

'Where could he have gone?' George asked.

They enquired of neighbours but no-one knew.

'Probably going to scour the country for Tobias, poor tormented man,' Jane said. She shook her head. 'Even if he finds him, I doubt if he'll receive comfort. Let's get back home to a warm fire.'

Sarah stopped abruptly. She had glimpsed a sideways view of herself in the window. She took a step back and gazed at her reflection. Her eyes followed the contour of her body. She smiled. At last! Breasts! No wonder it had been a tussle to button her chemise this morning. The image smiling back at her was a delight. At five feet three inches and, possibly a half, she was growing into a graceful young lady. Her butchered hair had grown back to its former glory and she had learnt how to keep it neatly under her cap. Her complexion was pure peaches and cream.

Her smile turned into a scowl. She didn't like the rest of what she saw: untidy, slovenly, hunched shoulders. No wonder she couldn't grow breasts. Look at you, she remonstrated with herself, and you wanted to be a dancer.

The hairs on the back of her neck tingled as she sensed someone was watching her. She bent forward and rubbed an imaginary spot from the pane of glass, stepped back, nodded in satisfaction and proceeded down the stairs polishing the oak banister with a dusting cloth as she went.

In the attic room, Sarah practised deportment. She hoped it wasn't sinful for the Bible to crash to the floor so many times but it was the only book they had.

'Head up, shoulders back, smile,' she repeated over and over. Divested of her restrictive clothing, and clad only in her night shirt, it was easier to pull her shoulders back. But it was another thing to keep the book balanced on her head.

'Are you sure this is necessary, Lizzie?'

Lizzie Hedges was stretched out on her bed, hands behind her head, and kicking her legs in the air to Sarah's walking rhythm. She rolled over and studied Sarah's performance.

'I've seen young Miss being taught by that la-de-dah Frenchie. She made her walk with **THREE** books on her head. Mind you, she had a bit more space than you have, Sarah, so it would be a mite easier to balance.

But you're getting the hang of it. Take the steps slowly and point your toe.'

Sarah obeyed. Arms relaxed at her side, she pointed her toe and moved cautiously forward. One step, two steps, three steps. Then she had to turn as she ran out of floor space and once more the Bible slid off her head.

'It still won't do any good unless I can get a bigger day dress,' Sarah moaned.

'Why don't you ask Mrs Bumstead. She's not a bad soul. There is a cupboard on the second floor that's got lots of uniforms in it. There must be one that'd fit you. Go on, ask her.'

They sat at the table. Mr Paget, always at the end backing onto the double doors that gave entry to the proper part of the house. Mrs Bumstead, always at the opposite end near to the outer door. On one side sat young Dick Griggs, who wore a uniform and called himself a footman but did whatever Mr Paget told him. Alongside him was Wilf Abery, a ruddy faced man with wrinkly iron grey hair, a general handyman who did all the heavy work outside and in. And much to Mrs Bumstead's annoyance, only ever came to table with the sleeves of his hair shirt rolled up, exposing his brown sinewy arms. Lizzie and Sarah sat facing them - after they had served food to the others.

Under cast down eyes, Sarah looked around the table. Most had finished. Only Wilf was still wiping his plate.

'Mrs Bumstead,' Sarah began then coughed hesitantly.

'What is it girl? Speak out.'

'I was wondering when we'd get new uniforms.'

'New uniforms! The ones we've got are perfectly satisfactory.'

'Yes, of course they are. No disrespect. What I

meant, Mrs Bumstead was, is there a **different** one I could have? I think I have outgrown this one.'

Wilf gave a raucous laugh. 'Lass is right and no mistake. No room for her new bosom.'

Sarah's delicate complexion changed dramatically to vivid scarlet. Mrs Bumstead tut-tutted. Dick Griggs opened his mouth to say something but changed his mind and poked a crust of bread into the space.

Mr Paget snapped his fingers. 'Another glass of stout, girl.'

Lizzie leapt to the occasion.

Mrs Bumstead hissed down the table. 'See me in my room later.'

Sarah finished serving the apple pie but she was too despondent to eat any pudding herself. At half past nine, she tapped on Mrs Bumstead's door. 'Wonder how much will be stopped from my wages this time for being cheeky,' she thought.

She had been in the room lots of times before and was always struck by how untidy everything was. Clothes heaped up; odd saucers containing odd buttons or pins. Yet Mrs Bumstead was so fussy in the kitchen and scullery. 'A place for everything and everything in its place,' she was frequently saying. Mrs Bumstead eyed Sarah up and down before rising from her chair and standing close to her.

'Take off your dress.'

Sarah obeyed.

'Loosen your under garments.'

Again she did as she was told.

Mrs Bumstead held a piece of string in her hands which she wrapped about Sarah's chest.

'Don't wriggle, girl. Mmm. Sit there a minute.'

The housekeeper disappeared and Sarah slumped down on the chair and wept. She had been so proud this morning when she saw her new shape. Now she felt humiliated and ashamed because she had been forced to display her breasts. It wasn't her fault they had rounded out. She couldn't stop them from growing, could she?

'Whatever are you snivelling for? Here, try these on.'

A cascade of garments descended onto the floor in front of Sarah.

'This first,' Mrs Bumstead handed her a cotton chemise and then two woollen dresses, one mid-blue and one light brown, then a grey cotton dress and a dark green linen dress.

As she donned each item, Sarah twirled round to display them. Her eyes were shining with delight.

'They are all a bit on the large size,' Mrs Bumstead began but Sarah interrupted her.

'They suit just fine, really they do.'

'I was about to say, miss, that it won't notice as you will be tying your apron over them.' But her smile belied the rebuke. 'You've been doing very well in recent months, girl. Mind you, you are still on the clumsy side at times but I reckon I can make something of you. How old are you now? Fourteen?'

Sarah nodded.

'The grey dress will be worn in the mornings, the dark green in the late afternoon and evening. The woollen ones will be for autumn and winter months, brown in the morning, blue for afternoons and evenings. Make sure you hang them up and brush each one after you've worn it. Now, get along with you. I've got to have some shut eye.'

Sarah gathered up all the clothes into her arms. Mrs Bumstead opened the door for her. Sarah quickly turned and planted a kiss on Mrs Bumstead's cheek.

'My word! Whatever next?'

She hugged the dresses close to her as she ran up the narrow back stairs. Gurgling with excitement she collapsed onto the low bed. Lizzie had tucked down for the night but stirred as Sarah yelped with delight.

'Look, Lizzie! Look!'

Sarah held each one against her to show them off.

'What she give you all them for?'

'Lighter shades for morning, darker for afternoons and evenings.' Sarah pirouetted in the small space between them 'I'm to be trained for a parlour maid. What do you think of that?'

As she twirled about, she saw Lizzie's face crumble. She squatted on the end of the bed.

'Oh, Lizzie, I'm sorry. I know you've been here longer than me and you are older, so it should have been you Lizzie. I'll see Mrs Bumstead first thing and say you should be trained before me.'

'Course, not, me lovely! Course it's got to be you. Don't you say no such thing to the old dragon. Anyway, can you see me in a parlour. I ain't cut out for it. But don't you come uppity with me. I shan't stand for that!'

'I'd never get uppity with you, Lizzie. You're the best friend I've got. Next to my sister Laura, I love you the best.'

Chapter 14

Placards shouted the result: Liberal Landslide! Newspaper headlines declared: The General Election of 1906 has seen the Tories - who'd been in power since 1886 with only a slight break - swept out of office by an overwhelming popular vote.

On the evening of polling, Laura and Eddie hovered on the fringe of the political meetings in West Ham Park. Each candidate sought to gain the attention of the passers-by while opposition supporters heckled and barracked the speaker. The Tory and Liberal groups were about the same size but the newly formed Labour Party had gathered a substantial crowd to hear their candidate.

'If you were able to vote, Eddie, which one would you choose?'

'Now there's a Labour man standing, I'd vote for him but the trouble with politicians, Laurie, is that they talk too much and do too little. Listen to them now, saying what they will do if they're elected. If they do get in, ask 'em in six months time if they will keep their promises and most will deny they ever promised anything.

She looked up at him as he talked so earnestly.

'A man's got to be twenty-one before he can vote and

that's more than five years away so I don't think I'll worry my head about it now,' he laughed.

As they strolled away, another group came marching towards the party meetings.

'**VOTES FOR WOMEN!** They shouted. There were nearly fifty women in the group, many carrying WSPU placards and thrusting them high in the air. Their high pitched voices carried across the open space. '**VOTES FOR WOMEN'** drowned out most of the men.

Laura and Eddie dodged out of the way but stopped to enjoy the fun as each tried to outdo the other. It finished up as a deafening sound so they went home.

George always brought home a newspaper which someone had discarded. Sometimes it was a day old but it still gave him the news. Laura had never been particularly interested in reading a newspaper, she preferred her poetry books, but the political meetings had interested her and she wondered what would be reported in the newspapers.

'May I look at your paper, Pa?'

'Of course, girlie. But it doesn't have much about ladies' fashions in it.'

She looked up surprised at his words.

'Oh,' she smiled, putting down the fur trimming she was applying to a hat. 'No, I don't suppose it does, Pa. I'd like to read about the election. Do you think it will make a difference now the Liberals are in power?'

'Whatever do you know about the Liberals and the like?'

'Eddie and I listened to some of the meetings in the park last week. Eddie said he wouldn't trust any of them. Neither the Tories, nor Liberals but he said if he had a vote it would go to the Labour man.'

'Did he now? Well, the lad's right. Not Liberal. Not Conservative. They won't lift a finger to help the working class. Working class have got to do it for themselves.'

Her father's words brought a painful reminder. 'Mr Garvey said education was the key to unlocking the door of the poverty cell.'

'Ah, David! I miss him. Yes, learning and workers getting together in unions to gain better conditions and wages. And having Labour Members to ensure Parliament pass fair laws. That's the way forward. East end of London is where it all started. Did you know Keir Hardie was first elected to Parliament by West Ham? Our own Borough put a Labour man in Government.' A sly smile spread across his face as he gazed at his daughter. 'Who would you vote for, girlie?'

'But it's only men who vote, Pa. Although last week there were women in the park demanding votes for women.'

'Ah, yes, but they're just the posh ones. It's working women who can change things through the unions. Unions are important. Did you know as far back as 1888, it was the girls of Bryant and Mays match factory who went on strike to improve their working conditions. So many of them got phossy jaw.' George gazed into the distance. 'Yes, I miss David Garvey. Many a night we'd sit talking until the dawn came up and I'd missed me bed.'

'More fool you,' Jane said fiercely as she marched into the kitchen. 'Always on about the working class. Just talk. What good does talk do?'

'But, Jane, you can't keep your head in the sand all the time.'

'Head in the sand, indeed! You're filling the child's head with a lot of rubbish!'

'Its not rubbish,' George retorted. 'And Laura isn't a child. She's a working girl.'

Laura stared at her parents. Quarrelling over nothing!

For a moment there was silence in the small space

then George passed the day's paper to Laura and busied himself cleaning his boots with an old newspaper. Jane returned to the scullery.

Laura read through the report on the front page. Twenty-nine Labour Party representatives were returned as Members of Parliament, largely due to the support of the growing Trade Union movement. The Women's Social and Political Union – ah, yes, the WSPU banner Laura had seen- began militant tactics to ensure the Liberal Government took women's demands seriously.

They were walking out for their meal break when she heard her name called.

'Stringer!'

Laura turned back to face Johnson, the overseer.

'Mr Pilgrim wants you, girl.'

'Here! What's her want her for?' Kate asked.

'Well if she hurries along there she'll find out won't she?' Johnson replied.

The command to appear before Mr Pilgrim didn't fill her with dread. Not now. A year ago she would have trembled in her boots but now she was thirteen and a half, Laura was legally employed.

There was a grunted response to her knock and she entered the clerk's office. He didn't look up from his papers.

'The overseer gives a good report of you, er...' He shuffled the papers and scanned the register, '...er, Stringer, isn't it?'

Laura felt an overwhelming urge to reply: 'Well it was when I came in,' but thought better of it and merely nodded.

'Overseer says you've been tried out occasionally at the bench and have proved satisfactory. The company is expanding and the owners have authorised three additional benches to be put in place. You will be tried out for a fortnight.'

He reshuffled the papers over the register and prepared to write. He dipped the nib into the inkwell and the pen was suspended in mid air as Laura asked:

'What will my pay be, sir?'

He raised his head and his eyes glittered behind his pince-nez.

'Two shillings and thruppence,' he said between clenched teeth.

'Thank you, sir. And as you will need someone to take over my duties, I should like to tell you Daisy Sudson has learned the job very well.'

Two large black blobs fell onto the polished surface of his desk. Laura gave a quick curtsy and left the office before Mr Pilgrim gave his reply.

She kept a poker face and squatted down between Maisie and Kate.

'So? What's up?' Kate asked.

'He hasn't given you the push, has he?' Maisie asked putting her arm round Laura.

She could contain herself no longer. A huge grin spread from ear to ear.

'I'm going to get a bench! Well, I'm to be tried out for a fortnight when they bring in the extra benches.'

'About time,' Kate retorted. 'The skinflint's been using you for months.'

'I don't mind, Kate. I had to learn.' She munched one large piece of bread and nibbled the corner off the second piece before looking up. Daisy was standing by the iron gates. Laura waved to her and she skipped over and took the proffered bread and danced away again.

'I did say to Mr Pilgrim he would need someone to replace me and Daisy Sudson knew the ropes. I hope he gives her the job.'

'You cheeky monkey,' Kate laughed. 'I bet he nearly swallowed his Adam's apple.'

'That was a bit forward of you, Laura,' Maisie added.

'Why? I just thought, well, she was already in the workshop.'

'She can't read nor write, nor nothing,' Kate said. 'Can't add up, neither, that's why he can diddle her every pay day. He won't give her your job, love. Nice of you to try.'

'What do you mean, diddles her?' Laura asked in a shocked tone.

'You watch on pay day,' Kate said and tapped the side of her nose.

As soon as they were paid off on Saturday, most workers hastily left the premises. Today, a few hovered by the gates; some stood chatting not far from the pay line. Daisy was the last to approach the table. The coppers were lined up at the edge. Johnson's eyes flickered toward Mr Pilgrim but he said nothing.

'Here you are, missy.'

Daisy's grubby fingers were about to pluck up the coins when Laura stayed her hand.

'Beg pardon, sir. I think you have made a mistake. Those last two coins are ha'pennies. They should be pennies.'

The yard was suddenly silent. Mr Pilgrim's pince-nez fell from his face. His eyes were venomous. He tapped the gold frame of the glasses against his fingers, magnifying the clenched knuckles.

'Dear me, so they are. Very observant of you, Stringer. You should have spotted that, Johnson.'

Mr Pilgrim retrieved the two small coins and dipped into the soft leather pouch to produce two pennies which he laid on the table.

Laura put on an endearing smile before she released Daisy's hand.

They walked out together. At the corner, as they said goodbye, Daisy hugged her.

'Ta for getting me the extra money. Real good of you.'

'It's not extra, Daisy, just what you were entitled to.'

'I'll do me best. I shan't let you down.'

'Oh, I don't know that you've got the runners job, Daisy. Your wages today is the amount you should have been receiving all the time.'

'I don't mind what job I do, Miss, if I'm to get extra coppers. Ta-ta.'

Rearrangement of the workshop began the following week. To accommodate the four extra benches, the existing two lines of six were turned side on to make a square of four each side. Positioned at each corner was a tier of three shelves each one segmented to take buttons, studs, buckles of different shapes and sizes. There was no need for a run around girl. Mr Pilgrim had made sure of that. Bench hands could top up their own supplies. Also removed were the three stoves. It was no longer necessary to ladle from large tubs of glue into their own tin cans. Gas pipes were laid along the floor and in the middle of the square of four benches gas rings held smaller glue pots.

To her delight, Laura was placed between Kate and Maisie. She kept a close watch on her companions and followed their routine. Kate was quick but a bit slap-dash whereas Maisie turned out a neat job every time. The materials held a fascination for Laura: the moiré silk used for lining bags, came in a range of delicate colours its shimmering water wave glinting silver. Soft calf leathers were warm to the touch. The most important part of the job was gluing. Too little and the silk bubbled on the cardboard interface; too much, and it soaked through the fine fabric marking it with brown blotches. Gluing the leather onto the outside was just as tortuous; there must be no hint of a smudge on the finished product.

'You'll get the hang of it, love,' Maisie reassured her. 'Just try to get a rhythm to the process. See.'

She place a cut piece of leather onto her work paper, dipped her brush into the glue pot, shook it gently twice, smoothed the brush across the leather in straight even strokes, overlapping the edge. Repeated the process with the cut cardboard. Next she lifted an identically shaped piece of silk, held it by the extreme edges and wafted it onto the glued surface from bottom to top and smoothed it with a rounded stone. With each action, her head nodded in time to an unheard melody.

Yes Laura decided, she would follow Maisie's routine.

In the warm spring and summer months it was pleasant enough sitting on the flag stones outside the gates but when it was windy or wet, Laura would hurry off down the road. She had discovered the place last Christmas and regularly made her way there when the weather was bad. Now the cold winds were blowing up for winter once again, she set off for her special eating place. The last shreds of leaves swirled about her feet as she pushed open the side gates and slipped into the church yard. At the back of the cathedral two large stone tombs stood under the bare branches of an elm tree, its thick trunk bulging between them. A narrow ledge ran round the base of one tomb; the other tomb had a pointed roof jutting out. Laura squatted down on the ledge of the tomb closest to the tree trunk and received a measure of protection from the overhanging roof of the other.

'Good afternoon, my dear. I enjoy seeing you again, my dear, but it must mean winter is fast upon us.'

Laura looked up into the kindly eyes of the verger.

'You remember me from last year?' she asked in amazement.

'Of course I do. How could I forget such a charming little church mouse - so quiet and considerate? Come in when you've finished. The choir's practising.'

She reached into her cloth for another slice of bread and chewed the corner. It was nice to be remembered. The verger had found her crouched down by the low wall to get some protection from the wind. As he had approached she thought it was to dismiss her from the grave yard. Instead, he had told her there was a better place and led her to the tombs by the tree. He had said food must not be taken into the church, but after she had eaten she was welcome to sit inside. Three or four days each week she would make her way to St Paul's and quickly eat her bread and jam and hurry inside. The verger sat at the back and signalled Laura to join him. They would talk in whispers or, if the choir was there, or the organist, just silently enjoy the music.

In her musings she had idly nibbled the bread causing crumbs to fall to the ground. About her feet several threadbare sparrows were enjoying a feast. She dribbled a few more crumbs for them.

'I know you're hungry, birdies, but so am I, she said, swallowing the last piece.

Icy crystals were in the wind stinging her face and she ran into the comfort of the back pews and the soothing sounds of the young boys' voices blending in harmony.

'You went off smart like,' Maisie said to Laura as the gates reopened at one o'clock. 'Where did you go?'

Kate sidled alongside Laura and linked arms. She grinned across at Maisie.

'Off to meet her young man, I shouldn't wonder.'

'What young man?'

They still walked arm in arm.

'Her young man.' Kate jerked her head towards

Laura. 'I see them last week. At the station it was. Canoodling they was.'

Laura pulled away. Her cheeks reddened.

'We were not canoodling. He's just a friend.' she protested.

'Come on, lasses,' Johnson chided them. 'Stop your jawing and get on with your work.'

Laura hung her cloak and bonnet on her peg and hurried to her bench. She wasn't sure what was meant by canoodling. She met Eddie most Sundays and they'd walk and talk. It was such a relaxed meeting. She held his arm but that was just what every gentleman would do when escorting a lady. Was that canoodling? Laura gave up.

The afternoon passed in busy occupation. An important order was behind schedule because silk supplies had been delayed. To complete on time, the owners had fitted in extra benches and hired four freelance workers who were on piece rates. They brought their own tools in neat fitted leather rolls. One man had a glass polishing ball that shone with internal glints.

'False tiger eye,' he told Laura. 'The coloured streaks inside the glass are flat. See.' He twirled the ball between his fingers. 'If its was a real tiger eye, they would sparkle and reflect outward in the light. And if I owned one this large, I wouldn't be working at Garsten's,' he laughed.

When the bell sounded at seven o'clock, Laura stretched her back with relief. She felt pleased with herself; she had kept up a steady rate and not one had been rejected. The girls were subdued as they struggled to push weary arms into coat armholes or raise them to bonnet strings. Mellow gaslight softened the frosted pavements but the cold seeped through thin soled boots.

'I went to St Paul's.'

'Eh?'

'I went to St Paul's,' Laura repeated. 'I often go there. I sit in the church yard to eat, then I go inside. It's so high you can hardly make out the tiny windows. Except, I don't suppose they are tiny it's just that they look small from the ground. It's such a big place, there are lots of dark corners. But I like the singing.'

'So it wasn't the young man today,' Kate said with exaggerated disappointment.

Laura had to laugh. 'I'm not old enough to have a young man. Eddie works for the Great Eastern at the Stratford depot. I knew he had to collect some tools from Liverpool Street station and we arranged to meet. To travel home together. Certainly not canoodling.'

'I know you wasn't,' Kate said. 'I was just joshing you.'

'Is that your church? Did you go to St Paul's to pray?' Maisie asked.

'Oh, I didn't go to pray. I just go inside to get warm. I don't think that's sinful, do you? It was the verger who said I could. I didn't think about it being a church because it's such a big building.'

'Ours is a nice little church building,' Maisie said. 'It's bright and ever so friendly. Why don't you come along one Sunday? I'm sure you'd like it.'

'Now don't go trying to turn our little Laura into a psalm singing sister who spouts about Jesus saving us all the time. One of you is bad enough but to have one at each bench beside me hollerin' Hallelujah! Is more than a mortal can stand.'

'Kate! How can you say such a thing. I've never said...' Maisie was close to tears.

Kate flung her arms around her friend and hugged her fiercely.

'You soppy muggins! I never said it for to be the truth. I thought you'd knowed it. Course you never said no Hallelujahs at me.'

As they clung to each other they were jostled by

pedestrians pushing past them into the station entrance. Laura was bemused by their actions. Tall, willowy seventeen year old Maisie was quiet and timid. Buxom, assured sixteen year old Kate dominated her in a nice way. From the moment she started at Garsten's Laura was aware of the close bond between these girls although they seemed quite opposite characters. They never had cross words, unlike many others in the work room. They looked out for one another. Thirteen year old Laura had been pleased to be included in their company.

'I must go or I'll miss my train,' Laura said, clutching the return half of her ticket.

'All right, love,' Kate answered. 'We're off to get the tram now.'

'I meant what I said about coming to our Mission Hall, Laura. I do hope you'll come one Sunday.'

She thought about it on the way home. As a child she had been on the Sunday school outings but never attended the Sunday school. At regular school they had been taught about the scriptures and each morning had assembled in the hall for prayers for the Monarch and they would sing a few hymns before rushing off to their classes. In history, she had learnt about Catholics and Protestants; the Crusades and the Martyrs. But what did you go to church for? She wasn't sure. Of course, you had to get married in a church and buried from a church. But you didn't do this every week!

As the train pulled into Stratford station, powdery snow dusted the platform. Although there was no wind, the chill atmosphere numbed her cheeks making all thoughts disappear as she hurried home to the warmth of the range and something hot inside her. Ma usually had a pot on the hob simmering a meat bone, with potatoes bobbing in it, or dumplings. Georgie was always glad to see her. Her arrival provided an excuse to pause in his task of helping with the washing; he had substituted for Laura in holding sheets for mangling, or folding dry washing into piles for Ma's customers. Best of all was the greeting from Pa when he came home from the *Thatched House*; a hug and a kiss and she enjoyed the moist smell of malt from his lips. Mostly, he kept his promise to Jane: one hour from opening time at half past six and then home. Sometimes, as Laura passed the door, George would come out and they'd walk home together, her small hand warmed in his grasp. When Ma went into the scullery for her nightly wash, George would mention a topic in the paper and they would discuss it until Ma returned to the kitchen.

When all the work was done, Laura and Georgie would go to their room. She'd tuck him up, kiss him goodnight. There was a contentment about their family life that, for Laura, was only marred by the absence of Sarah. It was months since she had written in her book another imaginary letter to Sarah full of tit bits of daily happenings or even when all she would say was: just an ordinary day today,

The sheer grind of daily routine left little space for imagination. Winter was especially bleak. It was dark when Laura got up at six o'clock and scurried along the gloomy passageway to the kitchen. A meagre warmth remained from the range where Jane had stirred the embers at three o'clock to heat a pan for George's tea. Shivering in the icy scullery, Laura stripped off her bodice and pantaloons and washed under her arms and between her legs. It was dark when she ran to Stratford Station to buy the tuppenny workman's ticket to Liverpool Street. It was dark walking along Aldersgate Street to get to Garston's for the factory gates to open at five to eight. Sometimes it was even dark at the midday break if there was fog or there were snow clouds overhead. And it was dark when Laura made her way home when the factory shut at seven o'clock. She was drained of energy and after supper when the range was damped down the warmest place was bed.

It was different when spring came. Sunlight not only brightened the day but it lifted the spirits also. Laura found herself skipping along the pavements, leaping over cracks. If she accidentally stepped on one, she would immediately cross her fingers and twirl about twice to ward off disaster. Her travelling companions watched her with amusement. There were six or seven girls who regularly caught the same train each morning and struck up friendly acquaintances. Two girls worked in the feather curling factory in Fore Street, but they had to work by candle light.

Maisie greeted her warmly.

'Glad you got here early today. I want to ask you something.'

She linked her arm with Laura's and strolled along the factory perimeter. The appearance of the factory had changed since the time Laura had started her employment. The top half of the brick wall was demolished and replaced with railings, and the solid iron doors inset in the wall had been removed and gates installed. The workers concluded it was easier to observe them through railings than solid brick. The inner courtyard was unchanged; deep ruts made by the iron wheels of the carts bringing in the hides still caught out the unwary walker.

'I've been taking lessons at the Mission. You know, I told you about the Baptist Mission Hall in Mile End. Where I go of a Sunday?'

'What d'you mean, you've taken lessons? What sort of lessons?'

Maisie was silent for a moment and trailed her hand along the railings.

'It's difficult to put into words. You see, you have

to feel it in here.' She tapped on her chest. 'You have to renounce the Devil and believe in the Lord Jesus Christ and be born again.'

Laura laughed. 'Maisie! How can you be born again? Once you're born, you're born.'

She felt Maisie's hand tighten on her arm as she looked at her reddening face, Laura realised how tactless she had been.

'I'm sorry,' she said softly, 'it sounded odd, that's all.'

The gates opened and they joined the others slowly tramping into the factory.

'Will you tell me more when we break? Please, Maisie?'

She smiled at her and Maisie nodded.

As she glued and moulded and trimmed the pieces, Laura's mind was ranging over all the ways in which one could be born again. It was a fascinating subject. She must remember to discuss it with Pa. She wondered if Pa knew about being born again.

St Paul's had been deserted at the first sign of warmer days. Although Laura still wandered down to the church yard if she wanted to have some time to herself, today she was happy to squat with Kate and Maisie.

'Has she asked you then? Are you coming to see her?' Kate asked between bites.

'I hadn't finished telling Laura about the classes.'

Kate shrugged and steadily chewed three chunks of bread in quick succession.

'The Mission appoints examiners to see if we understand the Bible and if we are ready to receive the Holy Sacrament of Baptism. Well, I'm ready and I'm going to be baptised in two Sundays' time, the twenty-sixth of May. I'd like my dearest friends to be present. Oh...'

She held up her hand as Laura was about to protest.

'You don't have to belong to the Mission. You don't have to belong to any church. You just come to watch, so to speak. There will be three other members of the Mission who will speak for me; one Godfather and two Godmothers, so there won't be any call upon you to say anything. I just want you to see me, that's all.' Maisie's voice trailed off wistfully.

Laura's heart thumped loudly in her chest and she felt an unexplained surge of pride.

'I'm very pleased you've asked me, Maisie, and I shall certainly attend,' she said gravely. 'Two weeks' time, you say?'

The days passed quickly and soon it was the twenty-sixth of May. Laura had rummaged in the oddments bundle on Mrs Pickles' stall but nothing had caught her eye. Nothing that would be worthy of the occasion of Maisie's church service. She glanced along the stall. In the middle was a roll of soft linen cloth in a delicate shade of lavender. Exactly right but it was tuppence a yard. Mentally she counted the knots in her petti-coat. Two and a half yards would be enough to make a costume to fit her small figure. Laura delighted in the extravagance.

She finished sewing it late Saturday night. The skirt fell straight over her slim hips then flared gently for the last six inches. The jacket, too, flared slightly at the back but the front was smooth held by one large button. She had found a grubby straw hat in the market and gently washed it until it revealed its true cream colour. She had folded scraps of lavender linen into the petals and stitched them together to form a rose which she pinned onto the hat. The ties of a cream satin blouse fell over the lapels of the jacket matching the hat.

'You look a real treat, girlie.'

George gazed at her with pride. Even Jane nodded her approval.

'But I think the rosette on the hat goes more with a wedding than a baptism.'

'Oh do you really think so, Ma?'

'Well I'm no judge of religious matters but-'

'I think she's grand,' George interrupted.

For a moment Laura hesitated, took off the hat and was about to remove the rose when George stayed her hand.

'Leave it be, lass. If the churchifiers don't like it more's the pity.'

She reached up and kissed him. At the gate she looked back and waved. Around the corner, she was surprised to see Eddie.

'I know you said I couldn't come to the Mission as I wasn't invited but as Sunday's the only day we see one another...'

He took her hands and held her at arms length.

'Laurie, you are beautiful.'

'Eddie, you daft thing. I'm too short to be beautiful.'

'You're a treat for the eyes. And, Miss Laurie, let me tell you, you are growing. Look.' He stretched out his arm. 'You used to walk underneath, now look at you. You'd bump into my arm.'

With surprised delight, Laura found his words to be true.

'That's such a pretty get up you've made for yourself but I'm afraid it's going to get wet.'

He scurried her into a doorway as raindrops wetted the pathway. In the confined space they pressed against each other. Laura's head was under his chin. Eddie sucked in the sweet smell of her hair, her flesh. It filled his nostrils, he was light headed and dizzy. He felt he was floating. Something was happening inside him. His stomach churned over, a sweat broke out on his skin; he felt as if his blood was bubbling through his veins. He fought for breath. It puzzled him. He had loved Laura from the moment he had met her as a school girl. Why should her closeness now, disturb him so much? But he saw she was no longer a school girl; she had grown into a young woman. Now, it was something more than warm affection. He desired her.

Laura unaware of his sexual arousal, raised her skirt an inch or two from the ground and studied her well worn black boots, lovingly polished to a brilliant shine by Pa.

'It's only a small heel. So, I suppose you're right.' She raised her head and smiled at him. 'I have grown, haven't I?

He roughly pushed past her and ran to the end of the road. He gulped for breath. 'Tram's coming,' Eddie called back.

It clattered along the iron rails and nosed into the waiting bay. Eddie held Laura's arm and helped her board.

'Meet you tonight and you can tell me all about it, Laurie. Ta-ta.'

He darted away before she could answer.

I expect he's cross because he couldn't come, she thought. But it wasn't for me to say yes or no.

As she alighted from the tram, the last dregs of the rain cloud pattered down on her straw hat. Outside Mission Hall a group gathered about the doorway. Laura searched for Kate's friendly face.

'Good afternoon my dear. And welcome to the mission. It is a most auspicious day you have chosen to join us. Three of our dear sisters are to receive the Holy Sacrament.'

'Yes, I know. I have come to see my friend Maisie Tucker get baptised,' Laura replied eagerly.

'This is a sacred service, Miss. Not some frivolous happening.'

'I meant no disrespect, sir. I am happy for my friend as this means much to her.'

He tipped his hat. 'Beg pardon, miss,' and walked away.

Kate grabbed her arm. 'Can't take my eyes off you a minute before you take up with some young fella-me-lad.'

Laura laughed. 'I certainly wasn't getting off with him.'

They waited until all the others had filed into the church and then followed behind to sit in the back pew. The normally ebullient Kate was subdued by the quiet atmosphere.

Laura noticed people knelt before taking their seats. 'I think we should kneel and say a prayer,' she whispered.

Kate fell to her knees beside Laura. 'What do I say in a prayer?' she asked.

'Just say you hope everything goes well for Maisie.'

Kate beamed at her. 'That I do, love.'

After a short service and a hymn, the baptism began.

Dearly beloved, forasmuch as all men are conceived and born in sin (and that which is born of the flesh is flesh) and they that are in the flesh cannot please God, but live in sin, committing many actual transgressions; and that our Saviour Christ saith None can enter the kingdom of God except he be regenerate and born anew of Water and of the Holy Ghost.

Laura and Kate tried to follow the words in the prayer book they were handed as they entered the church. But they soon lost the place and simply did whatever the congregation did. They stood up when the others stood up, sat when they did and knelt when they did.

Maisie and the other two girls who were to be baptised came forward from the front pew and stood before the priest.

'Well-beloved, who are come hither desiring to receive holy baptism, ye have heard how the congregation hath prayed that our Lord Jesus Christ would vouchsafe to receive you and bless you, to release you of your sins, to give you the kingdom of heaven and everlasting life.'

The priest then called forward each girl in turn. Maisie was the last one.

'Dost thou renounce the devil and all his works; the vain pomp and glory of the world, with all covetous desires of the same, and the carnal desires of the flesh, so that thou wilt not follow, nor be led by them?'

'I renounce them all,' Maisie replied in a clear voice.

At the end of the questions and responses, the three girls left the body of the church. The organ played softly.

'Is that the end?' Kate whispered.

'I don't think so. Look.'

Laura pointed to the side of the church. Behind the stone font blue velvet curtains were suspended from a brass rail. A church official opened the curtains revealing a sunken rectangle. From a side door came the three girls to be baptised. They were each dressed in a plain white smock. The priest and another official, in turn took each girl by the arm, led her down the few steps and dipped her into the water: 'I Baptise thee in the Name of the Father and the Son and of the Holy Ghost. Amen.'

When the tram drew into the kerb, Laura expected to see Eddie waiting there. She hoped he would be for she wanted to tell him all about the Mission and the service and Maisie being dipped in the Holy Water. At the corner of Burgess Road she looked about but the street was deserted.

In an alley beside the pork butchers shop on the opposite side, Eddie crouched, hidden from view. As Laura stepped off the tram, his heart gave a lurch at the sight of her. He ached to rush to her side just to walk with her but he was afraid she would somehow know what was in his heart: he wanted to hold her close, touch her skin. He watched her disappear before leaving his hiding place.

All afternoon, thoughts had turned over and over in his mind. What he felt - was it normal? Or was it evil? How could you know? He wished there was someone he could talk to. But there was no-one to confide in; no brothers, no father. Had his father felt like this about his mother? The shrewish face of his widowed mother drifted into his mind's eye. His father's image was blurred; Eddie had been eight years old when his father had been killed on the railway.

'If I don't see Laurie for week or two, this feeling may have eased off,' he reasoned. 'Then it'll be just as it always was with us.'

Chapter 15

Summer was fickle. Just when you thought the weather was set fair, Nature changed her mind. All week it had been stifling. Laura had taken to wearing a spiced lavender bag tied round her neck. It was pleasant to breath the sweet herb instead of the pungent smell of sweating bodies and glue.

'It ain't so bad for you,' a girl said as they rocked toward London town on the Great Eastern. 'All you get up your nose is smells. We get strands of feathers. You can't damp 'em too much else they won't curl. And in this hot weather feathers stick to everything.'

Now it was Saturday afternoon, with her wages in her bag, Laura had wanted to wander among the stalls along the Broadway. And what happens? It's windy and raining. She pushed through a group sheltering under the awning by the china and glass stall. Someone bumped into her forcing her dangerously close to a finely balanced pyramid of tea cups.

'Beg pardon, miss,' he said.

The voiced thrilled her. She turned and smiled at her assailant.

Eddie's surprised expression dissolved into a broad grin, his eyes sparkled in pleasure.

They were motionless as they gazed at each other.

'If you ain't buying,' the stall keeper poked Eddie in the back, 'then don't block the way for them that does.'

At that moment, an elderly lady, her grey hair twirled into a bun on top of her head, caught hold of Eddie's arm.

'I've been calling you. The rain's stopped and I want to get this shopping over and done with.'

As he was pulled away, he mouthed: 'Tomorrow' and was swallowed up in the crowd.

Laura skipped along dodging puddles, her head buzzing with his voice; his face mirrored in her memory. Two Sundays she had waited by the water trough. Time and again she had traced every letter of the chiselled inscription: Metropolitan Drinking Fountain and Cattle Trough Association. Even if he had chores to do for his Ma, always in the past he had found ways of getting word to her. Three Sundays, nothing, not a word. And she did miss him. There was a void in her life. She had made excuses for him but finally came to the unhappy conclusion that perhaps he had been forbidden to see her. Although they lived near to one another Laura had never been to Eddie's house. Whenever she had been on the other side of Leytonstone Road, she deliberately avoided Argyle Road. Something Eddie let slip once, made her realise Mrs Sawyer did not know of their friendship so she couldn't have forbidden him to see her. Finally Laura had given up the weekly vigil. She came to a dismal conclusion: it must be that Eddie didn't want to see her.

And now, today, when she wasn't expecting it, she had seen him again. He had smiled. The smile lingered in her memory. She'd see him tomorrow.

At Mrs Pickles' stall, Laura fingered remnants of silks in a daydream.

'Anything special you're looking for today, missy? I kept a few bits back in case you come by. Here.'

She delved under the stall and handed over a brown paper bag.

'If you think you can make use of 'em, I'll let you have 'em at a bargain price as always, dearie. Two three the lot.'

Laura handed over the coins in a trance and hadn't even looked into the paper bag.

'No, dearie. I said tuppence three farthings. You give me three farthings and forgot the coppers. That ain't no good,' Mrs Pickles laughed.

All Laura could see was Eddie's face as his lips made exaggerated movements to say: tomorrow. It was an eternity until tomorrow.

She sat at the table sorting the scraps of material. Eddie filled her thoughts. She remembered Kate's words about being her young man. She liked the sound of it. Well, she didn't know any other young men except Georgie and he didn't count. It's like Shakespeare's play, she mused: Romeo and Juliet. Juliet was fourteen like me, well I'm nearly fifteen. I can't remember how old Romeo was but I expect he was almost eighteen, like Eddie. And our families are against us. That wasn't really true, she reasoned. Although she had never invited Eddie in, she always told Ma and Pa where she had been with Eddie. The very first time, Ma had taken her into the scullery and cautioned her. 'You're a young woman and he's a young man. He must never take liberties with you. You understand?' She had nodded but hadn't really understood.

'Well, will you? Laura! Will you? You're not listening to me are you?' Georgie shouted at her crossly.

'I'm sorry, Georgie dear, what were you asking me?'

'I asked if you'd get me a job in London town near

you. I know there's nothing for a lad at your place but there must be other factories around there.'

'But you haven't left school yet, Georgie. What are you talking about? You were only twelve in June. You can't leave until next year.'

'You did. So why can't I? All my mates have left and got jobs. Jack Forest got a good one with Whitbreads in Chiswell Street. Even Percy has been taken on at the tram depot, sort of apprentice he says.'

Jane called them to help her bring in the last pieces of washing. After the clouds had cleared, daylight had lasted long into the summer evening. Jane had dragged a stool out into the yard and spent a pleasant hour or so just gazing into space with Lucky curled up at her feet and purring contentedly.

They folded the dried clothing into neat piles. Laura and Georgie said goodnight and went to their room.

'You will look out for me, won't you Laura? See if you can find me a good spot.'

'I'll see.'

She stretched out on top of the bed cover to keep cool. She wondered what she should wear tomorrow. What colour suited her best? There was that light brown cotton dress with the large cream collar. That was nice. Or the lavender costume she had made for Maisie's church service. That was the last time she had seen Eddie. Colours, shades, hues, wafted through her mind and she drifted into sleep.

Roughly she was wrenched from slumber.

'Laura!'

She awoke at Jane's urgent whisper.

'Father's not home. It's past eleven o'clock. I don't know what could have happened. Get up, will you?'

Laura pulled on her grey twill dress and thrust her bare feet into cold boots. Her eyes adjusted from the dark passage to the opal glow of gaslight. Jane sat at the table with her head in her hands.

'Don't fret Ma. I expect he's gossiping with his cronies and forgot the time.'

'The *Thatched House* would have shut half an hour since.' Jane stood up.

'But I'm going round there to see if anyone is about. You stay here for now.'

A coal slipped in the range fire and sent an eerie red glow into the kitchen. Laura suddenly shivered and stood close to the warmth. Ma seemed to have been gone such a long time. At last she heard the front door close and heard Jane's tread along the passage. Light fell on her face, freckles vivid against her pallor. Laura rushed to he side.

;Ma, what is it? Is Pa all right?'

'He's at the Police Station. Arrested!'

Jane slumped into a chair. Her eyes stared into space.

Laura drew her chair alongside Jane and sat in silence. Questions tumbled about in her brain but she must wait until Ma was ready to tell her what had happened. The gas mantle flared suddenly washing the room in garish light before smoking into extinction. Laura hastily turned off the gas supply, pulled back the curtain and raised the window. Stars twinkled in the soft blue sky.

In the shadowy light, Laura gained courage to press her mother for answers.

'Tell me what you found out, Ma. What happened? What did Pa do for the police to arrest him?'

'He was in a fight. A drunken brawl,' she said savagely.

'Pa! In a fight?' Laura said, astonished. Her father was the mildest of men. Never a cross word; never a fierce temper. He could never have raised his fists.

'It can't be true, Ma.'

'The landlord was sweeping out the public bar. He told me.' She spat out the words.

Laura ran back to her room and collected her shawl. Jane still sat at the table transfixed.

'Ma, I'm going to the Police Station. I must find out what's happened to Pa.'

Jane made no reply and Laura quickly left the house. It was already tomorrow but Laura pushed the thought from her mind. Most of the streets were deserted. On a corner, a night watchman kept guard over a hole in the road; his brazier damped down until breakfast time. A policeman patrolling his beat, called after her to hurry home like a good girl. She reached the Broadway and drew breath. The water cart cleaning the streets gave her time to rehearse what she would say.

Quietly she pushed open the swing door and crossed the small area to another set of doors. Down three steps and she was in front of the counter. A policeman sat at the back writing. Laura gave a light cough.

'I never hear you come in, miss. You gave me a fright, you did.'

It was a pleasant voice and he smiled.

'It's very late. What can I do for you, miss?'

Laura returned his smile. 'It's my father, sir. Mr George Stringer. I understand he was, arrested.' The last word was barely audible.

The policeman turned away and brought a heavy ledger to the counter. 'George Stringer, you say.' His finger traced up the lines, each event entered in a neat hand.

'Yes, here 'tis. Nine thirty seven, Constable Corchoran and Constable Derwent entered the station with the accused, George Stringer, arrested outside the *Thatched House*, drunk and disorderly having been involved in a fist fight.' He looked up into Laura's concerned face. 'Don't worry, miss. He'll sleep it off in the cell and be up before the Magistrate Monday morning. He'll be bound over for sure, as he has no previous record.'

'It's true, sir, he has never been in trouble before. Please, sir, I should like to take him home with me.'

'I'm sorry, lass, he's got to stay until Monday morning. The law's the law.'

'I believe, sir, there is something called bail, isn't there?'

'What's the point of it? He might as well stay here.'

'No, sir. I want him home this night.'

She hadn't meant her voice to sound so defiant; she had meant to be pleading.

'Look, lass. The lowest bail is half a guinea and there is...'

Laura bobbed down below the counter and undid knots in her petticoat.

'Here, sir.' She counted out five shilling pieces, ten sixpenny pieces, three pennies, two ha'pennies and five farthings. She quickly retrieved one farthing.

'I'll get the Station Sergeant, miss. Please wait here.'

Her gaze was on the minute had of the large wall clock. She watched it tick round and round. Half past one in the morning; she had never been out so late. A key grated in a lock. She turned round and stifled a sob as she watched her father brought up from the cells. George's eye was bluish black and so swollen he couldn't' see out of it. His mouth was bruised and there was congealed blood around the lips.

They stood side by side at the counter.

The Station Sergeant looked sternly at George. 'You understand you must present yourself to the Magistrate at eight o'clock on Monday morning. Failure to do so will result in forfeiture of the bail bond registered by, er...' he glanced down at the record book, 'by Miss Laura Selina Stringer.'

She took his arm and led him out into the fresh

night air. The sky remained light and the stars were losing their brilliance as dawn crept close. Her hand slid down to grasp his; her fingers pressed into his palm in compassion.

Jane was still sitting at the table as they came into the kitchen. Her eyes took in the state of his injuries. Without a word she stood up and got water and cloths. Gently she soaked away the crusted blood from his lips and around his eye. He flinched slightly but said nothing. A pad soaked in salt was placed under the bruised eye. Laura eased him out of the chair and helped him off with his coat.

No-one had spoken since they had left the police station. Now, as the first strands of daylight streaked the sky, Jane led the way along the passage to their rooms. 'There are a few hours left for sleep,' she said.

After a fitful sleep Laura got up. Georgie was snoring contentedly oblivious of the night's events. On the kitchen table were the piles of freshly laundered shirts, night shirts and linens awaiting collection. Blowing on the line, was the start of a new load. Jane was into her usual Sunday routine: in the scullery standing at the sink up to her elbows in suds. Working Tuesday, Thursday and Saturdays at the Ranelah Road lodging house meant getting customers' wash done on Sundays and Mondays and ironed on Wednesdays and Fridays. She heard Laura open the door.

'Mrs Pidgeon will be first to call, she's all right. But Mrs Henson owes a shilling from last week. Don't hand over the laundry until she's settled. The iron's heating on the hob. Just give that top shirt another rub over the collar.'

'Yes, Ma.'

Laura picked up the holder and lifted the iron off the heat. Her head ached and the iron seemed extra heavy. Her spittle sizzled on the hot base and she rubbed it first on an old cloth and then spread out the shirt collar. Backwards and forwards, backwards and forwards.

'Where did you get it?' Ma asked making her jump. She looked enquiringly at Jane.

'The half guinea. Where did you get it?'

'I saved it, Ma'

Jane eyed her suspiciously.

'Oh, it wasn't from my wages, Ma. I hand over to you the four and six Garsten's pay me and you give me back a shilling for fares. I saved it from what the women paid me for trimming a hat or stitching up a hem. They pay me in coppers and Mary changes it into silver for me. I'm saving up for a sewing machine.'

Jane made no comment and returned to the sink. Laura didn't think it was wrong to keep it for herself.

Georgie sauntered into the kitchen.

'Hello, Sis. Hello, Ma,' he called into the scullery. He yawned and stretched. 'I'm hungry.'

'You're always hungry. Oh, Georgie,' Laura scolded, 'you didn't go to bed with your socks on did you? You always run a hole in them like that.'

Georgie gazed down at his feet, the top of the sock flapping beyond his toes.

'Suppose I must've done.'

He bent down to take them off and caught sight of his father coming down the hallway.

'Cor! Look at Pa!'

In an instant Jane leapt from the scullery and brought the palm of her hand sharply round Georgie's left ear. Georgie let our a wild yell. A few minutes later Mrs Milton was leaning over the bannister.

'Is someone hurt, Mrs Stringer?'

'Nothing to worry about, Mrs Milton,' Jane replied.

George, Jane and Laura stood silent like statues. Georgie squatted on the floor rubbing his ear. A single rap at the door brought them to life. Laura folded the first pile of laundry and tied it with strong. She forced a smile onto her face and went to answer the door.

Jane stacked the rest of the washing onto the chest and brought out the bread and jam. The four of them sat at the table.

Gradually the pile of washing diminished as Laura handed them over and received payment. Even Mrs Henson paid what was owed. And no-one mentioned the fight or what happened last night; perhaps word hadn't yet got out.

In a valiant attempt, Georgie had kept the tears back but his face showed his hurt. George looked at his son. He cleared his throat.

'I was in a bit of a scrap last night, lad. I made a fool of myself and upset your Ma and your sister.' He looked across at Jane. 'I'm truly sorry. Tell me what you want me to do.'

'There's nothing you can do now,' Jane sighed. 'Except to keep it to ourselves.'

A loud knock at the door startled them. For a moment they sat quite still, perhaps hoping the caller would go away. Laura held her breath. Then the single knock came again.

'There's no more washing to be collected,' Jane said in dismay.

'I'll go, Ma,' Georgie said.

A chattering of voices and feet running along the passage. Then the door flew open and Sarah dashed into the room.

Laura rushed to her sister and hugged her close.

'When no-one answered my knock I thought you'd gone away without telling.'

'Oh, Sarah, as if we would do such a thing,' Laura laughed and gave her another hug.

The colour had drained from Jane's face. 'What's wrong girl?' she demanded. 'Have you lost your position?'

Sarah put her hands on her hips and turned to face her mother.

'That's a fine welcome I must say. Can't I come home to see my family? I haven't been home for months and months and that's all you say to me.'

'Have you been dismissed?' Jane persisted.

'No, Ma, I have not! I get a day off now and again, you know. But I don't get enough money to pay the tram fare home regularly. They keep taking fines for breakage's out of my wages. Oh, it's really awful, Laura.'

'But I thought you were a parlour maid now, Sarah.'

'A fancy name, Laura, that's all. Parlour maid in the afternoon but I still have to get up at five to clean out the grates.'

As she moved farther into the room, Sarah caught sight of her father's face.

'Oh, Pa,' she cried as she ran to him. 'Oh, your poor face, dear Pa,' she held his battered head between her hands and caressed the torn flesh with gentle kisses.

His arms came up and hugged Sarah in a fierce embrace in recognition of her compassion. Tears filled his eyes.

'I don't know how I got into the fight, really I don't, lass,' George's voice wavered. 'I'd had the usual pint or two with me mates in the Thatch. We were standing in the Public talking about all sorts of things. Several Irish navvies were there, I expect from the road works beyond the Broadway. It got that we said one thing and they said the opposite, or we'd say something and they would argue. None of it meant much, we were just joshing each other. Next thing I knew was they were pushing and shoving that poor old codger from the across the road at Number Nine. I don't know what happened after that. I was out on the pavement along with some others when the police came. I wasn't quick enough on me pins and I was nabbed.'

Although he was still clutching Sarah in his arms, George's eyes were on Jane and his words were directed at her.

'That's all there was to it,' he added lamely.

'You two girls go and gossip in your room while I get us something to eat. And Georgie, see what Lucky is doing in the yard.'

After the children had been dismissed, Jane drew her chair nearer to George. She looked at his injured face, a face she loved and adored, now swollen and scarred. Jane leant her head on his shoulder, his arm cuddled her close.

'Oh my dearest husband. Sometimes you do give my poor heart such a big jolt. What will happen tomorrow?'.

'Most likely I'll be bound over. There could be a fine.'

Laura made Sarah describe every room in the house, each stick of furniture, who was in the household and what they had to eat. Sarah's descriptions were always prefaced by Ugh and followed by whatever derogatory term she could find.

'It can't be that bad, Sarah, really it can't'

'But I tell you it is.'

'I know it wasn't good at first. But I thought you liked it after you were given the duties of a parlour maid. On the few times I've managed to see you, you never said it was bad. You and, what's the name of the other girl?'

'Lizzie. Lizzie Hedges.'

'I thought you and Lizzie enjoyed working together.'

'I like Lizzie well enough. But the work is something awful, Laura. I tell you straight, it's more than a body can stand. That's why I wanted to come home today to make sure I saw you. Oh, Laura, please will you find me a job with you. Oh, it doesn't have to be right away but I want a job where I can earn a bit of money and meet people. Like you say you do, travelling on the train every day and having a proper pay day at the end of the week. Oh, please, Laura. Say you'll look out something for me. Anything will do. I know I can't do the same as you. Well, you've done it for two years or more. Please, Laura.'

'Wasn't there a document that Ma signed for you to go into service? It said you were, articled I think it was, articled for a number of years.'

'Only until my sixteenth birthday. And that's next February. I have to give three months' notice to Mr and Mrs Whitaker, through Mrs Bumstead of course. Say you'll look out something for me, Laura, and I can give in my notice from October. Please, Laura.'

Yesterday it was Georgie wheedling for her to get a job lined up for him, Laura thought wryly. Now it was Sarah. All the family seemed beset with problems. How she longed to confide in Eddie. Had he waited for her at their usual meeting place? Was he concerned because she hadn't come? Then a miserable thought struck her: perhaps he hadn't gone there, either. But he'd said: tomorrow.

'What do you say, Laura? You'll be able to sort it out with Ma. I'd best be making my way to the tram now. Old Red Nose - that's Mr Paget - will be watching the clock for certain. A minute beyond my time and I'll be stopped another sixpence,' Sarah laughed. 'Not for long though, eh Laura?'

After another poor night's sleep, Laura accompanied her father to the Magistrate's Court. They were told to be there at eight o'clock but Laura, determined to be early, arrived at seven thirty. They sat on the steps until the bailiff pulled open the heavy oak doors. Two officials escorted them to the side entrance of the court. They were told to sit on the long pews.

'When your name is called, stand up and accompany the police sergeant into the court and stand in front of the Magistrate's bench.'

'May I come, too, sir?' Laura asked.

'Who are you?'

'I'm his daughter.'

Another constable came from the court and recognised Laura.

'You're the persistent young lady who put up the Bail Bond, aren't you lass?'

'Yes, sir.'

'Well, you will be required to attend the Magistrate, too.' He winked at her. 'I'll put you right, miss. Don't worry. I'm certain it will come right.'

Two other names were called before them but finally George stood at the wooden rail. The policeman spoke up for George and it was over in a matter of minutes.

'There, said it would be all right. Bound over for a year. Which means,' and he glared at George, 'which means you must behave yourself. I'm sorry about the fine, lass. It will be taken out of your bond money. The balance can be collected at the cashier's counter through the door to the left. Goodbye to you, and good luck.'

It was good to be outside in the fresh air. Laura filled her lungs, she felt as if she'd been holding her breath. She took George's arm and they walked in silence along the Broadway. As they neared the church the clock chimed out the half hour.

'I must get on to work, Pa. Will you be going home now?'

'That's it, girlie, you get off to work. I expect you'll lose some pay for lateness and there's the fine. But I'll make it up to you, girlie, I promise you I will.'

'Don't fret about the money, Pa. Will you be all right?'

'I'll be off home. I expect your Ma will find some job

to occupy me today and I'll be back in line tomorrow morning.'

The gates were locked. Suspended from the brick supports was a rope. Laura gripped it firmly and pulled. A great bell tolled out. The doors were flung open and Jack Armstrong, head down, hurried to the gates. He inserted the key and swung them open before he saw Laura standing there.

'Cor! Thought you was me deliveries come. Wasn't due until ten thirty. Here! You shouldn't come inside. You know the rules. You have to stay out until midday.'

'I'm in and I'm staying in.'

Laura slipped behind him and ran to the factory door.

'They'll know it was me what let you in,' Jack called in dismay.

She dodged past Mr Pilgrim's window without being seen and made her way into the work area. Laura walked sedately across the floor to the overseer's cubicle.

'I know it is an hour into work time, sir.'

Johnson looked up startled.

'But may I go to my bench, sir? I understand my pay will be affected by my arriving after start of work. I will explain the reason for my lateness when we break at midday so as not to take up any more of the company's time now.'

Johnson's mouth had gaped open as Laura spoke. He was astonished at her daring and simply nodded.

She quickly settled at her bench and pulled cut leathers and silks onto her work area.

'How did you get in, you cheeky monkey?' Kate whispered. 'What happened to make you late. Nothing bad, I hope.'

'No, nothing bad, dear Kate,' Laura whispered.

She thought about what she would tell her friends

and decided to tell them the truth about Pa. But she
was uncertain what to say to Mr Johnson. Perhaps
half truth, about attending court this morning but
not the real reason. The routine of gluing card and
leather and smoothing silk had become second nature
to Laura. Her mind filled with all sorts of things and
didn't affect her output; now she wove a believable
account of why she was late. She thought about Eddie
and determined that without fail next Sunday she
would be at the water trough.

Each day seemed to have twice as many hours in it
and the weekend was as far away as the moon. Now,
at last, it was Sunday. Laura awoke from sleep, excitement tingling through her. She puzzled about what to
wear. Should she put on the lilac outfit? Laura held
it against her and dodged and stretched to see all of
herself in the small mottled mirror suspended from
a nail on the wall. It was the only really smart style
of clothing she had. She looked again. No, something
more simple today. Laura's dresses were folded over
a rope stretched across the corner of the room, all
created from cheap remnants by her skilful sewing.
She decided on the dark red one with the large pink
collar and pink cuffs fastened with a red button.
Household chores and eating were accomplished in a
trance.

'If you polish that plate any more, girlie, you'll rub
off the pattern.'

'Pa's speaking to you, Laura. Can't you hear him
and you are in my way.'

Georgie struggled into the kitchen carrying a
bundle of aired washing.

Laura laughed and ruffled his hair as he passed.

She hurried through the back streets taking a
devious route. Should she come into Leytonstone Road
and walk to the horse trough from the left or should
she go farther on and come to it from the right? A

tram was approaching and she stepped behind it to cross onto the opposite side. Her gaze focussed on the oblong stone container. A carrier held the reins of his horse as it dipped its head into water. No-one else was there. Laura crossed back onto the other side. From behind the cart a tall figure came into view. She stood still. Her heart raced but her feet refused to move over the pavement. With a great effort she placed one boot ahead then the next, left, right, left, right. Her legs responded to brain's command.

At last she reached the trough. They stood smiling at each other.

'Hello,' Laura's voice was barely audible.

'Hello,' Eddie replied as he held out his hand.

Her hand nestled in his palm. The world about her became a distant vision blurred at the edges. There was no time nor place, they were enveloped in a bubble drifting through space. Silently they walked together; an overwhelming happiness filled Laura blotting out the past. This was how it would be for all the years to come.

They walked as far as West Ham Park and Eddie steered her to an iron seat. He took her face in his hands.

'I love you, Laurie, with all my heart. Say you'll be mine, darling Laurie.'

Tears filled her eyes and trickled down her cheek. His thumb brushed them away.

'What is it, dearest? Have I said something wrong? I know we're young, but...'

Laura put her finger on his lips. 'Oh, you silly darling. Nothing's wrong. Everything is wonderful.'

They sat looking at each other, His eyes slowly scanned her face, storing each minute detail into his memory: flecks of amber glinted in her left eye, a minute emerald flash in the right one, adding a lustrous sparkle to eyes that shone; tiny freckles near the tip of her nose; the outline of her upper lip which curved into a perfect bow. How he longed to taste the sweetness there.

Laura blushed and cast down her eyes under such penetrating scrutiny. Eddie moved closer to her and his arm circled her shoulder. Gradually he drew her to his side and she rested her head against his chest. It was their first physical contact. A flood of sensations swept through Laura's body. Wrists tingled, hunger lurched through her stomach, dull aches alternated with sharp stabbing pains. It was all very strange but wonderful. Was Eddie experiencing the same excitement? She raised her head to look at him. His lips came down on her mouth in a gentle kiss.

Whistles and shouts interrupted their caresses. Four lads had been knocking a ball about on the far side of the grass. With each kick the game moved sideways until they were near the bench. Laura and Eddie were so absorbed in themselves they were not aware of the four boys observing them.

'That weren't much of a smacker,' one said.

'I seen better with the coal horse!' another jeered.

Eddie grasped Laura's hand as then ran toward the park gates. They fell against the railing, helpless with laughter. An elderly couple dressed in black passed by. The lady sniffed and tossed her head at them, the gentleman held up his large Bible as if to ward off any disease or insanity that may emanate from such weird people.

After a moment, they made their way home. Neither said a word, there was no need. All too soon, it seemed to Laura, they had arrived at her gate.

Georgie sat on the step, whacking a stick on the flag stone and counting.

'Fifty-seven, fifty-eight. Oh, it's you. Said to Ma, I expect you were with him,' Georgie nodded towards Eddie.

Georgie didn't like Eddie. Since he came on the scene, Laura had scant time for her little brother.

He continued striking the ground. 'Ma was looking for you but I said no use looking in the street as you were sure to be canoodling in the park.'

Laura reached down and wrenched the stick from his hand.

'I've a good mind to give you a hiding with this. Ma knew very well I was meeting Eddie so you didn't tell her something she didn't already know.'

She threw the stick away. She was aware of a sharpness in her tongue and Laura was determined nothing should spoil such a wonderful day. She smiled and reached down to ruffle his hair.

'Come on, little brother, time for supper. Let's go in.'

Georgie grinned in response and pushed open the door. On the threshold Laura turned back to wave goodbye to Eddie.

He nodded. 'Same time next week, Laurie,' he called softly before dashing off down the road.

She was drowsy but couldn't sleep. Lying on her back, Laura stretched up her arms and wound them about her head. A soft mewing escaped her lips. Pictures danced through her mind: the two of them walking through the park; the two of them sitting on the bench. A place of their own, cooking supper for Eddie when he came home from the railway yard. Babies! Two or three. Growing old with Eddie, both grey and stooped. She giggled.

'Give over, Laura,' Georgie mumbled. 'I got to get my sleep.'

She snuggled down under the cover. Marriage was a serious thing, it needed a lot of thought. Not that she and Eddie would be wed for many a year but it had to be right. She wanted it to be right.

When the bell sounded for midday meal break,

Laura moved quickly ahead of Kate and walked beside Maisie. 'It's ever so important, please Maisie.'

'Of course, dearie,' she whispered in answer. 'I'll be over the road looking in the draper's window.'

'What's all the mystery about?'

'No mystery Kate. I'll tell you later on,' Laura called as she skipped down the road.

Her bread and jam forgotten, Maisie listened to every word Laura said. Gradually a smile spread across her face.

'Oh Laura, I'm so glad. I can see you've thought it out. Come to church on Sunday, Laura, and meet our Minister and he will explain everything to you. Your learning will take some time, may be almost a year but it will be worth it, you'll see.'

Kate stood on the corner chatting with lads from the iron foundry. She watched Laura and Maisie walk arm in arm on the opposite side of the road. They crossed to Garsten's gates. Kate ran ahead and blocked their way.

Hand on her hips, she demanded: 'Well! What's the mystery?'

Laura laughed, 'I told you there was no mystery, Kate.' She leant forward and flung her arms about Kate's neck. 'I wanted to ask Maisie about learning the Bible and being baptised.'

'Eh?' Kate spluttered.

Laura stood between her friends and linked arms. 'You have heard me talk about my young man...'

'Worn our ears down, you have, talking of your young man.'

'Shush, Kate, let her tell us in her own way.'

Laura blushed and smiled. 'My young man, Eddie, has asked me to be, well, special. You know, walking out together. Some day we'll be wed. I have this feeling, I can't explain it, but it has to mean more than cooking and washing for a man and having babies. When I get married in the church I want the blessing to be real.'

She let go of their arms and held her head. 'Such a lot of words. It doesn't make sense to me so it must be all gibberish to you.'

The gates opened signalling the start of the afternoon's grind. Laura hurried to her work place and busied herself with routine. As she had drifted into sleep last night, she had remembered Maisie's baptism. Peace and tranquillity had spread over all present not just those confirming their faith. Somehow, all were uplifted. Because of her happiness with Eddie, she wanted the same lightness of spirit she had seen in the congregation that day. It had been straight forward in her thoughts but speaking out loud seemed to muddle it up.

'I hope I can make sense of it to Eddie,' Laura thought.

Chapter 16

August Bank Holiday Monday was just two days away and still there was no sign of summer a-coming in. Just rain and more rain.

Head bent against the wet onslaught, Laura ran toward the station. She clutched the oiled cloth tightly about her shoulders. Sarah had laughed at first. 'Don't bend over or someone will take you for a table,' she'd said but soon changed her tune when she saw how dry it kept Laura's clothes. She begged Laura to find another piece in the market and make her a rain cape. The station entrance was ahead and Laura gratefully sheltered under the archway. Some of the usual travellers were on the platform, others queued at the ticket office. She nodded to various acquaintances. From the group of girls waiting for the train, one saw Laura and waved and hurried to stand beside her in the queue.

'Have you heard about Rose Bullen?' she whispered.

Laura was busy sorting out coins for the fare and didn't answer.

The girl plucked at her sleeve.

'Just a minute,' Laura said. 'A ha'penny has slipped to the bottom of my bag.'

She was proud of the patchwork bag she had made

from scraps of discarded leather and drawn together with a cord but with all those seams, small items wriggled underneath hidden from view.

'Here it is! Three tupenny workman's returns Liverpool Street, please.'

The clerk scooped up the coins and replaced them with three pieces of cardboard.

'Why do you always buy tickets for your brother and sister?'

'They can't run as fast as me,' Laura replied.

'Leave 'em to get their own and if they miss the ten past seven that's their look out.'

Laura smiled and moved back to the entrance to look for Sarah and Georgie. It was no hardship to run ahead and get the tickets. Laura liked doing it. When Garsten's took a lease on the warehouse next door and began setting up equipment, Laura asked if they would be needing new hands. Just before Christmas she had written a joyous letter to Sarah telling her to give in her notice terminating on her sixteenth birthday; in February there would be a job for her at Garsten's. Soon, Sarah was home sharing the bed with Laura once again. Sarah working with Laura, left only Georgie as the miserable one.

'He's doing no good at school, Ma and he'd be leaving in the summer anyway. Let him leave at Easter and I'll find him something in the city near us.' Laura had no difficulty in getting him placed at Jantsen and Nicholson's paint factory in Falcon Street.

'Trains nearly here,' the girl said accusingly as Sarah and Georgie tumbled into the station.

'Look, Laura, the rain's ruined my hat.'

Sarah shook her head and droplets of water scattered about. Large red cherries tied into the silk band of the black straw hat drooped despondently onto the brim.

'You knew it was raining, Sarah. Why did you put it on instead of your bonnet?'

'I'm meeting Clarence at the pie shop at ten past twelve.'

'Clarence!' Laura said in astonishment. 'I thought his name was Billy.'

'Billy works at the iron foundry. Clarence is an apprentice at the upholsterer's. I see them both,' Sarah giggled, 'not at the same time, of course.'

They walked out to the platform and Georgie turned one way to join the men's group and Laura and Sarah headed for the young women but the girl blocked their way.

'Rose Bullen had a baby,' she blurted out. She turned back to the group. 'I've just told them. They didn't know either.'

'Working up to the last minute, she was. On her way home, when it happened.'

The girl drew Sarah and Laura into the group.

'I don't understand how it could have happened,' another girl said. 'She wasn't married.'

'Gawd love us!' the first girl screeched. 'Don't tell me you still think babies come from under the gooseberry bushes,' she jeered.

Her laughter had attracted attention and the young men turned toward them. Several girls shifted awkwardly and looked down at the ground.

'Do you know how babies come?' one asked timidly.

'Course, I do. The man's got the key and the woman's got the keyhole.'

'What key?'

'You know, duckie. His Jimmy Riddler.'

For a moment there was an embarrassed silence.

'That's nonsense,' one said hesitantly. 'Where has a woman got a keyhole?'

'Between her legs, yer daft ninny! And the man

inserts his key and unlocks her virginity,' the girl said
with a raucous laugh.

'That's dirty.'

'Course, it's not dirty. Well, sometimes it might be.
But 'ow do yer think you come to be standing 'ere.
Only because yer Pa put his key in yer Ma's keyhole.'

With relief, Laura saw the engine along the track,
steam billowed from its squat funnel, and the whistle
sounded the approach of the train. Passengers hurried
forward, the nearest one grasped a handle and opened
the door. Laura contrived to be at the back with Sarah
and two of the youngest girls and were level with a different compartment. As they sat down Laura saw the
girls were upset.

'Don't be concerned with what she was saying. She
likes to say naughty things. Thinks it makes her ever
so grown up. Put her words out of your mind.'

'It doesn't have to be like that,' Sarah said. 'It can
be dreamy and exciting, gentle and fiery, but loving.'
Her voice was husky, her violet eyes held a mistiness
as they gazed into the distance.

'Sarah Matilda that's disgraceful behaviour,' Laura
hissed. 'When I am trying to calm these girls.' She
paused and stared at her sister. 'How do you know
about such things? Oh, Sarah, you haven't...'

Sarah dug Laura in the ribs. 'No I haven't, sister!
How could **YOU** say such a thing?'

'You said it with such feeling, I just wondered.'

'The young mistress at Midmellian had books and
periodicals which she gave to Lizzie and me and we'd
read them in our attic room then dream of a gallant
young officer galloping off with us.' She smiled at such
foolishness but her sigh denied it was foolish. 'And
what about you and Eddie?'

Laura laughed in response. 'I deserved that. Like
you, dear Sarah, I know it will be beautiful when the

time comes. And that time, when we are married, is a long way off.'

Four o'clock each Friday afternoon was Jane's special time. A time for herself. Now all the children were working, the house was quiet until half past seven. Of course, George was home from market at two in the afternoon but slept for an hour or two. Jane would wake him with a cup of tea, he'd read the paper before adjourning to the *Thatched House*. But Friday nights he never stayed there long.

As usual she checked the bolt was across on the scullery door. She drew the pins from her bun and shook her hair free. It had dulled a little from the amber gold of her youth but it still had a glossy sheen. Slowly she took off each layer of clothing until she was standing naked. Two pans of water had been boiled on the range and carried through to the scullery. The first one was emptied into a bowl and cooled with water from the tap. A soaked cloth was dabbed with soap until a frothy lather had gathered, then Jane spread the cloth first over her face, then arms, chest, legs, thighs, back - as far as she could reach. Before each area, the cloth was re-soaped until every inch of her was cleansed and rinsed off in cold water. Jane reached up and took a small jar from the shelf. The second pan of hot water was emptied into the bowl to which was added several drops of essence from the jar. A sweet scent filled the small cramped space. Jane dipped a clean cloth in to the spiced water and slowly moistened under her arms, under her breasts, between her legs. The freshness filled her nostrils.

Often in the past, as she had stood in naked cleanliness, she would hold the grey dress against her skin. With the silk, clinging to her firm breasts and taut stomach she would be transported back to Brighton all those years ago. In her mind she saw the reaction of the lift attendant as she had stood resplendent in the shimmering grey with pearl clasps at the shoulder. The cotton bag was hanging on the back of the door now. But it would go back into its secret place not to come out again. She looked down at her body. Her figure had thickened, the delicate material would no longer cover her large breasts and round belly. She smiled to herself; it was of no consequence. That life was a false one; she had what she wanted.

Fresh pantaloons and crisp bodice covered her washed body. Jane heard George come into the kitchen and quickly completed her dressing. For the moment she put the cotton bag in with the customer's orders which were ready for collection on Sunday. She would remove it after George had gone out and put it back in the box by her bed.

'I'll just put the water on to make us a nice cup of tea, dear.'

Jane took two china cups and saucers from the shelf. For just her and George, she always used the best cups. George picked up his paper. Hot water was poured onto the tea leaves in the large brown pot and Jane gave them a vigorous stir. She held the cup in her hand and reached across George to put it on the table. Her bosom came close to his face in deliberate provocation. The warmth of her flesh had enhanced the perfume. Greedily, he drank in her aroma. She knew she had aroused him. She turned back to the stove and brought her own cup to the table. Not a word was said as they sat sipping tea and looking at each other. Each glance stimulated desire. George summoned all his willpower to suppress his ardour. Jane ached with expectancy.

George broke the spell, could stand it no long. He grabbed his cap and rushed out of the front door. She smiled to herself. He would remember her tantalising smell later tonight. In bed. In an effort to return to normality, Jane set plates on the table in readiness for the children's supper.

Stamping feet broke into a run. Georgie burst into the kitchen.

'Ma! Say we can all go, please say yes.'

He put his arms about her and kissed each cheek. Jane pushed him away but Georgie clung onto her arm.

'Away with you. What's all this about?'

Georgie led Jane to her rocking chair and made her sit down.

'Well, Mr Birch, you know, landlord of the *Thatched House*, well, he has arranged a trip by charabanc. MOTOR charabanc,' he emphasised. 'Can we go, Ma, please. It's to the seaside! Percy told me. He and his Pa are going. Let's go, too.'

He had gabbled so fast he finally ran out of breath.

Jane held her hands over her ears.

'Laura, Sarah. One of you. Will your please tell me what this is all about?'

'Well,' Laura began, 'on Bank Holiday Monday, a motor charabanc is leaving the *Thatched House* at half past eight and will drive al the way to the seaside at Margate.'

Her voice had started in a matter of fact way, now it held a tinge of excitement. 'There are still some places left and, Oh! Ma! It would be nice if we could all go. You and Pa, all of us. It will cost nine pence each...'

'Ninepence! Good gracious girl, nine pence for each one of us!'

'Ma, we can pay for ourselves and I'll treat you and Pa, if only you'll say you'll come.'

'Come and eat your supper.'

Sarah started to protest. 'You haven't said...'

'Not another word,' Jane said sternly.

One by one, they washed their hands and walked dejectedly back to the table. Normally they would all eat together but on Friday nights Jane served the children on their own. A plate of cold mutton sat in the centre of the table. Although the pangs of hunger were strong, none had the will to eat. Jane turned back to the stove and lifted out steaming potatoes. She carried the dish to the table.

'We'll talk to Father when he comes in,' she said.

Laura was the first to fill her plate. She knew how to handle Pa.

They were all anxious to help with chores and tidied away quickly to await George's return.

Week nights, George would spend a couple of hours, may be from six until eight, in the public bar with his mates. But not Fridays, never so long on Fridays. Saturdays were different and special.

His eye was on the large clock over the bar. He was eager to be off home and quickly swilled the dregs of his ale and bid good night. His long strides soon covered the short distance between pub and home. He would have a few words with the children about their day, send them off to bed and then he and Jane would sup together before retiring for the night.

George stopped abruptly after stepping into the kitchen. The children were seated round the table all staring at him. Jane stood behind them, her face impassive.

'Something up? What is it?'

Jane prodded Georgie. 'Georgie has something to say.'

'But I thought Laura was going to ask. Please, Laura. You ask.'

George flopped down in his chair. Just when he was buoyed up with expectations, some problem comes along to spoil it all.

'Well, what is it?' His voice was unusually harsh. 'Come on girl, spit it out whatever it is you want to say.'

Tears began to glisten in her eyes. She hadn't expected her father to be so gruff. Laura had hoped to wheedle agreement out of him. She stood up.

'Well, father. The, er... Mr Birch of the *Thatched House*...'

George shot his head up. 'What about the *Thatched House*?'

'Mr Birch has laid on a motor charabanc to take customers to the seaside at Margate on Bank Holiday Monday. It costs ninepence for each person and we should like to go. We can pay for ourselves and I should like to pay for you and Ma if you will say you'll come.' She ran to his side. 'Please, Pa. Please say we can all go together.'

A deep sigh of relief escaped George's lips. 'You gave me a fright, girl. All so serious. Tell me again. I was anxious as to what it should be I wasn't listening clearly.'

As he listened attentively to the details of the trip, his fear receded and his heartbeat levelled to normal. His night with Jane would not be spoilt. He raised his eyes and looked at Jane but she gave no hint of what she thought about the trip.

'Charabanc trip, eh? There was a list with names on it, behind the bar, I suppose it showed those who'd booked a seat. I did wonder about it, meself.'

Laura clapped her hands for joy.

'If your mother is in agreement, then I think we should go.'

There was such pandemonium in the kitchen that they didn't hear the tap at the door.

Mrs Milton, mob cap perched on her grey head, peered round the corner.

'Beg pardon, I'm sure. But I afeared when I heard all the noise, I thought something terrible had happened.' She dropped a curtsey to George. 'I didn't know you was in, sir,' and quickly closed the door.

It was several minutes before their laughter subsided.

'No more of this tonight,' Jane said sternly. 'Off to bed with you.'

'I'd best run up to the Thatch and book our places, Ma,' Georgie said. He held out his hand to Laura for money.

'Thank you all the same, girlie. It was kind of you but I shall pay for mother and me. Come on lad, I'll walk with you to be quick about it.'

Jane filled the pans with water, ready for the morning and put them on the range with the teapot alongside then hurried the girls off to bed. She damped down the fire before she retired to the small back room. Her night-gown lay folded on the box beside the bed. But this was the one night in the week when it wouldn't be needed until morning.

Her hair released from it's tight knot fell about her bare shoulders. She heard the front door close and father and son say goodnight. She slipped under the sheet. George stood at the side of the bed and folded each item of clothing in the order to be put on in the morning. The bed creaked as he got in beside her. For several minutes they lay still. Jane smiled to herself, she knew what she had to do. She moved onto her side, with her hands she gently nestled his head between her breasts. When she heard his breathing quicken, she placed her leg over his, pressed against his stomach and began a slow rocking motion. George reared up in a fervour of desire. Squeals of delight escaped Jane's lips with each surging movement. After the climax, she would lie in his arms for a while until the yearning returned and she would twine her legs with his to revive the feeling. And again they were swept along with their emotions. Once more Jane titil-lated him into vibrant action to be absorbed in delir-ium. As the passion subsided, she lay contented at his side. George tried to stimulate her one more time but she was already drifting off into dreams.

At the usual time, Jane stirred from sleep. She slipped out of bed and put on her night-gown. Thin early morning light filtered through the yard window. She looked down at the slumbering figure in the bed, his head turned toward her space. Tousled hair framed his face. The furrows in his brow were less deeply etched nowadays. Perhaps their more settled life had eased the burden off his slight shoulders. She gazed lovingly at this dear man, her husband. In spite of Matilda's misgivings, their marriage had lasted; eighteen years it was in June. And their bond was greater now than ever it had been. George rolled over on to his back; he would wake soon. She hastened from the room. Jane stirred the kitchen fire into life. In the scullery she unbolted the back door and stepped out into the fresh morning air. Lucky came from beside the lavatory and wove in and out of her legs. She reached down and stroked him.

'Well puss my lad, have you had a good night, too?'

For answer, he purred even louder.

George was washing at the sink when she returned. She made the tea and set it to brew; cut two thick slices of mutton and placed it between pieces of bread then wrapped it in a cloth. George drank the tea she had put before him and pocketed his breakfast. Not a word was said; there was nothing to say. George was off to market.

Jane moved back to the scullery and picked out the cotton bag from customer's washing. She carried it back to the bedroom and hid it at the back of her bedside box. She climbed into bed for another hour's rest. She hugged herself in pleasure. Their exhilaration knew no bounds. In the early days there was always the fear of pregnancy and, at the last moment, Jane would pull away from George; he would be hurt and frustrated and she would be unfulfilled. But as each year passed with no more babies in the end she gave herself completely to George. She did wonder, a little guiltily, whether the destruction of his seed all those years ago had made it impossible to conceive.

So much the better for our life now, she thought.

No more time for thinking, work was waiting. Money was all right but work at the young men's hostel was tiresome. I've a good mind to give it up, Jane thought. Now all the children were bringing in a wage it wasn't necessary. She resolved to hand in her notice.

It was half past four, later than she thought. Laura ran through the back streets out into Leytonstone Road. The thoroughfare was thronged with people. She dodged between them to reach the water trough. She looked around to seek out the familiar tall figure but Eddie was nowhere in sight. Her mouth was dry and she bent under the drinking fountain.

'Serve you right if I pushed you in.'

Laura twirled about and grinned happily at Eddie.

'I see little enough of you as it is, without you being late,' he grumbled. 'What with Sarah always being with you when you come off the train from work, and all this time you keep spending at church. When have you got time for me?'

She linked her arm with his. 'Ah don't begrudge me Sarah's company. I've had little enough of it. When we were little, she was always sent to Granny Goult, then she was put into domestic service. I'm sorry I was late, dearest. We were making the final arrangements at church. You know I am to be baptised next month. Then there won't be any more Bible lessons in the afternoon. I'll still be attending the morning service, of course.'

Eddie squeezed her arm in forgiveness. 'I know, Laurie.'

Although there had been no rain today, puddles

still remained on the pavement. Laughing, each tried to make the other step into one until they collided in the middle of a deep pool splashing other passers-by. They hastily skipped into an alley.

As his laughter subsided, Eddie pulled her close to him.

'It's bank Holiday Monday tomorrow. A whole day, my sweetheart. What shall we do?'

Laura took a deep breath. 'Please don't be angry but I can't see you tomorrow.'

He released his hold on her.

'All of us, Ma and Pa, Sarah, Georgie and me, we're going on a charabanc ride to the seaside. I've never seen the sea, Eddie. Fancy that, the seaside. It's a motor charabanc. From the *Thatched House*. It leaves at half past eight but I don't know what time it gets back so I can't promise to meet you then.'

Her voice trailed off. The excitement of the trip was waning. She would rather not go than lose Eddie.

For a moment, he said nothing. Tears welled in Laura's eyes. As the first droplet spilled onto her cheek, Eddie's thumb brushed it away as he had done once before.

'Well, it would be a pity for you to miss a trip to the seaside especially as you've never seen the sea. I'll find out from the landlord what time he reckons the motor will be back and I'll be waiting for you. So I'll know you've got back all right. Now, I ain't going to spend any more of this day in fighting, Miss Stringer, so come on. Let's go and look at the fair.'

Laura gazed rapturously at him. He clasped her hand and in an uneven way ran beside her in the direction of the fair. The sound of the hurdy-gurdy was drawing a crowd. Painted horses rose up and down on the roundabout.

'Appenny a ride,' the showman shouted.

'It's eight o'clock! Now have you got everything?' Laura asked.

Sarah was rummaging in a drawer.

'What are you looking for?'

'I can only find one pink glove.'

'Well get another pair.'

'They won't match my dress,' Sarah moaned.

'Sarah! We are going to the seaside not taking tea with the King and Queen. Get another pair.'

Although the sky was opaque, it didn't look as if it was full of rain clouds. Laura was sure it was going to be a lovely day. She left Sarah holding three pairs of gloves against her pink cambric dress and joined her mother in the kitchen.

Jane was loading food into a basket.

'I've cut the bread and there was a bit of mutton left over. I've put in a piece of cheese and some apples. I don't know what to do about something to drink.'

'May be the Thatch has put in a keg of ale,' Georgie said.

'Well, there'll be lots of taverns when we get to Margate,' George put in. 'We can call in for a glass of ale. Come on then. Let's be off. Where's that sister of yours, girlie?'

Laura ran up the passage. 'If you don't come now, Sarah, we'll leave you behind.'

'Do these look all right?'

She held out a pair of dark blue silk gloves.

'Yes, dear. Come on.'

Outside the *Thatched House* a small group had gathered. Jane and George led the family to join them.

'How do. Looks like we're in for a nice day.'

A horn sounded and a cheer went up at the charabanc drew alongside. Everyone clambered aboard; there were a few double seats down the middle and the rest sat on benches along each side. Their jolly spirits subsided as they descended into a dark hole just after leaving Stratford.

'Only the Blackwall Tunnel,' the driver called over his shoulder. 'We're under the Thames.'

The farther they got from London, so it seemed the skies got clearer. By one o'clock the journey was nearly over. And there wasn't a cloud to blot out the sun.

'There's the sea!' called the driver.

Everyone lurched forward to catch their first sighting of the sea, slewing the coach sideways. Some youngsters tumbled to the floor but no-one was hurt. The driver turned onto the coast road and drove alongside the beach. He parked in a side turning.

'Now then, one and all. We are at the seaside and we are here to enjoy ourselves.'

'Yes,' came the reply.

'But I got to get this vehicle back to the terminus yard so we must be saying our farewells to Margate at half past four.'

George helped Jane down and she took his arm. Sarah, Laura and Georgie linked arms and walked behind them.

'Oh, isn't this nice. So warm,' Sarah said as she loosened the top button of her dress.

George paused and sucked in the salty air.

'Takes me back to when I was a boy.'

'Have you been to the seaside before, Pa?' Laura asked.

'To this very place, I have, girlie. I came with my father.'

'Good gracious, George! Look!' Jane pointed to the waves rolling in on the sand.

Standing in the water were a group of young people. The two women were clothed in tunics with frilled skirts and the two young men were dressed in yellow and black striped costumes extending to the knee.

One young man bobbed down and swam farther out into the sea; The others followed.

'How exciting!' exclaimed Laura. 'I should like to do that. I wonder if it is difficult to learn. Can you do that, Pa? Did you do it when you came with your Pa?'

'Lor' no! We were working, father and me.' He turned to look back toward the road. 'See those,' he pointed.

'Those big sheds do you mean, Pa?'

'They are bathing machines. Father would sell his nag and the cart, and we'd leave mother with the young 'uns and we'd get on the boat in London and come down river. He'd buy another horse and we would work the bathing machines. Ladies would walk up the little steps at the back of the machine. Inside they'd change their clothes, then father and me would lead the horse down the beach and into the sea. We'd go out as far as we could - sometimes I had to sit on the wheel hub else the water'd be over my head. Turn the horse around, and then the ladies would come down the steps into the sea for a dip. When they got back inside they'd bang on the side and we'd lead the horse back up the beach. We'd stay for the month of August, then sell this horse and do the journey again in reverse like.'

He looked wistfully at the rotting wooden cabins. 'Certainly brought it all back to me seeing them again.'

'May we take off our shoes and stockings, Ma? Please. So we can walk on the sand,' Sarah pleaded.

After a slight hesitation, Jane nodded and soon Sarah, Laura and Georgie were slithering across the sands. They ran down to the water's edge and dodged back before a wave caught them. Once they knocked into each other in their haste; first Georgie fell tripping up Sarah who grabbed hold of Laura's arm to save herself. It only had the effect of tumbling Laura down with Sarah still clinging to her arm. Helpless with laughter, they scrabbled along the sand just as the water trickled over their feet.

George found an iron bench beside a laid out flower bed and Jane opened her basket of food.

'Come on children! Have something to eat.'

'Aren't these pretty flowers. Do you know what they're called, Pa?'

'Yes dearie, they're pansies. Pansies for constancy.'

'What does that mean?'

'It's just a saying, girlie.'

'One day, I shall have a garden and grow pretty pansies,' Laura said.

After they had satisfied their hunger they walked along the promenade.

'Music!' Sarah said. 'Listen! A band's playing. Oh, let's go and hear them.'

In a circular projection above the beach sat musicians in gold braided uniforms, instruments glinting in the sunlight as their hands moved up and down in time to the rhythm of the tune. They had drawn a good crowd. Most of the charabanc party were there. As the piece ended to the applause of the audience, the conductor turned round.

'Now then, ladies and gentlemen. You seemed to like that one of Ella Retford's and some of you were singing. Let's try it again and all join in. I'll help you along.'

He turned back to the band and raised his baton to start the introduction: um-pa-pah.

'Ready! She's a lassie from Lancashire
Just a lassie from Lancashire
She's the lassie that I love dear - oh so dear.
Though she dresses in clogs and shawl
She's the prettiest of them all
None could be fairer or rarer than Sarah
My lass from Lancashire.
That's it, come on, sing up.'

The crowd joined in and the sound swelled across the beach. George's clear tenor voice took up the song. He sang the tuneful notes with gusto which the conductor acknowledged with a broad smile. It was good to hear him. Jane thought, such a long time since she had heard him sing. She poked him in fun as he changed Lancashire to London and Sarah to Jane and, for everyone to see, pointed his finger at Jane. All too soon the performance was over.

'Best make our way back, don't you think?' one of the men said to George.

'But it's early yet,' protested Sarah.

'Well, we've a fair walk back to where the driver told us to meet,' George said. 'Come along.'

The driver counted everyone into the charabanc and he started up the engine.

Sitting together, George still held Jane's arm. 'We've had a good day, mother.' As he gazed into her eyes, Jane felt young again. He leaned across to the long bench. 'Georgie, did you and the girls enjoy for first trip to the seaside?'

'Yes, Pa,' Laura answered. 'A day I'll never forget.' Jane was pensive. She saw again Sarah, Laura and Georgie rolling on the sands: young adults playing as children. Something that hadn't been possible when they were children.

Someone was whistling softly, the tune the band had played. Several more joined in humming quietly. The muted melody drifted through the coach, careful not to disturb passengers' musings on the wondrous events of the day.

From the coach window, Laura could see the tall figure standing under the gas lamp outside the *Thatched House*. He touched his cap to George and Jane as they stepped off then reached up both arms to help Laura down.

'Had a good day, Laurie?'

She smiled up at him and nodded.

'Even though I wasn't with you?' he chided her and held her arm close to his.

The group turned the corner into Burgess Road. Georgie and Sarah called back over their shoulders to Eddie all that they had done. At the gate, Jane ushered them up the pathway. Laura and Eddie hesitated.

Jane smiled. 'Just five minutes, Eddie, that's all. It's work tomorrow.'

'Thanks Mrs Stringer. Five minutes and no more, I promise.'

As Jane pushed the door to, she glimpsed Eddie clasp Laura in his arms and kiss her. On tip toe Laura's arms linked behind his neck returning his embrace. The fifteen year old child was adult once again.

Strands of September fog swirled across the yard or spiralled heavenwards. A real blackberry morning, Great Aunt had called it. Laura remembered the early morning hikes up the lane picking the berries still damp with mist.

Laura stirred herself to get a move on. Today was her special day. The new dress she had made was more the colour of sloe berries with their powdered bloom. Its simple style was only enhanced by a small white lace collar. The church service would begin at half past ten. She would go ahead on her own. Eddie had said he would follow with Sarah. Laura had asked Pa and Ma to come but knew what their answer would be. Pa protested he was as god-fearing as the next man but never felt comfortable inside a church. And Ma said she couldn't understand why Laura couldn't just attend the church without having to go through the palaver of being dipped in water, but wished her well.

The tram rocked along Whitechapel Road. She got off ahead of the stop and walked the rest of the way to the Mission church. As she entered the building,

Laura remembered how nervous and ill at ease she had been when she came to Maisie's baptism. Now she knew most of the congregation and felt composed. She took her place in the front pew. The service proceeded; Laura knew every word and repeated it in her mind... 'be regenerate and born anew of Water and the Holy Ghost...that our Lord Jesus Christ would vouchsafe to receive you and bless you, to release you of your sins, to give you the kingdom of heaven and everlasting life.'

She was called forward and Laura answered: 'I renounce them all.' She walked through the side door and slipped out of her blue dress and donned the simple white shift. She re-entered; the priest and churchman held her arms and led her down the steps into the cool, clear water.

'I baptise thee in the name of the Father and the Son and the Holy Ghost. Amen.'

She slipped below the water and as she emerged she felt a lightness within her and a great happiness spread through her body. She felt she wanted to laugh and cry all at once.

Outside the church she met Sarah and Eddie. Laura kissed Sarah and Eddie and linked arms with each of them as she walked silently to the tram stop.

Chapter 17

Her heart beat fast as she approached the door. Through the patterned amber glass Laura could see Mr Pilgrim at his desk. She straightened her shoulders and knocked firmly. The shadowy figure raised its head. It seemed an eternity before the voice called:
'Come!'
Nearing the desk she half curtsied and nodded, 'I should like to put before you, Sir, a proposal from the bench hands.'
His eyes squinted and his pallor neared magenta.
'I've told you before there will be no unions in this establishment.'
'But, Mr Pilgrim, that is not the proposal.'
'The owners have been most generous and put in the extra facilities you demanded.'
'Asked for, Sir,' Laura politely corrected.
How it had happened, Laura didn't know but she had become the spokeswoman for the workers. It probably started after she had been put in charge of her block of six benches. She had protested to Johnson that Maisie and Kate and others had been there much longer. Not that there was any more money to the job. And when the blocks had been increased to ten, Laura was surprised workers actually asked to be with her

team, even men! Any problems, they came to Laura and asked her to get permission from Johnson to go to Mr Pilgrim. First, it was about the scraps of leather on the floor. As each worker was responsible for keeping his bench area clean, what they swept up, could they keep? Yes, it was agreed. Next, it was aprons. The upholstery workers across the road had aprons, could they have aprons to protect their clothes especially as the glue was hard to remove. In due course, heavy jute aprons were provided one per employee and the worker was expected to launder his own apron. Laura took hers home each week to wash; some didn't - she had had to chide Kate once or twice for a dirty apron.

It was a disgrace, they had said, extending the factory but still only one lavatory for everyone. 'Go and ask Mr Pilgrim,' they'd said, 'ask if the builders could put in a couple of lavatory pans for the girls in one cubicle and two urinals and a pan for the men in a separate cubicle.' And as the connecting wall was knocked down, new toilets were installed. Of course, you still had to ask permission to leave your bench to go to the lavatory and the visit was timed by Johnson.

Laura cleared her throat. 'The bench hands should like to have a little more time on Saturday, Sir and ask if it would be possible to leave at one o'clock instead of two o'clock.'

Mr Pilgrim began spluttering with rage. Laura hastily continued with her request.

'In order to have that extra hour, we should like to work until eight o'clock on Friday night. May I ask you, Mr Pilgrim, to consider this request.'

She returned on her heels and left his office. In the corridor, Laura blew out a deep breath. She had rehearsed what she wanted to say over and over again and hoped she hadn't left out anything. She made her way back to the work floor and signalled to Johnson she was back at her bench. She placed the fine grained crocodile leather onto the board in front of her and began smoothing it with the glass handle. The action calmed her.

As the bell sounded for the midday break, Johnson was the first to ask her.

'What did he say, lass? Will he agree?'

She was surrounded by eager faces.

'I don't know. I just said what we wanted and asked him, to consider it.

'He'll let us know.'

Johnson patted her shoulder. 'I reckon it'll be all right.'

He strolled off whistling. Johnson was proud of his protégé. Laura was the best worker Garsten's had ever had; always turned out a neat job. And he made sure the management knew. Not just Mr Pilgrim. Whenever the bosses came into the factory, Johnson would find a way of mentioning Laura's name. All the special orders, urgent ones, or delicate jobs, were given to her because they knew it would be completed on time without a blemish. That was why Johnson had suggested Laura be spokesman for the workers; Mr Pilgrim wouldn't refuse her requests in case she upped and left.

At the end of the month the notice was posted at the entrance:

Garsten and Company Limited has graciously deemed to change the factory working hours for the benefit of the employees.

With effect from Monday, 8th of February 1909, the hours of work at this establishment shall be as follows:

Monday 8 A.M. to 7 P.M.   Tuesday 8 A.M. to 7 P.M.
Wednesday 8 A.M. to 7 P.M. Thursday 8 A.M. To 7 P.M.
Friday 8 A.M. To 8 P.M.   Saturday 8 A.M. To 1 P.M.

Bench inspection will be made at 12.50 and wages will be paid at five minutes to one.

Johnson grinned at Laura and nodded. Everyone seemed pleased. Moving an hour from one day to the next made little difference to Laura except she would be an hour later at the public baths on a Friday and perhaps the water wouldn't be as hot. But it would still be worth the thruppence it cost to lie in the bath, soap all over to feel really clean and step out into a fresh towel.

Jane was enjoying being a lady of leisure, well not exactly leisure, she still took in washing from regulars like Mrs Pidgeon and Mrs Henson and sometimes a few casuals but she didn't have to go out. She could do the washing when she liked as long as it was ready for Sunday collections.

She looked up as Laura came in.

'Did you get what you wanted?'

'Yes, look. Isn't it lovely?'

A pale green silk ribbon was draped over her fingers.

'And look! Aren't these beautiful?'

In her palm were a dozen tiny red buttons that glinted like rubies. She left them on the table and hurried away to her room to return carrying a folded sheet. She got her needle and thread and opened out the sheet. The skirt of the dress was of pale green satin backed silk with high ruching at the back; the bodice, of a finer silk, was of the same colour but had red roses the size of pennies scattered irregularly in the pattern. Laura attached the ribbon to the neck edge of the dress and stitched the tiny red buttons along the curve above the bust. She displayed it over her arms.

'Eh, girlie. That's just grand.'

'Pa! You startled me. I didn't hear you come in. It's for Sarah's seventeenth birthday next Wednesday. I think the colour will suit her perfectly.'

'She is a dazzling beauty and no mistake,' George said with pride.

'With far too many young men running after her. And she doesn't always play fair with them,' Jane said. 'I wish you'd speak to her, father. She shouldn't accept their gifts.'

George laughed. 'If they're daft enough to spend their wages on the lass, that's their look out.'

'But what do they want in return, George?' That's when the troubles starts.'

'I'm sure our girl knows what's right and what's wrong.'

Laura scooped up the dress and hurried out.

Although she had been walking out with Eddie since she was fourteen, Jane had no qualms about Laura. Laura had her head screwed on the right way. Eddie had asked her to marry him when she was eighteen and he would be twenty-one but Laura refused saying he must finish his apprenticeship first. His seven year indenture would not be concluded until he was twenty-three. There was only one man for Laura and she was content to wait for him. But Sarah flitted from one young man to the next without hesitation.

Laura hid the dress away until next week. Sarah was easy to suit for a birthday present but what could she give Eddie?

'Laura!' Jane called. 'Come to the market with me and see what bargains we can get for our dinners.'

Through the bustling avenue of stalls, Jane selected her wares and Laura gazed at the trinket sellers' wares but there was nothing suitable as a gift for Eddie.

'I think I might look in Boardman's or Roberts's, Ma, if you don't need me for a while.'

'Don't be too long, I've just bought us herrings for supper. Meet me at the pork butcher in half an hour.'

In the department stores, she idly turned over gloves, and scarves and ties but none seemed to be the right kind of gift. At the leather counter she saw an elegant pigskin wallet. Just the thing; similar to ones made at Garsten's for suppliers to royalty. But Laura gulped at the price tag: four and sixpence! A whole week's wages! She walked away but each time her steps took her back to the counter and at last she succumbed. With the package neatly wrapped she hurried to meet her mother.

Torches flared along the line of stalls casting giant wavering shadows among the goods.

'Come on, girl. You take this bag for me. I've got a nice bit of roasting pork for tomorrow and trotters for in the week. Let's get home; this chill is eating into my bones.'

She pulled George's muffler tightly about her throat and set out for home at a brisk pace.

While Jane gutted the herring for supper, Laura crept away to her room with Eddie's present. She would try to see him on Tuesday, to give him her gift. Or, perhaps she should hand it to him on Monday night for him to open on his birthday before he went to work. The trouble was, how to get it to him or get word to him to meet her. Eddie lived with his widowed mother. Since her friendship with Eddie began, Laura had not met Mrs Sawyer. Oh, she had seen her that time in the market but Eddie had never taken her to his house. Even Jane commented on it saying when a boy and girl started walking out each visited the other's home so parents could see for themselves the sort of company they were keeping. Eddie said his mother's health wasn't good, and she was easily upset by visitors. Laura had said she would welcome the chance to befriend Mrs Sawyer; she could do things for her. But Eddie said, No. She was sure his mother was aware of their relationship but perhaps denied it existed, not wanting to lose Eddie. Yet they were betrothed! Eddie even wanted to wed when he was twenty -one, before his apprenticeship ended. Surely, Eddie had told his mother? Or had he?

Jane carried in a pan and set it on the range.

'George! What are you doing with that dirty newspaper on the table? It had the fish in it!'

'It's The Times. The toff's newspaper. I don't often get a chance to read a paper like that.'

'Give it here. I need it to wrap up the heads and innards.'

'Just let me finish this bit. Well, I'll be blowed! I'm sure it is! Jane, here, Look at this!' He pointed to a picture. 'Isn't this your brother, Jane?'

Slowly Jane came to stand beside George and leant over his shoulder.

The picture was of an elegantly dressed man, holding a top hat, accompanied by a beautiful woman and a young boy in the courtyard of Buckingham Palace.

'Says here the King has made him a Viscount so he is now the Right Honourable, the Viscount Grant, to be addressed as My Lord. And his nine year old son is the Honourable Algenon.'

'Algenon! Poor child!' Jane commented. 'For goodness sake, what did Arthur do to deserve to be given a title?'

'Something about foreign trade. Apparently he was in the Tory government when Balfour was Prime Minister. He was second to the Marquis of Lansdown, the Foreign Secretary. Seems he lost his seat when the Liberals got into power with Mr Asquith as Prime Minister.'

Jane's forefinger traced the outline of Arthur's face. 'It is strange, when I was a child he was always the most caring of my two brothers. If I got a scratch, it was Arthur took care of me. When I was sick in bed, he would come to read to me. We would play together, but James being older, was less of a companion. Yet, it was Arthur who turned his back on us.'

George's voice was barely audible. 'That's because you married me, Jane.'

Jane moved from his side to stand in front of him.

'And I wouldn't have it any other way. Now give me that paper.'

She playfully snatched it from his hand but immediately passed it back.

'Don't let the oily bit get on to the table now.'

Soon dripping was sizzling in the pan and a cloud of pungent smoke drifted across the kitchen as Jane tossed in the floured fish.

Laura had prevailed upon Georgie to wait at the top of Argyle Road on Monday night and hand over the package to Eddie when he came home from the railway yards. Now she had to wait until Sunday to know whether he liked his present. But Sarah had thought her dress was the prettiest she had ever seen.

'Laura, it's lovely!' she exclaimed as the undid the soft paper wrapping. 'I shall wear it on Saturday.'

'Where are you going with Clarence?'

'No, Laura, not Clarence. I've finished with him. He was such a wet fish. La-de-dahing about but no manners.'

'So, who is it now?' Laura asked.

'His name's Stanley. He's a salesman. Does ever so well. He knows how to treat a girl, he does. Didn't you see him the other night as we got off the train? He raised his hat to us and said good evening.'

'I cannot keep up with all the beaux, Sarah.'

'All my beaux! You soppy thing. But Stanley is nice. I wonder what he'll give me for my birthday.'

'Well, he's taking you out on Saturday, isn't that enough?'

'Oh, Laura, it's ever so exciting. We're going to the picture palace in the Broadway.'

For Sarah, her rendezvous was just four days away. Laura would have to wait until Sunday to see Eddie.

Coming out of the factory gates at midday on Friday, Laura felt someone tug at her cape. She turned around.

'Daisy! Daisy Sudson. How good it is to see you. How are you? You look well.'

'Oo, that I am, Miss. And ever so happy.'

Laura had felt uneasy when Garsten's not only did away with the run about girl job - she had so wanted Daisy to have it - but they also cut out the stacker-up and then the sweeper's job, so Daisy was dismissed.

'Where are you working now, Daisy?'

'I'm at the fur place just off Chapel Street. I get good wages, thanks to you.'

'What do you mean?'

'You showed me what the coins were and I learnt 'em.'

'I'm sure you're worth every penny you get.'

'I'm on an errand now, Miss, so I mustn't stay long. But as I was down this way I thought I'd wait a piece until you come out so I can tell you.' She paused and smiled at Laura, her face split in half with the grin. 'Me and Jack, you know, Jack Armstrong as was at Garsten's, well me and Jack are to be wed Sunday fortnight.'

'Daisy! That is wonderful news.' Laura hugged the girl. 'I am really pleased for you both. Where does Jack work?'

'He's a 'prentice!' Daisy said proudly. ''Prenticed to the umbrella maker in the Strand. He's being taught all about spokes and 'ferrils' and the like.'

'Please give my congratulations and good wishes to Jack.'

'Yes indeed I will, Miss. And we've got ourselves two lovely rooms over the Golden Goose in Mile End. Jack's a pot man there of evenings and the landlord, being a widower now, says he has no use for all them rooms.

Must hurry along now, Miss, but I just wanted to tell you, you being a real good friend to me. Ta-ta.'

Her spindly legs leapt high in the air, swirling her petticoats nearly up to her knees as she hastened back to work.

'Who was that funny thing you were talking to?' Sarah asked.

'That was Daisy Sudson. She worked here when I first came to Garsten's. A dear, good soul. She told me she is to marry a chap who also worked here at one time. I suppose Jack must be seventeen or eighteen now.'

'I don't want to stop to eat now, Laura, I want to see if any shop has green gloves to match my dress. I can buy them tomorrow.'

'You'll be starving by supper time.'

'I'll nibble something at my bench,' Sarah whispered.

'No you won't, Sarah Stringer! You know it's forbidden. You may mark the leathers.'

'I shan't. In any event, I'm only cutting cottons off those queer strap things. Why a man should want to put his watch on his hand instead of in his pocket, is beyond me. See you later.'

Laura was glad she was kept on bags and cases. At first Garsten's ignored the trend of small watches being attached to the wrist saying the fashion wouldn't last. Men would always wear waistcoats and so have pockets to keep their timepieces on chains linked through a button hole. But when the custom didn't disappear, they quickly marketed a leather wrist strap.

Johnson rang the bell at ten minutes to one. Quickly, materials being worked on were removed to the under shelf. If the top layer of thin cardboard was heavily soiled with glue it was removed - but woe betide the worker who had to replace his cardboard. Mostly, it was simply turned over to present a dry, cleaner surface for the following week's work. Laura walked around her block of ten benches, smoothing her hand across each work area. All was well, she held up her hand. Others soon followed and Johnson rang the second bell for closing.

They filed out into the courtyard and stood in line while Johnson set up a table and chair just inside the double doors. Mr Pilgrim then appeared with the ledger.

As soon as they were paid, the workers scattered.

'I saw a sweet pair of gloves in that little shop in the Strand. I think I'll go and get them.'

'You've already got several pairs of gloves, Sarah. Save your money for something else later on. Come on, I want to get home.'

Sarah sulked on the train home but by the time it arrived at Stratford she had other ideas for her pay.

She looked truly beautiful as she stood in the doorway and twirled about as George commanded. At seventeen she had attained a height of five feet four inches, two inches taller than sixteen year old Laura. Mellow gaslight highlighted golden curls pulled high on her head so that thick bunches hung behind her ears.

'Here, let me put this on you,' Laura said and slid the ribbon about Sarah's neck and fastened it with a small pin.

'Do I look all right?' Sarah asked timidly.

Even Georgie joined in the approval. Sarah drew the thick shawl about her shoulders and hurried up the passage way.

'Well, mother, our young 'uns are growing up so fast I can hardly recognise them. My! Our Sarah was bonny! Her young man will be the envy of all the other mashers tonight and no mistake.

After the supper was cleared away, Laura sat at the table sewing fragments of suede together for a bag, then discarded them in favour of reading George's newspaper. Jane had dozed off in her rocking chair. The front door closed.

Jane roused herself. 'Is that her?'

'No, Ma. Just Pa back from the Thatched.'

'Not in yet?' George asked on his way through the scullery to the lavatory.

Laura looked at the small carriage clock on the mantle shelf. Ten o'clock. It was a bit slow, it regularly lost time and Laura was always putting it right by the church clock but it was a lovely ornament, especially as Pa had brought it home.

'You're tired, dearest,' George said. 'You go off to your bed. I'll wait up for Sarah. You, too, girlie.'

'No, I'll stay.'

George held the paper in his hands but wasn't reading. Laura fiddled with the patches but her eyes were on the mantle clock. It said twenty past eleven but the church clock had chimed the half hour some time back. At last Laura's sharp ears heard the front door being opened and pushed to. No footsteps came down the hall. Then Laura detected the sound of a doorknob clicking.

'Was that her?' George asked.

'Yes, Pa. She has gone straight to the bedroom,' she whispered, 'probably thought we were all in bed.' She winked at her father. 'I'll go and get her.'

Laura tip-toed to their room. She was about to turn up the gas lamp when she heard Sarah's stifled sob.

'Please! Please don't put the light on.'

Involuntarily, Laura's hand had turned the key higher illuminating Sarah collapsed on the bed.

'Oh, my dearest. What's the matter?'

She gently clasped Sarah's shoulder to sit her up. Laura gasped in shock. The red roses on the green silk bodice were indistinguishable from blood blotches where the material hadn't been ripped. Sarah's once white shoulders were bluish green and scratched. Teeth marks, visible on her breast, had drawn blood.

'Dear Lord! I must get the doctor to you. I'll tell Pa, he's...'

'NO!'

The anguished sob that came from her sister chilled Laura.

'I'll just go and tell Pa to go to bed.'

Sarah fiercely clutched her arm.

'Don't fret, my sweet. I shan't say anything to him.'

She ushered her father out of the room. She filled a bowl with warm water and found clean rags. In the kitchen cupboard she located the iodine bottle and returned to the bedroom.

Skilfully, Laura removed the dress, its tattered shreds dangled from her hands. Sarah's chemise and pantaloons were torn.

Laura stood beside the bed, her heart pounding.

'Sarah, dearest,' she whispered. 'Did he...interfere with you?'

Only increased sobbing was her answer.

Georgie stirred in his truckle bed in the corner.

'What's up, sis? Wha'sa time?'

'Shush!' Laura lightly skipped to his side. 'Nothing to concern you. I just need the light on for a while. You've got plenty of time for sleeping.' She kissed him and tucked in the blanket.

Nearly an hour later, Laura was doing the same for Sarah. The bloodied and torn clothing she hid in her sewing box. She took off her own clothes and pulled on her night gown. There was a single chime from the clock but whether it was half twelve, one o'clock or half past one, she didn't know. She slipped in beside Sarah's shivering body and cuddled her close.

She left her sister lying in bed, neither had had much sleep. Jane was stirring the range into life and George was at the sink. Laura made them sit at the table while she told them as much as she had learned from Sarah between violent shudders.

'I think we should have the doctor look at her, Ma.'

George was banging his fists on the table. 'Just let me get my hands on the blighter. I'll wring his neck for him.'

'Now, George, keep your temper. Losing it won't help Sarah and we must do what's best for Sarah.'

'But if he's sullied her,' his fists smashed the air, 'he'll answer for it.'

Jane put her hands over his to stop them pounding the table.

'Doctor Shugar is the nearest, Laura. Through the alley. I know he's a Jew but women hereabouts say he's a good doctor. I know it's a Sunday but it's not his Sabbath. Go for him. I'll make a drop of broth and see if she'll take some. Have you got some silver to show him?'

After three days in bed, Laura made her go back to work. 'Normal everyday things are best,' she insisted, 'to force bad memories to the back of the mind.' Scratches and bruises were powdered over but there was nothing to hide the haunted stare of her eyes.

Beautiful violet eyes were transformed into tiny black specks. Sarah's physical injuries healed in a few weeks but the mental scars were deep. Rarely did she speak, only nodded when addressed; she huddled in the corner of the railway carriage to and from work and, after a scant meal, would creep away to bed where she would curl up and hug herself.

Life around her carried on as normal but Sarah felt she wasn't part of it.

Laura had tried to persuade her to go to the Easter Sunday service at the mission hall but she just shook her head. When she came out from the church she was delighted to see Eddie waiting there.

'Had a bit of time in hand so thought I'd come along this way to meet you.'

'I'm so pleased you did, dearest. It's a lovely day, let's walk back.'

She linked her arm through his and they strolled in silence. It was good just to be with him, there was no need to speak. Often it seemed they interpreted each other's thoughts and would merely smile or nod, no words were necessary.

'You're troubled Laurie. Is it Sarah?'

'I wish I could do something for her. It is as if she has crawled into a shell. Sarah seems to think she was to blame for what happened. Says she was dressed too prettily.' There was a catch in her voice.

'That blackguard is the one to blame,' Eddie spluttered. 'He is responsible for what he has done to Sarah.' He paused and turned to look at Laura. 'Seeing as she's in the family way, and being if he could've been found, would your Pa have made him wed Sarah?'

'Gracious me, no! Father said a man like that could never deserve a girl like Sarah. When she begins to show. I'll take her to Great Aunt Laura's place. She'll be comfortable there and when her time comes the child will be place in an orphanage. Sarah says she doesn't want to see the baby's face.'

Poor Sarah. She remembered when Rose Bullen had an illegitimate baby and the tittle tattle among the travelling girls; Sarah couldn't endure that. Unable to control her tears any longer, Laura sobbed into her hands. Eddie drew her into a closed shop doorway and held her close until she had cried herself out. She reached into her bag and drew out a handkerchief and dabbed her face. Blinking her reddened puffy eyes, she smiled up at Eddie. He grinned back and quickly kissed the tip of her nose.

'Tell you what, Laurie. Let's go up West. To Hyde Park. One of my mates at the yard said Arthur Henderson,

you know, the Leader of the Labour Party, was going
to have a soap box at Speaker's Corner. I'd like to hear
what he has to say. Wouldn't you?'

A tram was approaching and Eddie hurried Laura
across the road. They changed trams in the city. Along
the Strand and around Trafalgar Square, Laura was
captivated by the buildings and statues, especially the
tall column with Nelson atop. Her gaze darted about
and her fingers pointed in all directions. Happily,
Eddie had taken her mind off Sarah's plight.

There was a large crowd assembled in the north-
east corner of the park; some were absorbed by the
words of the speaker telling them of Oriental medi-
cines; others lingered by a man reciting religious texts.
But the largest throng surrounded a mild mannered,
grey haired man of medium build. The speaker was
inspiring; the mood of the crowds almost tangible.
There was an expectancy among the people, believing
the words of the orator that a new day was dawning.

'Trade unions are the weapons of the workers.'
'Unity is strength.'

It was exciting to be a part of the movement and
Laura was buoyed up by the enthusiastic audience.

'I've joined the union,' Eddie said. 'Daft not to.
They've got us all manner of better conditions and
pay.'

Laura smiled to herself. Garsten's didn't allow
unions, but work practices had been improved. She
took Eddie's hand as they wandered back to the tram
stop. It had been a good day.

Her first thoughts on reaching home were of
Sarah.

George looked up and smiled in greeting. Jane was
in her rocking chair, snoozing under a paper.

'She had a mouthful of soup and mashed potato
and took off to her bed,' George said in answer to her
query. 'Did you go for a walk, girlie?'

'Eddie met me and we went up West. To Speakers' Corner in Hyde Park.' Laura related the afternoon's events. 'And did you know the government has said when people are too old to work and can't earn any money for themselves they'll be paid an old age pension?'

'Yes, I read about it. The Liberals have got an able man in Lloyd George; they knew they had to do something to keep the popular vote and five shillings a week old age pension when you're seventy was the best they could come up with. Of course, not many will live to be seventy!'

'Who's seventy?' Jane asked stirring from beneath the paper.

'No-one, mother. And if you doze any more, you'll not sleep in your bed. Come on, lights out.'

Despite the new life growing inside her, Sarah was wasting away. Firm flesh cheeks had fallen away leaving taut skin almost transparent. Lustrous eyes were clouded and vacant.

'She don't look long for this world,' Kate whispered as they left for the day.

'Do they know what ails her?' Maisie asked.

'I dunno. Poor Laura looks worried sick about her. I reckon something is eating away inside her. They say she does her work, same as always, but like she was a mechanical doll. It's so sad when you think what a beauty...'

'Hush,' Maisie hissed. 'They're coming out now.'

'Well, it was like I said,' Kate spoke loudly, 'with the King's horse running in the Derby, no bloomin' jockey was going to pass him. So, of course, the King's horse won. Here, Laura, you going to the May fair at Wanstead on Saturday. They say it'll be the biggest ever.'

'Well, we certainly can't miss that, can we?' Laura smiled brightly. 'Yes, we'll be along there, won't

we Sarah? Tomorrow we'll arrange where to meet.
Goodbye.'

It was too far for Sarah to walk to Liverpool Street
Station as usual, so Laura guided her sister along
to Aldersgate Street Station, they could take the
Metropolitan for a couple of stops. Walking to the
station they passed Georgie and his pals.

'You carry on, I'll catch a later one, sis.'

Until it was evident Sarah was pregnant, they had
concealed from him the circumstances of his sister's
condition. The details embarrassed Georgie; he was
unable to look at Sarah. When he spoke to her, he
would look anywhere except at her.

There was a train waiting at the Great Eastern terminus. It was already crowded but many would alight
at Bethnal Green. The two girls stood in a cluster of
women and swayed in rhythm to the rocking carriage.
Approaching Bethnal Green the driver applied the
brakes abruptly sending passengers to one side like
a collapsed house of cards. Some landed on laps of
sitting passengers causing loud guffaws. It was a relief
when the train arrived at the platform.

'At last,' Laura said, 'we can sit down for a bit.'

She led Sarah to a seat.

'Are you all right, dearest?'

Sarah's face was ashen. Her breathing rapid. Laura
held her hand and gently rubbed it.

'Soon be home, now.'

The few stops seemed to take forever. Laura's gaze
never left her sister's face. Several times Sarah seemed
to lose consciousness. As it pulled in, Laura was ready
with the door handle and quickly stepped down. If only
Georgie had come home with us, she thought. I need
someone to help. She turned back into the carriage.
Sarah had recovered sufficiently to respond to Laura's
urging and eased herself onto level ground. With an

agonising effort she put one foot in front of the other and walked out the station holding onto Laura's arm.

'Hello, Laurie, sweetheart.'

'Oh, Eddie! My darling! You just don't know how glad I am you're here to meet me.'

Before she realised it, Sarah's hold on her arm slid away as she crumpled into a heap on the pavement. As she knelt beside her sister, Laura saw blood stained clothes. Eddie crouched beside her. He lifted the pathetic bundle that was Sarah and hurried into the roadway. His urgent shout brought a cab alongside. Laura heard him direct the driver to the hospital.

'You stay with her, lass.' Eddie said, 'and I'll fetch your Ma and Pa.'

White starched aprons paraded past Laura but had no news for her. Once the nurses had seen Sarah's condition she had been whisked away leaving Laura sitting alone on the bench in the corridor. She was numb, if a thought came she swept it out; she knew she should pray but her mind was blank. Presently, she felt a hand touch hers.

'Is there any news, girlie?' George asked, his rough voice breaking with emotion.

Laura shook her head.

'That lad of yours has money to waste,' Jane said. 'Brought us here in a Han'some!'

Along the corridor came two men in white coats and a nurse. Laura's heart beat faster than ever. One man smiled. Sarah was alive!

'She has lost the child,' he said gravely. 'But she is young. She will need rest and care. And fattening up a bit,' he laughed. 'She will be released tomorrow, some time after rounds at three o'clock.'

It seemed the miscarriage had not only taken the child from her womb but also a great weight from Sarah's shoulders. The stigma of the rape had been removed.

341

On, Sunday, George borrowed his brother's horse and cart and Laura placed bedding on the boards to make Sarah comfortable for the journey to Great Aunt's farm. Laura sat on the cross board with George. She remembered a similar journey all those years ago when she had been the patient. Pa had come to take her home to hear the doctor's verdict on whether or not she was blind.

It was hard to recognise the lane leading to the farm. Of course, there was no farm now. Only the new housing estate. There were so many roads criss-crossing each other; so many plots lined out, it was a veritable maze. Laura located the cottage but there were no dogs to greet them. George tethered the horse in the roadway while Laura raced up the newly laid out path to the door.

'Who is it? Who's there?' came Great Aunt's querulous voice.

Laura tried the door handle and was surprised to find it locked.

'Me, Great Aunt, your namesake, Laura.'

She heard the bolt being drawn and key turned. She was not prepared for the sight of the frail, stooped old lady who squinted up at her.

'Eh? Who's that, d'you say?'

'It's Laura. And I have Pa and Sarah with me.' She flung her arms about the old lady's neck and smothered her with kisses.

'Sarah's not been well, Aunt. We thought she could rest here and perhaps the country air would make her well again.'

'There's no country air left abouts here. Just houses and more houses. Why do you folks only come calling when you want something?' she grumbled.

A pang of conscience hit Laura. It was true she had not visited the farm since...when was it? She had come with David Garvey. My goodness! That was three years ago!

'I'm sorry, aunt, we have neglected our visits to you. Cousin Martha wrote to mother with the good news of your ownership of this cottage and a bit of land.'

'Don't see nothing of Martha, neither, not since her hubby lost his legs. Cut off by tram wheels.' She spread her arms wide. 'All gone now, the lot of 'em. I'm like an island and the sea of houses is coming ever closer. But me and Daniel ain't going to budge.'

George placed Sarah on the cushioned window seat. Beads of perspiration glistened on her forehead and deep ridges between her eyes told of her pain.

'Good god, man!' Great Aunt's voice was hoarse. 'Did you bring her here to die?'

'No, aunt, she is not going to die,' Laura said fiercely. 'She has had a terrible internal injury but it will heal.'

'You...bring...Fairy Princess.'

The voice startled them; the words barely distinguishable. They hadn't heard Daniel come into the kitchen. With no fields to work, he had grown fat. His large head was now almost completely bald. There was still a rustic hue to his skin but there were folds of flesh spilling over his shirt collar. He stood beside the seat and gazed down at Sarah. He put a tentative hand on the rich golden curls surrounding the small white face.

'I can't look after her,' Great Aunt said irritably. 'It's enough having to take care of me and Danny.'

'Me. Danny care for Fairy Princess. Me, aunt, me do it.'

Danny bent down and put his head close to Sarah. 'Princess. You tell. I do it.'

Danny's flabby face split in a wide grin. She held out her hand and Danny held it gently between his large palms. Sarah smiled.

Chapter 18

Jane adjusted the hat, tilting the wide brim down over her forehead shading pale sandy freckles that peppered her face. She gazed at her reflection in the scullery mirror. Each side of the hat rolled back over the top to expose her amber gold hair; she loosened strands from the restricting bun and looped them over her ears. The hat didn't fit well on such fine hair; she didn't have the luxuriance of Sarah's hair. It had been a silly, extravagant purchase. She anchored it into place with an elaborate hat pin, an even more silly and extravagant purchase.

The purple dress with black braid scalloped along the hem edge fitted well, especially the gathered material bunched up at the back - it disguised large hips. Laura had repaired it perfectly. She always had an eye for a bargain. It was on a reject's stall in the market as there was a tear from the neckline across the shoulder. Her answer was to cover it with a high collar, the latest thing in fashion. The purple and black collar reached up and complemented the black hat. And she had found a short black cape on the second hand stall that steam had restored to its fine textured serge.

Jane nodded at her image. Now she really looked like a lady of leisure. Start the year right, she had said, when the bells ushered in Nineteen Hundred and Ten. After years of having her hands constantly in hot soapy water, her rough reddened skin had gradually returned to normal when she gave up the last of her washing customers just after Sarah's eighteenth birthday. Her mind went back to the past when once before she had nice hands. Then it had taken raw potato, lemon juice, goose grease rubbed into palms, between fingers and over the backs to produce lady's hands suitable to greet the fashionable ladies of Brighton. This time, just by doing less washing they regained their texture.

It wasn't necessary, she decided, not with four bringing in a wage. The only trouble was, it meant there were many hours in the day with nothing to do. How long did it take to sweep and mop over linoleum floors and beat three rush mats? Or to dust a couple of mantle shelves? Once or twice she had invited neighbours in for a chat over a pot of tea but they were always inquisitive. She had tried the Mother's Union at the church but hadn't seen eye to eye with the ladies there. In the past three months she had been into every shop in Stratford so many times she could find her way about blindfolded. There was nothing new. Except the hat. She had seen it last Tuesday and by Thursday had made up her mind to have it even though it meant dipping into next fortnight's rent money. Now she needed somewhere to parade her new finery. An advertisement in George's paper had given her the answer. Today was going to be different. She was going up West. A new store built by the American, George Selfridge, had opened last year in Oxford Street. There were special sales items to celebrate its first anniversary.

Standing on the opposite pavement, she stared at the building. It was certainly very stylish. Tall columns perched above high windows. Jane crossed over and strolled along the frontage looking at the neat displays; one or two items draped in an unusual setting. At the entrance, the liveried doorman saluted her, stepped forward and grasped the long brass rail to open the wide door.

It was certainly an educational visit, too. Jane was mildly shocked at some of the new materials used for under garments, as well as the shapes. She bought hairpins at twice the price in the Stratford shops, but they were packaged so beautifully with a coloured tie. Even half a yard of ribbon was wrapped in smart paper. She called a halt to her spending before all the rent money disappeared. But it had been a lovely day.

The doorman must have seen her approaching the exit for he had the door open and stood to attention.

'Thank you,' Jane said and stepped past him into the street and nearly collided with an incoming customer.

'I do beg your pardon, Madam,' the gentleman said.

He raised his hat in apology and Jane looked into the face of Arthur.

'Forgive me,' he said 'I am sure we have met but I cannot recall your name. Most ungallant, I'm afraid.'

The doorman was watching the proceedings. He looked closely at Jane's face. Was she offended by the man's effrontery?

Jane looked at her brother for a moment then turned back to the attendant. The silver three penny bit in her gloved hand was the tram fare home, instead she passed it to the doorman.

'Thank you, my lady. May I call you a carriage?'

'No. It is a pleasant day. I shall walk.'

She started toward the roadway, then deliberately changed course and walked in front of Arthur. In that instant, he recognised her.

'Such a grand lady,' the doorman said.

It was as much as she could do to keep a straight face. She wanted to laugh out loud but people would think she was a lunatic! It had been so funny! At first, when they had stood face to face, she had felt a renewal of the love they had shared in childhood. She almost reached out to take his hand in welcoming greeting. Until he had asked who she was! Her mind rolled back the years to when she was pregnant and had been taken into his photographic studio.

'Don't you dare have your baby here,' he had said with such venom that crushed any youthful bond. She hadn't thought about him in years; even seeing his picture in the paper last year and reading of his elevated position had not stirred resentment; there was no feeling at all. But today, seeing him, standing beside him, she wanted to heal the rift between them. When it was apparent she - his sister - had been wiped from his memory she knew there was no purpose in announcing who she was. It would only have caused a scene; for she had no doubt he would have slighted her to give him the advantage. Jane realised he would never forgive her for preferring George to Oliver Steadall. Yet, Matilda, although she had been disappointed, had understood the undying love each gave to the other. The very thought of George sent a quiver of excitement running through her. Jane had intended strolling down Regent Street but instead hurried along the road home. She'd pick up the tram at a later stop for less fare.

She had to smile as the picture of Arthur's face danced in front of her eyes. He had been so charming to the unknown lady, raising his hat, giving a slight bow. Until he knew it was his sister! Then the mask was whipped away; his face purpling with anger.

'My word!' George exclaimed. 'You're a handsome woman, Mrs Stringer.'

She had stepped off the tram and was nearing the

corner when the voice startled her. Guiltily, a hand reached up and touched the side of her hat. She had thought to be indoors with the hat hidden away before George got home.

George took her hands and held her at arms length.

'You look a real treat and no mistake.'

He folded her arm over his and they walked along together.

'It's a very nice hat,' he whispered, 'and just the sort I should like to buy you, if you'll let me.'

Jane stopped in her tracks. Her quizzical gaze made George wriggle uneasily.

'I know what you're going to say, how is it I've got money to spare to buy you a hat. But it's a rarity when I can, so just accept it, can't you?'

Jane's eyes didn't leave his face. Under her scrutiny, a deep blush crept up from his neck. He gripped her arm and forced her to walk toward their gate.

'It's like this. Ever since last year - do you remember - I told you about the bloke at the market as takes bets,' he tightened his grip, 'and we backed Minoru, the King's horse in the Derby and it won. You remember I gave you the half crown winnings. Well, once a fortnight, I put a tanner on with him. Never any more than a tanner. Sometimes I lose the lot, sometimes I get me money back and sometimes, like yesterday, I pick up a tidy sum.'

He held open the gate, grinned at her and touched his cap.

'Now Mrs Stringer, where have you been today in all your finery. Meeting your fancy man eh?'

Jane laughed. 'As a matter of fact, I have. I'll tell you about him later. And the hat cost three and eleven pence and the hat pin cost one and tuppence three farthings. I hope your winnings will run to it.'

Over a cup of tea, she related her chance meeting with Arthur.

'The look on his face!' Jane's bubbling laughter filled the room. 'It was a picture!'

George took hand. 'Do you miss seeing your kin folk, Jane?'

She kissed her finger and put it on his lips.

'I have the best kin folk in all the world and they're sitting here with me right now.'

They sat in comfortable silence, looking at each other and holding hands, each filled with a myriad of loving thoughts.

At the supper table, the girls were agog to hear about Selfridges and admired the way customer's purchases were wrapped.

'Let's go there after work on Saturday, shall we, Sarah?' Laura asked.

'I don't know. It all sounds a bit grand,' Sarah replied.

Her figure had regained its normal weight to give a well rounded shape to her body. Bloom had returned to her cheeks and all outward scars had healed. But she still reacted like a scared rabbit; eyes, large as saucers, looked out on a world she felt she wasn't part of.

'There'd be time, Sarah.' Laura persisted. 'Eddie doesn't come for us until seven o'clock.'

To help Sarah return to a normal life, Eddie had suggested each Saturday night he take out both sisters, to the Music Hall, or the picture palace or to a pie shop - whatever they fancied. 'We'll still have Sundays just for ourselves, Laurie,' he said. If it was possible to love him more, Laura would. How kind and thoughtful he had been.

'I know, tomorrow we'll ask Kate and Maisie if they'd like to come with us, Sarah. We'll make an outing of it. But,' she wagged her finger at her sister, 'I'll only allow you to buy one thing.'

Laura was looking forward to Saturday's visit. She particularly wanted to look at the fashions to see if there was anything she could copy. Laura didn't need to take a sketch pad, she had a retentive memory. With a practised eye she would look at seams and shaping, which colours were used for contrast. She still sewed everything by hand; her savings were growing but hadn't quite reached the price of a treadle machine.

It was announced from the Palace at two thirty in the afternoon.

Friday, 6th May, Nineteen Hundred and Ten.

King Edward the seventh died in his sleep this morning.

His second son ascends the throne.

LONG LIVE KING GEORGE THE FIFTH.

There was less public demonstration of mourning for Edward than there had been for his mother, Victoria. Of course, she had reigned for over sixty years and Edward just for nine. But it did rather spoil the Saturday shopping spree. At Selfridges, all fashionable gowns had been removed and stark, black ensemble filled the stands.

'Cor! It's a bit dreary, isn't it? Kate said.

'And very disappointing,' Laura added.

'How long d'you think it'll be before things get back to normal? Do any of you remember what it was like last time? Kate asked.

Laura smiled. 'Do you remember, Sarah? Granny Goult died at the same time as Queen Victoria. Ma made us black arm bands and everyone thought we were very loyal until we said it was for our granny.

Black bordered newspapers reported another death some days later: The Lady with the Lamp, Angel of the Crimea, Florence Nightingale died in her seventieth year.

'There's bound to be a third,' George said.

Until the mourning period was over, department stores and dress shops displayed only gloomy merchandise. Jane found it very dull. Nothing to be extravagant about. Instead, she was spending her time patching vests and combinations and darning socks. They wouldn't have passed inspection with a seamstress as Jane cobbled the holes. But it filled in the time until George came in from market.

'I met the postman at the gate,' George said, 'and he gave me this letter for you.'

'For me! Jane exclaimed. 'Now who on earth would be writing to me?'

'Well, it's official like as the name and address aren't written with pen and ink but made by one of those type writing machines. Look.'

Jane took the envelope and held it in her hand as if weighing it. She turned it over several times until George burst out.

'For goodness sake, Jane, tear it open and read it.'

She took a knife from the drawer and carefully slit the envelope along the top edge and removed a single sheet of paper covered in the same typescript.

'It is from the matron of an asylum in Birmingham. She says James died last Sunday.' Jane held the paper in her hand 'Poor, lonely man. You said there'd be a third.'

'What's that, mother?'

'You said there would be a third death.'

Her decision was made in minutes. The funeral was to be on Thursday, the ninth of June at three o'clock. Today was Wednesday.

'How much do you think the train fare would be? To Birmingham.'

'You're thinking you'd like to be in attendance at the funeral, are you? Train fare's hard to fathom. Sometimes they have specials on. I shouldn't think it'd be more than seven and six return. But there'll be lodgings as well. Ten bob should cover the lot.'

Ten shillings! But she was determined to go and began putting a few things into a bag for the journey.

'I know you're saving up for that sewing machine you've been talking about, Laura, but you manage very well with needle and thread. And it will be just a loan,' Jane said. Laura couldn't refuse the request to finance Jane's journey to the funeral of her eldest brother. But she knew in her heart the money wouldn't be returned. Small amounts lent in the past had been forgotten and ten shillings would definitely slip the memory. The longed for sewing machine retreated into the distant future.

George kissed her goodbye as he left for market. Jane stirred in her sleep.

'What time is it? Oh, goodness, George! I've over-slept. I've not made tea for you.'

'No matter, lass. You've tossed and turned most of the night and you could do with a good nap. I've got everything,' he shook his bag of bread. 'I wish you God speed, mother.'

As soon as the girls and Georgie had left for work, Jane put on the purple dress with the black braid and the extravagant black hat.

Several porters came forward to assist the smartly dressed lady as she entered St Pancras Station. Jane released her grasp on the small valise and followed the man into the booking hall. The porter took the ticket and led her forward, pausing for the inspector to make a neat triangular clip in the ticket, then onto the platform.

At the far end, the engine painted in the dark maroon of the Midland Railway jerkily emitted puffs of white smoke anxious to be off. The porter found her a seat and placed her bag in the overhead rack. Jane passed him a silver thrupenny piece.

'Thank you, M'lady,' he said as he stepped down and slammed shut the carriage door.

Until this moment, Jane's mind had been filled with planning the trip. Now she was on the train and it was steaming out of London on the journey north, her thoughts slipped unbidden to the last train journey she had made. Southward then to Brighton. Memories rushing one on top another: the tang of salty air, the music in the Pavilion, the grey silk dress caressing her skin, Horace's passionate breath on her cheek. Her gloved hand brushed her forehead, guiltily wiping the remembrances away. Jane focussed her mind on James but it was hard to visualise his face. Even when she dwelt on childhood times, his face was a blur. Arthur's was clear. But then she had seen him only the other day. Or was it because James was dead? Involuntarily she pulled George's face into her mind but this, too, was unclear.

She jumped up in a moment of panic and slid open the door onto the corridor to lean on the rail by the window.

'Is anything the matter, Madam?'

'No,' Jane reassured the ticket inspector. 'I wasn't sure how far we were.'

'We're running to time and should be coming into Birmingham in about twenty minutes, Madam,' he said and passed on along the corridor.

Jane settled back in her seat and composed herself. The funeral was to be at three o'clock but the matron hadn't said whether it was to be at the asylum. If it wasn't, how long was the journey from the asylum to the graveyard? Still, there had been no delays, she should find her way in good time. Time enough afterwards to look for somewhere to stay overnight. Perhaps matron might know of a reasonably priced bed.

Beads of perspiration danced on her brow. After leaving Snow Hill Station and crossing the canal, it had been an uphill climb to the institution and she had hurried. Jane reached out and pulled the iron rod beside the heavy oak doors. She heard the bell resounding inside.

After a long wait, bolts were drawn and a small frightened face peered out.

'I am Mrs Stringer.'

The door was quickly pushed to. Jane moved her weight from one foot to the other. Impatiently, her hand reached up toward the bell pull but the door opened before she had grasped it.

'What do you want?' A voice asked from the hidden interior.

Quickly, Jane moved to the sparse opening and rested her hand on the door.

'I am Mrs Stringer. I have travelled from London for the funeral of my brother, Mr James Goult.'

There was a silent pause and on a rush of breath the voice said: 'I'll get matron.' The shadowy figure disappeared and before she realised it, Jane was shut out again.

At last the door was opened fully, and Jane was invited inside. One small skylight in the centre of the high domed ceiling cast a thin spindle of light on the stone flagged floor. The chill atmosphere against her moist body made her shiver. And, as the bolts slid into place on the doors, Jane was reminded of her days in the workhouse, and a wild terror filled her.

As she passed through a second set of double doors, her rapid breathing eased. Along the dimly lit passageway, sailing toward her, was a large portly woman who continually smoothed the crumpled apron across her stomach.

'I am the Matron. How may I help you?' She asked, a pleasant smile wrinkling her cheeks.

'I am Mrs Stringer. I hope I am still in time to attend my brother's funeral.'

'Your brother's funeral?' A frown replaced the smile. 'I do not understand. Why do you come here?'

'I thought the procession would start from here.' The blank expression on the woman's face had not changed. Jane's hand dipped into her pocket and removed the letter. 'Here. You write to me about James Goult. You said he died last Sunday and the funeral would be today at three o'clock. I got the nine fifty two from London this morning.'

'Oh, no! Oh, my dear, I am so sorry you've had such a journey. I said funeral but it is simply a pauper's burial. In one of his lucid moments, Mr Goult had left an address with me, your address, and he asked me to tell you when he had passed away. He knew he was dying, you see. It was simply a courtesy to let you know. All of those who come here have no families to speak of. Some have been committed here by their families. Often, they do not wish to hear of them again. Upon death, we merely have them interred in communal ground. No ceremony, nothing like that. There's no money for that.'

'It's not yet three o'clock. Is his body still here?'

Matron's stern countenance melted. 'I shall enquire, my dear.' She took Jane's hand in hers. There was empathy between the two women. 'Is it your wish to have a proper funeral for your brother?' she asked softly. 'I know a reasonably priced undertaker and it may be possible to get him to come here within the hour.'

'He had no money at all?' Jane asked.

'None whatsoever.'

Jane's mouth went dry. Even the simplest of funerals would cost six or seven pounds, may be even more. All she had in her purse was three and sixpence to pay for a bed and a bite to eat before using the return half of her ticket tomorrow. Yet, she could not contemplate the thought of a pauper's grave for James. She tried to remember how much Matilda's funeral had cost. But that was many years ago. Jane knew she had to agree to a regular funeral - Matilda would have wanted it.

'Please make arrangements for a very simple funeral for my brother. I have no money about me today but I shall write a draft on a London bank for the sum involved.'

It was a fitting use for the money. Matilda's money. There was some left. It hadn't been touched since the visit to Brighton. And James was Matilda's first born.

The Matron held Jane's arm in a comforting gesture. 'I shall send a messenger immediately. Come to my parlour and I shall prepare us some tea.'

'Please, Please, may I see my brother?'

She was led down stone steps to a basement room. The floor undulated from years of heavy feet treading the surface; the once white tiles on the walls were hair cracked and yellowed but it was clean and smelt fresh from pine oil. Marbled slabs ran the length of each wall and two marble slabs atop stone plinths stood in the middle. On one of these was a swaddled bundle.

Jane slowly approached the table.

'We wraps 'em like that for the pit, d'you see,' explained the servant girl, who had accompanied her. 'Keeps all the bits together like to put on the cart.'

The girl's voice was dimly heard, as Jane reached forward and began to unwind the bandages.

'No, missus! You mustn't do that. No, you mustn't!' The girls voice rose hysterically. 'It's a corpse. There'll be the wrath of God.' Sobbing she ran from the room, her clogs pounding upon the steps.

She had released most of the strips of cotton from the head as Matron descended.

'It is most unwise, Mrs Stringer. Death is not always kind.'

'I know,' Jane said, remembering the bitter, twisted

face of Granny Stringer; the tired, desolate face of Emily.

The final pieces were peeled away revealing James' head. She gazed at the gross features: thickened lips, flabby cheeks fallen away, blotchy skin stretched tightly across the once fine nose. Jane's hand lifted a strand of hair from his forehead. She tried desperately to match this face with the one she had known as a child; or the face of the man in the sitting room at the time of Matilda's birthday; or on his daughter's wedding day. Or, even the face of the man anxiously purchasing quack remedies for his sick wife.

Slowly she rewound the bandages. She smiled. She had remembered her brother's face.

Everyone had been most kind. The undertaker gave her a cut rate as the body was already prepared. And he had a second hand oak coffin from a burial where the deceased had expressed a desire to be laid in the same chest as her husband. Matron and two servants stood beside Jane at the graveside.

Overnight accommodation was found for her with a niece of the Matron and Jane had gratefully fallen onto the feather mattress, fully clothed. Now she was aboard the train speeding south. There should have been sadness at the passing of her brother but Jane could not feel such emotion. They had never been close, none of them: James, Arthur and her. Were her own children - Sarah, Laura and Georgie - were they close to each other? She could not say. George was so different. He regularly jawed with his brother Will over a pint at the Baker's Arms. And many an afternoon he'd go off to Whips' Cross Hospital to see his youngest sister Kathleen Selina. She wasn't called that nowadays. Since she became a nun she was Sister Anthony. Jane found it hard to call a woman by a man's name and still said Kathleen. But she was a good soul and worked at the hospital as a nursing orderly.

George's dear face swam into her consciousness. And the thought of him gave her a warm glow. Soon she would be nestling in his arms, receiving sweetness from his lips. The soporific clickety-clack rhythm of the wheels lulled her into sleep.

As she alighted from the train, Jane was conscious of the crumpled state of her dress and wished she had removed it before resting last night. At the end of the platform she passed a door with frosted glass and lettered in gold: Ladies' Waiting Room and Services. She stepped inside and moved through the next door, down a short flight of steps into the washroom. Jane tapped at each door of the three water closets. All vacant. With a thankful sigh, she quickly divested herself of the heavy purple dress and plunged her face into a basin of cold water. Holding the dress taut against the wall, she sprinkled droplets of water on the skirt at the back and smoothed it down with a gloved hand. She repeated the action for the front of the skirt and both sides of the bodice and sleeves. It looked better and felt fresher against her skin. She had just put it back on as the attendant returned.

'Good day, madam, I'm sorry I wasn't present when you entered. May I be of service?'

'It was hot and stuffy on the train,' Jane said, 'I needed to dab cold water on my brow.'

'Of course. May I offer a fresh towel for a penny?'

Jane declined the offer and left the station. She took a tram across town. It was a long time since she had come to this part of London and was unsure whether it was on the left or right side of Lombard Street. Having gone in the wrong direction she retraced her steps and approached the building. The top hatted liveried doorman showed her to a leather bench.

'Good afternoon, Mrs Stringer.'

Jane stared at the ginger haired man. He wasn't the one she had seen before.

NOT ALL LUCK IS BAD

He grasped her elbow and steered her toward an open doorway.

'Jenkins is my name. Mr Blenkinsop has retired and I have taken over his duties. How may I help you?'

Carefully, Jane explained she required a withdrawal from her account. An amount of five guineas to be paid to the undertaker and two guineas to Matron.

'Here are their names and addresses, if you would be so kind as to send them drafts they may cash locally.'

The business was transacted within minutes and she was ready to leave.

'You know, Mrs Stringer. You really shouldn't leave that money in a drawing account. It is clear you do not require access to funds. Your last withdrawal was,' he consulted a ledger. 'Good gracious! Ten years, almost. It could be put to better use in stocks or bonds that would increase in value. If I might be allowed to advise you about investments...'

'No thank you Mr Jenkins. I wish the money to decrease, not increase. Good day.'

Wearily, Jane made her way to the tram stop. After several changes, she finally arrived at Maryland Point. Even the walk home was tiring and took far longer than usual. The door opened before she had time to insert the key in the lock.

'I was in the girls' room looking out the window, Jane. Saw you turn the corner.' He took the bag from her hand. 'How are you, dearest?'

In the seclusion of the darkened passage, Jane reached up and twined her arms about his neck. She hungrily pressed her lips to his.

'All the better for seeing you,' she answered breathlessly.

'Give over! George whispered. 'Mrs Milton's upstairs you know.'

He opened the door to their room and deposited the

bag inside while Jane carried on to the kitchen. A pan of water was bubbling on the range and the teapot was being warmed alongside.

'I thought you might like a cup when you got in, so I had it ready.'

They sipped their tea in silence for a while, then George cleared his throat.

'You got there all right, then? How was the journey?'

Jane moved from her side of the table and sat beside George. She took his hand and traced the veins with her finger. She told him of the journey and of her arrival at the institution but glossed over her panic at being in the place. She described unwinding the bandages to see James' face for the last time but refrained from saying why he was swathed in cloth and not embalmed. She told him how kind everyone had been, especially the Matron who had found accommodation for her. But she made no mention of her visit to day to the bank, for George knew nothing of the financial arrangements made by Frederick Bourne all those years ago and her resolve never to use the money for herself' solely for occasions Matilda would approve of.

George stroked her head and sighed in sympathy with that he thought was her deep sorrow at the loss of her brother.

'Laura says there's some cold mutton. Shall I get it for you, my love?'

'Yes. We'll have a bite now, then you can be off to the Thatched for a pint with your pals. She smiled. 'And, remember, it is Friday night.' She was amused to see a deep blush spread up from his neck. 'What's the matter, my husband?'

'I thought, perhaps...' He turned away to the scullery. 'I'll get us our supper.'

In the following weeks Jane found herself observing the children; watching them together. They were

NOT ALL LUCK IS BAD

closer in age than her and her brother; well not her and Arthur. When she was Georgie's age, fifteen, Arthur was seventeen, just as Laura was now. But Arthur had his life mapped out learning all he could about photographic plates and cameras at the Ilford film company with Alfred Harmon, and James was twenty-three already married for two years with a young son. Their father had been dead for seven years and Matilda had embarked on her dressmaking career. She supposed they could have been close had it been in their natures. Laura and Sarah had an affinity that would, Jane knew, endure beyond their youth. And the two girls were more than just fond of their gangling young brother. Like her father, Laura would always keep in touch with her brother and sister.

'What are you pondering on, love?' George asked.

'I was thinking how strange life is.'

'My word, Mrs Stringer, that is a deep thought! Too much for a poor old working man like me.'

'Away with you, husband. No, I was remembering my meeting with Arthur and then getting the news about James, that's all.'

He patted her hand in a sympathetic gesture and Jane immediately grasped his.

'I was also thinking, Mr Stringer, that it'd be nice to go out again. There's a Bank Holiday Monday coming up soon. All of us to go together. Like we did on that charabanc trip. Oh, I don't mean we have to go to the seaside. That'd cost too much but, say, to one of the fairgrounds. Laura can bring Eddie along, too. What do you say, George?'

'I like it fine. And I should like it to be to the seaside. What do you say to Southend-on-Sea? My father and me went down river on a boat from Tower Pier. It docked at the end of the longest pier in the world and we rode in gated wagons all the way back to the promenade.'

'But it would cost too much.'

'Not so much, my dear. I saw an advert about an excursion train being run by London Tilbury and Southend Railway. Just a minute.'

'Look. Here's what it says. Special day return leaving at nine thirty five from Fenchurch Street Station on Bank Holiday Monday. See. Four and ninepence. What do you say to that?'

'Well, it sounds all right. But will the young ones have the spare cash?'

George looked earnestly at Jane. 'Let's ask 'em, shall we?'

Before he finished speaking, he stumbled forward as the door pushed into his back and Georgie loped into the kitchen. His father turned round, tweaked the boy's nose and twisted him around in a joyous hug.

'Watch it, Pa!' the boy said smoothing his rumpled coat.

'Beg pardon, son. I was forgetting you're grown up now?' George said in mock humility. 'I was excited about our Bank Holiday trip.'

'But, George, we don't know...'Jane began to protest.

He just winked at her.

'Oh Ma, this letter was on the door mat. Will you give me the stamps?'

His hand reached forward and several inches of arm protruded out the end of his coat sleeve. Laura had let out all the hem there was.

'It's come a long way round the world, Ma. Look at all those markings on the envelope.'

Eagerly Jane slit the edge open and a sheet covered in an uneven handwriting fell onto the table. Eagerly she began to read it.

'Would you believe it, George? It's from Bessie. Mr and Mrs Kerridge, you know, Mrs Shipton as she was at Geity Lodgings. Well, they set up a small boarding house on an island called Bermuda. A lot of vessels call in there for refuelling so they have done well. Bessie stayed on with them until she got married. Fancy that! Bessie married.' Jane looked up from the letter. 'I do hope it is someone nice, she is such a good soul. She deserves the best.' She turned back to the page. 'She says: I met this very nice man. He has his own business, engineering, and his Works has the contract for the British Navy boats. And, it is so strange you won't believe this, Jane. But he knows you. Now what do you think of that?' Jane looked up at George. 'That certainly is strange.' Her gaze returned to the letter: We've been married four years but only last Christmas did we find out we both knew you. My husband once lodged with you, Jane. Reg Packard. Do you remember him?'

Jane raised her eyes from the paper and by chance met George's eyes. They were silent for a moment as they each peeled away the years from their memories.

Jane smiled. 'He was a good man and he has a good woman.' She turned back to the last few lines and quickly scanned the letter. 'She has a daughter whom she has called Bessie Jane. Oh, now! Isn't that nice of her.'

George stood beside her. 'You were saying, Jane, life is strange. I think you are right.'

It was a grey start to the August bank Holiday Monday but George predicted it was going to turn out nice. Sarah agreed with him especially as she had caught Georgie out in Pinch Punch First of the Month.

They entered Fenchurch Street Station; at the newsagent's a placard declared: CRIPPEN ARRESTED ABOARD MELROSE BY WIRELESS but George didn't stop to buy a paper, not today. While he went to the window to purchase all the tickets, Jane hurried toward the platform clasping the basket she had crammed with bread and a tin of luncheon tongue she had bought for one and thruppence which included a special opener; some apples and a bottle of beer for George. Georgie and Sarah skipped ahead of her as Laura and Eddie raced forward searching for an empty compartment. Now and again she lost sight of them in the throng.

'This'll do,' Eddie shouted and flung open the door. He stood on the step and waved frantically to Jane.

There was an old couple seated in the opposite corner and they greeted the family warmly as they all scrambled in. Before the train departed another family climbed in and as there was no corridor on the train the men took it in turns to stand.

When it arrived at Southend-on-Sea, the train doors were flung open to disgorge the holidaymakers all anxious to get to the seaside. It was a disappointment. The tide was out and all that was to be seen was grey rippled mud extending to the horizon. Not to be done out of a paddle, Eddie and Laura raced Sarah and Georgie across the warm, moist silt until they were no more than mere specks to Jane and George sitting in deck chairs on the promenade.

'Even if the sun didn't shine, it's been a lovely day,' Laura said as she strolled arm in arm with Eddie back to the station.

'Yes, lovely,' agreed Sarah,' especially as we won the race, didn't we, Georgie?'

Jane and George, at the rear of the group, listened to the good humoured argument as to who was the winner. George carried the now empty basket and hugged Jane's arm to his side.

Jane was looking at Eddie and Laura. She sighed. 'Do you think our Sarah will ever find a husband, George?'

'I hope so, my sweet.' George lifted Jane's hand to his lips and as he kissed her palm, he gazed into her eyes. 'Yes, I'm sure there's a man who'll love her enough to wipe out the past.

Chapter 19

Jane awoke with a start. She must have dozed off. It was dark. The heavy grey clouds had threatened snow but by midday only a light dusting of white covered rooftops and then evaporated. What was the time? The mantle clock had stopped. Where was George? She stood up and listened. Children's voices.

She walked to the foot of the stairs.

'Mrs Milton! Have you heard the clock chime? What time is it?

Jane didn't wait for an answer: the children's voices were louder now. She opened the front door.

'Are you home from school?' She asked the passing group.

'Course not! We don't start back until tomorrow. Teachers have still got a hangover from seeing in the New year,' the boy replied and the other children shrieked with laughter at his jest.

A neighbour came from down the road and Jane asked if she knew the time.

'It must be close on half past four,' she answered.

George should have been home two hours ago. Tuesdays were never busy days at the market. Jane returned to the kitchen and lit the gas lamp. She stirred the fire and watched the sparks rise up. She was anxious but, strangely not afraid. She sat in her rocking chair facing the door.

St Mary's church clock struck five followed by the muted echo of St Burnaby. Jane refilled the kettle and placed it near the hob. Impatiently, she walked along the passage into the children's room at the front. She stood in the dark behind the window. The gas lighter had lit the street lamps and above the houses was the glow of the electric lights in the main road. Several figures turned the corner and passed by, heads bent and hunched against the cold. Six o'clock chimed. At last came a form she recognised. He held the lapels of this jacket tight to his throat. He hurried. His gait was steady. Jane quickly left her hiding place and when the front door closed she was seated in her rocking chair.

'Evening, Jane.' George rubbed his hands and came close to the range. 'What a to do there has been! They wouldn't let the trams through.'

'Never seen anything like it. I walked from Spitalfields, through the short cuts I use to get to Whitechapel. I get on the tram as usual...'

'Now, George, go and wash first and I'll make us a cup of tea. When we are sat comfortable, you can tell me all about it.'

He was home! He was safe! Jane busied herself putting out their cups and rhythmically stirring the pot. Routine tasks settled her heart beat. When he stepped from the scullery, Jane's hand touched his damp cheeks.

'Ugh! You haven't dried properly.'

'Can't, not until I've had another shave. And I'm not going to do that until after a nice hot cup of tea.'

They sat facing each other and he relished the hot liquid as it warmed and revived him.

'It'll be in the papers tomorrow. Headline, I expect. As I said, all the usual passengers got on the tram and it set off. We got as far as the London Hospital and that was it. The police said nothing was to proceed beyond that point but didn't say why. Well, we sit on the tram for a bit then someone said there's a commotion ahead and we all got off to have a look see. The ruction is in Sidney Street. The police were holding back the crowds but down the road there was the fire brigade and soldiers! A bloke said they were Scots Guards. Apparently the trouble began when two foreigners barricaded themselves in a house. They had guns and they fired them at the police. The Home Secretary, Winston Churchill, was there overseeing things and, what you do think happened then?'

Jane smiled and shook her head. George was enjoying his story telling.

'The house went up in flames! With the foreigners still inside. Both died, no doubt about it, this bloke alongside me said. After that, they restart the trams and we got back on. It'll be in the papers tomorrow for sure. Fancy! Only three days into the New Year, what a start! Of course, Georgie and the girls won't have seen anything travelling on the train as they do. Won't they be surprised when I tell them!'

'Well, we don't want any more surprises like that for the rest of the year,' Jane replied.

George was treated to several pints at the *Thatched House* as he retold his story of how he was there at the siege of Sidney Street.

By the 19th of January, several inches of snow had fallen creating a white fairyland for the children but causing havoc for the grown-ups. Along the main roads, trams and carts and motor omnibuses had churned the pure white into dirty grey slush soiling the hems of skirts and trouser bottoms.

'Why can't the sun shine just once on my birthday,' Laura grumbled. 'It's either thick fog, or biting winds, rain, hail or snow.'

'You can share my birthday,' Georgie offered. 'But you ain't sharing my presents.'

'Who says you'll get any presents,' Laura retaliated. 'Thanks all the same.'

She tied a string about her waist and looped part of the skirt over it.

'You can't go out like that,' Sarah said staring at Laura's feet.

'Can and I shall. I'm not getting the bottom of my skirt wet and dirty. And all you can see is my boots. Come on or we'll miss the train.'

Lightly, she skipped through the puddles of melted snow and ran ahead to the station. No-one remarked on her appearance. Sitting in the carriage, with knees bent, her skirt hem was a decent level. Only when she was in the dry interior of the factory did she undo the string.

Laura pulled the shawl about her shoulders when she came from the scullery. No matter how cold it was she always untied her chemise to wash under her arms. Sometimes the stale odour from the girls at Garsten's was overpowering and she was determined never to cause offence. By a freak of nature she had no underarm hair and perspired only lightly. She paused at the foot of Georgie's bed to tickle his toes.

'Come on, sleepy head,' she whispered. 'Come on, we've got to sing to Sary.'

With his eyes still closed, Georgie tumbled out of bed and stretched out his arms. Laura guided him to the bottom of the double bed she shared with Sarah.

'Ready? Happy birthday to you, happy birthday to you, happy birthday to you dear sister, happy birthday to you.'

At the first notes, Sarah sat up and nodded her head in rhythm to the tune. Then she skipped out of bed and planted a wet noisy kiss on Georgie and Laura in turn. They were startled by a tapping at the window. Cautiously, Laura peeped behind the curtain. She let it drop in a hurry and pulled on the first dress that came to hand.

Quietly she opened the door. 'Oh my dearest one. How good it is to see you. But why...?'

She giggled as Eddie danced a jig, hopping from one foot to the other singing: 'I'm twenty-one today, I'm twenty-one today.'

'I know you are, dearest, but you'll get your gift tonight when we meet as arranged and not before.'

'I know we're to meet tonight but I want an answer from you now. Will you come to tea on Sunday? Will you?'

The invitation took her by surprise. To meet Mrs Sawyer at last! What had happened to bring about such a change? After all the years of her unofficial betrothal to Eddie, now, at last to meet his mother.

She saw the excitement in his face gradually fade at her lack of response. Laura stood on tiptoe and kissed his cheek.

'I shall be delighted to accept your kind invitation, sir,' she said with a deep curtsy.

The grin was back on his face as he leapt over the front gate and ran off down the road.

Nothing else filled her mind; despite her attempts to think of other things a voice in her head kept repeating: 'Two day's time. Two day's time.' It was hard to concentrate on her work. It was a special job she had been given two weeks ago and must be finished today. The very fine graining of lizard skin had to be matched perfectly for the colour to shade from charcoal through pale grey to ivory white. Laura had turned the skin every which way to get the best effect to set off the peaked flap of the handbag. It had been her suggestion for an angled flap sloping from one side rather than a point at the centre. She had selected a contrasting piece of skin to be stitched with the buckle fastening. It was nearly finished. A short handle dangled from gilt rings slotted into the side. A rich satin lining of smoke grey shimmered as the bag was opened. The bag was returned to Laura from the machine room and with a sharp knife she trimmed the corners into a neat curve.

I wonder what's behind the invitation to tea, she thought. Her heart raced. Will Eddie propose on Sunday? Will we marry soon? No, that can't be it. Eddie may be twenty-one but his apprenticeship doesn't end for another three years. That's when he'll be a proper engineer.

Daydreaming, Laura felt her knife slip. The cut was dangerously near the stitching. For several minutes she was unable to move her eyes from the curved shard of skin slashed from the seam; her hands were rigid on the bench. Slowly she got up from her seat and holding the bag before her like an altar offering she approached the raised plinth where Mr Johnson sat at his table.

'All finished, is it, missy?' He leant forward. 'You know this is to be a present to Princess Mary of Teck, Queen she'll be when King George is crowned.'

Laura opened her mouth to speak but no sound came out. Controlling her tears, she tried again.

'My hand slipped,' she said wretchedly.

'What!' he roared. And suddenly dozens of pairs of eyes were focused on the diminutive figure with arms outstretched toward the bulky frame of the man towering over her.

'Get back to work,' Johnson shouted to the room. 'It's not tools down time yet.'

He signalled to Laura. With heavy feet she ascended the three steps and laid down the bag. She pointed to the corner at the back of the bag where rather more had been trimmed away. Johnson turned the bag over and over. He ran his finger along the cut edges of the seams. Those along the edge of the gusset fitted on the left side were exact: an eighth of an inch. The gusset on the right side started as an eighth of an inch at the front but ended as a sixteenth on the back corner.

'Have you got a good eye, missy?'

Laura looked up surprised.

'Well, have you? Can you trim the other three corners the same?'

He had spoken so quietly, Laura was unsure if she had heard the foreman correctly. She frowned.

'You heard aright.' He leant forward, his whispered breath hot on her cheeks. 'Good eye, steady hand, clear mind.'

Laura picked up the bag and hurried back to her place. A burly Scot, who had the corner bench on her block, tilted backward on his stool as she passed.

'Are ye upset?' he hissed. 'Gi'e me the nod and I'll take him apart.'

She shook her head. At her bench, Laura carefully replaced the bag on the clean pasteboard. She studied the offending corner, gauged the depth between stitch and edge. Turned the bag over and with the rounded end of the stud punch, etched a thin line with her knife. She repeated the process with the other corners and, finally satisfied, applied pressure to the knife to release a curl of surplus lizard skin.

Johnson had sounded the closing bell. He removed his sleeve covers and donned his jacket. He stepped down onto the factory floor and began to walk in the direction of Laura's bench. As he did so, he became aware he was walking between two lines of workers. He sensed their hostility. He marvelled at the way this eighteen year old slip of a girl had won the devotion of the workers; young and old, men and women. He, too, had reason to be grateful to Laura for the harmonious atmosphere that prevailed. He was glad he had not caused her any distress.

Engrossed in the corrective work, Laura was unaware of the menace around her. She took the wax candle and first rubbed the raw edges then smoothed it over the seamed stitches. Her lips spread into a pleased grin.

Johnson's gaze had been fixed on Laura's hands watching each move and as she pushed back on her stool he walked briskly forward.

'Well done, Miss Stringer,' he called.

On each side of him the protective barrier melted and the tense situation was no more. Workers returned to their places and idly shuffled their tools before calling out cheerful farewells.

Lying in the tepid water at the bath house, Laura felt the tension of the day drain away. Rolling the bar of soap between her palms, the bright electric light coloured the small bubbles red and green and blue like jewels. Gas light hadn't created such treasures. It was scented soap, too. Other bathers were given the regulation bar of carbolic soap but the attendant produced a special bar from under the counter when Laura handed over her silver thrupenny piece.

Always on a Friday night, their meetings were brief. Eddie would be waiting outside the bath house to escort her home. They would linger for a while at the gate then Laura would shoo him away. There was work again tomorrow.

He said nothing more about the invitation to Sunday tea and Laura didn't mention it either. She reached into her bag for his birthday present.

'It isn't very much, my darling. We said we wouldn't squander our money, didn't we?'

Eddie unwrapped the soft tissue paper and held the artificial silk scarf between his fingers.

'Thank you, dearest Laurie. The best present I could have had.'

His arms slid beneath her coat to clasp her waist and his lips sought her mouth. Laura's hands linked behind his neck and eagerly returned his kiss. The warmth of his body against hers sent a quiver up her spine. Blood pounded in her ears shutting out all sound except the violent beating of her heart. She wanted more and more of him. His kisses rained down on her face, her neck, eagerly seeking the soft skin between her breasts. He pressed his loins against her impatiently forcing her thighs apart. Suddenly he released her and stepped back. He covered his face with his hands.

'Forgive me! Forgive me!' he sobbed. 'Oh dear God! What have I done?'

Laura grasped his hands, pulled them away from his cheeks and replaced them about her waist.

'My beloved,' she crooned. 'You have done nothing wrong.' She reached up, her lips tenderly traced his jaw line until they were close to his ear.

'I want it, too,' she whispered.

Gradually, he regained his composure. He understood how strong passion can overwhelm a man so much that he is beyond reason. And, for a fleeting moment, he understood that man with Sarah. He took Laura's hands.

'Waiting may be hard but I know when we are wed our union will be the sweetest paradise. Good night, my dearest one.'

Settling into the double bed beside Sarah, a warm glow filled her. Laura was so happy; happy in the sure knowledge of Eddie's love for her. Nothing- and no-one-could alter that.

Laura changed out of the dark serge coat she had worn for the mission service in the morning. Her outfit was laid out on the bed. Laura had been pleased with the light grey flannel suit she had made. Its style was copied from one in the window of Boardman's; three large buttons in the middle of the jacket at the point where the curving reveres ended and three small buttons on the seam line at the bottom of the skirt. A dark burgundy satin blouse with a deep frill at the neckline complimented the ensemble. Her long gold brown hair normally worn in a tight bun, was loosely swirled into a sausage onto the nape of her neck to hang below the narrow brimmed grey felt hat, banded with burgundy petersham. Eddie smiled approval as he offered her his arm. They walked in silence, content with the close presence of each other. At the bottom of Burgess Road they made their way through Granny's Alley out into Wingfield Road and on to Leytonstone Road. When they had crossed to the other side Eddie, like a true gentleman, changed his position to be on the road side. As they drew nearer to Argyle Road, Laura's heart beat just a little faster. These houses were set farther back from the road and had a neat tiled footcourt, some inset with raised flower beds. Most displayed fancy lace curtained windows upstairs and down to show single occupation - not let off in half houses. Eddie produced his key and opened the front door. They stepped into a wide passageway. A large mahogany coat and hat stand with umbrella receptacle, protruded into the space.

'We're here mother,' he called as he led the way and opened a door on the left.

Laura walked into the parlour. Mrs Sawyer, dressed in widow's weeds, was seated on a wooden chair with a curved back and arm rests. Laura moved forward her hand outstretched.

'I am most pleased to meet you, Mrs Sawyer,' Laura's smile twinkled her eyes.

No hand extended out in return. There was no expression of welcome in the large boned face. A nod of her head was the sum total of Mrs Sawyer's response. The rebuff almost stung Laura to tears.

'Shall I take your hat and coat Laurie?'

Laura was grateful for Eddie's sweet voice and turned her smile onto his dear face. She unbuttoned her coat and removed the pearl pin from her hat and handed them to Eddie. With speed he deposited them in the hallway and returned to escort Laura to an armchair.

'No Edward!' Mrs Sawyer's thin voice held authority.

Laura was startled at the use of his proper name. She'd never heard anyone call him Edward.

'In the chair facing me. I don't want to have to twist my head, not with my stiff neck.' She placed her hands each side of her neck as if to emphasise the point. All the time her eyes scrutinised Laura from head to foot.

Under the intense observation, Laura felt her cheeks redden and she meekly sat down on the bare wooden chair. For a few moments she stared at the floor, then deliberately gazed about the room. In the centre was an oak table so highly polished its surface reflected like a mirror each of the floral cups and saucers and small tea plates placed upon it. Silver teaspoons were laid alongside the matching sugar bowl with silver tongs peeping above the rim. Two straight backed armchairs covered in dark brown rep were each side of the hearth. A small corner piece, a glass fronted cabinet, displayed china boat ornaments. An extravagant well banked coal fire flamed and glowed in the open grate. Her eyes had quickly surveyed the room and came back to rest on the figure of Mrs Sawyer, whose face now wore an expression of smugness.

'My son tells me, Miss Stringer, you work in a factory. A leather factory, I believe.' Each time she spoke the word factory her nose wrinkled as if offended by a bad smell.

Laura sensed the afternoon was going to be a disaster. Long ago she had come to the conclusion it was Mrs Sawyer's refusal which had prevented their meeting but she was at a loss to understand why. Was it because she worked in a factory? She was unsure how to answer Mrs Sawyer, but before she had thought of what to say Eddie was brightly praising her.

'Laurie is Garsten's best worker. She gets all the important jobs, don't you dearest?'

The sound of his voice uttering that endearment released Laura from her misery. This was Eddie's birthday tea party and she would ensure it was a happy occasion.

'She's been working on a bag for no less a person-age than royalty!' he boasted to Laura's acute embar-rassment. 'She has charge of ten benches.'

'Edward, don't stand chattering. Fetch the tea.'

'Certainly, mother. Come on Laurie, you can help.'

Laura grinned at him. What a darling he was! He had contrived not to leave her alone with his mother. Laura carried in the two tier cake stand and Eddie brought in the steaming teapot. Mrs Sawyer had moved her chair closer to the table and Eddie put the pot in front of her. Laura returned to her allocated place and turned the chair to the table.

'It is very pretty china, Mrs Sawyer. My Grandmother had a similar tea set. I always loved the delicate pink roses twining about the cup.'

Mrs Sawyer was pouring the tea and her hand shook slightly. 'I doubt it was similar. This set was exclusive, a wedding present.'

Laura astutely ignored the interruption. 'My grandmother had her own dressmaking business in Leytonstone Road. Sometimes she would use a pattern but mostly she made up her own designs.'

'Laurie does that too, don't you? Take after your gran, I expect.' Eddie's voice held a note of pride. 'Do you remember Laurie? last year I think it was, we went to the Empire on your birthday, sat in the stalls that day, and do you remember that woman sitting next to you?'

Laura laughed. 'Oh yes! We were both wearing the same outfit. Except, of course, she had bought hers at many times the price mine had cost me to make.'

Laura relaxed and felt at ease. They laughed happily together at the shared memory until a shrill voice intervened.

'Pass the tea Edward.' She put the tea down and with exaggerated hand gestures declared: 'You'll never guess who called this morning Edward. Mrs Tucker! Yes Mrs Tucker and her daughter Lucy.' She glanced toward Laura. 'Such a beautiful girl, she and Edward were very close. Lucy has finished her education at that boarding school and is now home.'

'Don't remember her,' Eddie said in a noncommittal way and resumed his reminiscences.

Much as Laura enjoyed talking with Eddie, in his own home she had a pang of conscience about excluding his mother from their conversation.

'Mrs Sawyer, do you enjoy the theatre?'

'I am not well enough to go gallivanting about. Cut me a piece of cake Edward.' She passed over her plate, 'but we enjoy our life here, don't we Edward.'

Instead of answering her, Eddie began talking about his pals in the Stratford sheds which interested Laura and, of course Mrs Sawyer.

'Yes Edward will be a proper engineer. His father would be proud of him. He went into the sheds at fifteen as a wheel greaser, they spotted his talents for all things mechanical and, at seventeen was taken into a full apprenticeship, not just for steam engines, he's learnt all about other engines too.'

Laura saw how proud Mrs Sawyer was of her son and she nodded her head in agreement. She recognised that for years it had been just mother and son until Laura came along. *Two's company, three's a crowd.* The words rang in her head but, she must try to make Mrs Sawyer see it wouldn't be like that.

'Of course, Edward may be twenty one, but his apprenticeship doesn't end for another three years,' Mrs Sawyer said, a note of triumph in her voice.

Then tea was over.

'This has been a good time,' Eddie said as he helped Laura into her coat. 'We must do this regularly. What do you say mother? Let's make it once a month, I should like that.

It was settled. Although Mrs Sawyer had prevented their meeting in the past, it seemed now Eddie was a man - twenty one - he had insisted on inviting Laura for tea. Eddie was taking charge of his life. He made no mention of his mothers reluctance to welcome Laura, neither did he apologise for her behaviour. It was a matter of fact. As he closed the front door behind them, a black bonneted head peeped over the fence,

'This is your young lady then, is it? Are you going to introduce us son?'

'Of course I am. Laurie, this is Granny Scoiles...'

'None of that my lad. Be proper,' she reprimanded with a sly grin.

'Mrs Cecelia Scoiles, may I introduce Miss Laura Stringer.' The old lady's nut brown weathered face spread into a broad grin.

'You are quite right Eddie. She is lovely, I like her.' she leant over and patted Laura's hand resting on Eddies' arm, turned round and disappeared indoors.

'She's a good soul,' Eddie said as they strolled home. 'I've known her all my life. When Pa died on the railway, I was...mm... I must have been eight or so. Granny Scoiles looked after mother and me. She's a heart of gold. She's been very good to me.' He hugged Laura's arm. 'I'm special pleased she likes you.'

He opened the gate and Laura stepped through. With the safety of the iron railings between them, Eddie kissed her goodnight.

'I mean it you know. What I said about making it a regular tea party. You will come again, won't you?'

'Yes, dear Eddie. I'll come.'

It was the day before that was an ordeal for Laura. She fretted about what she could say to engage Mrs Sawyer in conversation, but once she was on Eddie's arm, walking toward Argyle Road, she didn't care if she sat dumb all afternoon. But, she didn't. She thought about the service at the mission and related the events of the morning. It wasn't meant to impress.

'Goodness gracious, Miss Stringer,' Mrs Sawyer exclaimed. 'We are not heathens here, you don't have to convert us you know.'

Again, the rebuff almost brought tears, but Laura swallowed hard. She determined to think of something else for next time.

Granny Scoiles must have been waiting behind the curtains for them. When Eddie held the gate open for Laura, the black bonneted head appeared.

'Good afternoon Eddie and Miss Laura.'

Laura could've hugged the old lady for calling her Laura and not Miss Stringer.

'My dear, you are looking bonny,' Granny Scoiles said as her beaming face appraised Laura. 'Such a lovely outfit you've got on. Eddie tells me how clever you are with your sewing. I wish you a pleasant afternoon,' and with that she disappeared.

Her words boosted Laura's confidence and it was nice to know Eddie spoke about her to the old lady. On each allotted Sunday, as they approached Eddie's home, they were met by Granny Scoiles in the usual way. Her warm friendly welcome was what Laura needed to see her through the tea party and somehow Granny Scoiles knew it.

Laura was spending Saturday afternoon altering a dress. She had bought it in the market - belonged to a duchess - the stall owner said. It was very pretty, bright blue tulle with occasional silver sequins on the skirt like stars in a summer night sky.

'I wish you'd change your mind and come with us next Thursday, Sarah. It promises to be a good evening. There'll be an orchestra and dancers and singers.'

To mark the occasion of the coronation of King George the Fifth on Thursday, the twenty second of June, West Ham Council had organised a special event in the Town Hall.

'It was kind of Eddie to say he would get another ticket but, I won't be doing any dancing.'

'I want to try this on. Sarah, come into our room and tell me what it is like at the back.'

Laura pulled off her cambric dress and stepped into the tulle dress. It felt cool and soft against her skin. Laura tied the sash at the back, drawing the front close about her neat waist.

'Sarah, is this part all right. Sarah! What are you looking at?'

'Soldiers in the street.'

'My goodness,' Laura exclaimed. 'We aren't going to be under siege are we? like Sidney Street?' she joined her sister at the window.

'See,' Sarah said. 'I saw them first at number nine, then they came out and went up to number seven. No-one answered their knock and now they are at number five. I wonder what they are canvassing for?'

'More likely looking for lodgings,' replied Laura.

'Ooh, look! They are coming over here.' They watched the two men pass through the gate and come up the path. Two loud raps of the door knocker.

'Should we answer it? What do you think?' Sarah asked. 'Mrs Milton doesn't always hear, does she.'

Curiosity got the better of them and they ran to the front door.

'Beg pardon, Madam. Er, Miss.' Both men scooped off their hats. As the dark haired man spoke, his eyes appreciated the vision before him.

'May I help you?' Laura asked.

'I do hope so.' For a moment he said nothing more, just stood gazing at the beautiful apparition before him.

Sarah, standing behind Laura, found herself under scrutiny from the pale blue eyes of the tall blond man.

'Well, what is it you want?' Laura asked.

'Ah yes,' he said straightening his shoulders. 'I am wondering if you know the whereabouts in this particular Burgess Road of a Mrs Jane Stringer?'

It was Laura's turn to stare. 'Mrs Jane Stringer,' she repeated stupidly. 'She's my mother.'

'Well, I'll be blowed! Fancy that! Now then, would you be Sarah or Laura?'

'What's going on?'' Jane asked coming along the passageway.

'Ma, this gentleman was asking...'

'Oh, no miss. Not gentleman. Only Officers are gentlemen. We're just foot soldiers. I'm Toby, Toby Goult.'

Jane frowned. It was strange to hear the name Goult. 'Well, Toby Goult, James' youngest. Don't keep them standing outside, girls. Do come in,'

She ushered them in.

'Laura, go and change your frock,' Jane whispered.

They all sat in the kitchen around the table.

'This is Samuel Hambleton, Sam, my mate. We're in the same troop. We've been abroad. Just got back to these shores. I went to the house opposite West Ham Park. Neighbours said my Ma had died some time ago.

I didn't know about it. Letters take a long time following you about in the army. The neighbours didn't know anything about Pa, where he'd moved to at all.'

Jane was sitting opposite Toby. She reached across and touched his hand. 'Yes, dear, your mother died five, no six years ago. And your dear father, my brother, died last year. I'm sorry, my dear.'

He listened reflectively as Jane told him she had been with her brother when Emily died. But she omitted to mention the squalor and degradation. Just as she left out where James was living when he died; only that she had travelled to Birmingham for the funeral.

'It wasn't possible to bring him back to London to rest beside his beloved wife,' Jane said.

Tobias nodded in acceptance of the facts. 'I hadn't kept in touch. I'm not good at letter writing. I joined up at sixteen and after training up north we were sent to the Sudan, weren't we Sam. We were there a couple of years and then moved up to Egypt where we've been ever since until called home for special duty.'

He turned eagerly to the girls. 'We are in the Sovereign's parade.' He said proudly. 'We're in the second squad behind the royal carriage. We're camped in Hyde Park and we drill every day but they gave us a pass for the weekend. We went to see Sam's Ma at Walthamstow and then I thought I might see if I could remember where you lived. And here we are.'

'We are pleased you remembered us,' Laura said. 'I'm sure I wouldn't have recognised you. But then, it was a long time ago when we last saw each other. At you sister Charlotte's wedding. I think I was ten,' she grinned at him.

'You've certainly blossomed since then, especially in what you were wearing just now,' he said cheekily.

'Oh, that's for the coronation. No, I don't mean I'm going to that,' she laughed. 'There's a do on at the Town Hall on Thursday evening.'

Jane made a pot of tea and set it on the table along with a fruit cake which she cut into generous portions.

Toby nudged Sam. 'Wakey, wakey! Lady's offering you a cup of tea.'

Since their arrival, Sam had not uttered a word. Sitting at the table, Laura was aware his concentration was on Sarah although he observed her from under lowered lids. When George arrived home from visiting his sister he was delighted with the visitors and eagerly questioned Tobias about the foreign lands where he had served under the flag. At first, Sam said a few words then relapsed into his silent study. Now Laura saw his devoted gaze evoked a response: a sly glance and a timid smile from Sarah.

'Dunno how long we'll be posted here after the coronation,' Toby said. 'There was talk of us going up to Scotland to give them a similar parade, in Edinburgh, I think. But no-one knows any more than that. We'll be in Hyde Park until Sunday, that's for sure. We up sticks at seven thirty to pastures new,' he laughed.

'The streets of London are very gay with miles of bunting,' Laura said. 'Sarah and I work in the city, I wonder if we'll be able to see any of the parade. Will it go anywhere near St Paul's?'

'I haven't bothered about where it's going. I just do left right left right until I'm told to stop. Do you know, Sam?'

As if caught out in a crime, Sam averted his eyes with a quick jerk of his head and stared at Jane.

'Beg pardon, missus?' he mumbled.

Tobias dug his elbow into Sam's ribs. 'It was me what asked you something. The girls want to see something of the parade on Thursday. Does it go near St Paul's?'

It was a cheering thought he might see her again. 'I know it goes by the Guildhall so it might come around St Paul's.' Sam openly smiled at Sarah. 'There's going

to be fireworks in Hyde Park in the evening. Would
you like to come to that?'

'Thursday evening is the do on at the Town Hall.
That's what my dress is for,' Laura replied.

Sarah's face quickly went from elation to
disappointment.

The silent rapport between Sam and Sarah had not
been lost on Tobias.

'Well, then, Sam, what do you say to us escorting
the ladies to the Town Hall, That is if all the tickets
haven't been sold.'

'I'm sure you could get tickets but I'm sorry to dis-
appoint you, cousin,' Laura grinned, 'I already have
my escort.'

This time it was Sam's bubble of happiness that
burst.

'And you, Miss Sarah,' he asked wretchedly, 'I
suppose you also have an escort?'

'No, I don't,' she relied eagerly, 'and neither does our
friend Vily Walters.'

Sarah's eyes pleaded with her sister not to say otherwise. Laura didn't. It was good to see Sarah returning to life.

'That's settled then,' Sam said with relief. 'What
time shall we call for you?'

Violet Walters, as she was called these days, was
keen to join the party. She'd just had a tiff with her
latest young man and an outing with a soldier was
just the sort of thing to bring him round. She came
across to show them the dress she'd bought.

'After you'd asked me on Sunday, I decided it called
for something special. I told them in the office I should
need the afternoon off to look for it,' she giggled. 'Mind
you, they're ever so good. Being the only lady employee
in the office has its advantages.' She demonstrated by
twisting her fingers. 'Well, it gets a bit boring typing
insurance schedules.'

She opened the box and shook out the dress.

'Oh, Violet,' Laura exclaimed. 'It's stunning.'

'I'll leave it here until Thursday,' she winked. 'Mother will only get upset if she sees the price ticket!'

Garsten's had graciously allowed the workers to leave the factory at five o'clock in honour of the King's coronation. There was almost a stampede to be first out of the gates.

Laura sponged herself down in the scullery to freshen up after the stuffy journey home and was quickly followed by Sarah. Violet came across at six o'clock. They were a most glamorous trio. Violet, the tallest by a couple of inches, in white crepe silk with a pearl encrusted bodice was dazzling; her honey blonde hair hung loose about her shoulders. Sarah was dressed in a pale rose pink satin. Laura added contrast in bright blue tulle.

The Town Hall was decorated with gold and silver cardboard crowns around the room. Tables and chairs lined the walls. The orchestra upon the stage was playing as they arrived. Toby was delighted with his companion for the evening and proudly showed Violet to a chair. Sam and Sarah sat demurely at the back. After the first half of entrainment by singers and a juggler, the orchestra leader announced it was time for dancing.

'Now, you young ones,' he said looking towards them especially, 'how about taking the floor with this latest hit The Gaby Glide. Let's see you do it.'

As soon as the music struck up, Violet was on her feet ignoring Toby's plea he didn't know it. Eddie swept Laura onto the floor and they began stepping out The Gaby Glide to the applause of the other dancers. Sam and Sarah refused to be drawn into the fun but clapped along with the rest. With such a receptive audience, the orchestra played one after the other of all the popular tunes and repeated one or two by request, especially Alexander's Ragtime Band.

It had been a good coronation day.

Chapter 20

Precisely at seven thirty on Sunday morning the tented encampment in Hyde Park disbanded. Most of the troops returned to their home barracks. But not all, much to Sarah's pleasure when she received a letter from Sam.

Dear Miss Sarah

I write to tell you I did not go back to Egypt with Toby and the rest of the detachment. Orders were waiting for me and I am posted to Salisbury for special gunnery training.

I shall not get leave for two or three months but when I do I should very much like to call on you if you will permit me.

Until then I should very much like to write to you. Of course, you do not have to write back. Not unless you want to.

Your obedient servant
Samuel Hambleton.

Often Laura caught sight of her sister rereading the letter and give a sweet contented sigh. By the end of

---

September when Sam was due on leave, Sarah had a package of letters tied up with ribbon.

George opened the door and welcomed him.

'Come in, lad. It is good to see you again. Come on through. Our girl is dressed and ready for you.'

Sam had discarded his soldier's uniform for a striped jacket and winged collar shirt. The bowler hat sat uneasily in his head and he swept if off as he faced Jane and Sarah.

'How do, Mrs Stringer. Hello, Miss Sarah,' he stammered and quickly looked at his boots.

'Off you go, now.' George said slapping Sam on the back. He then gripped his arm earnestly. 'Take care of her and don't be too late bringing her home.'

Laura had been helping set up the harvest tables at the Mission and got home about nine o'clock. She found George and Jane sitting grimly at the table.

'Don't be anxious. It's early yet. And Sam Hambleton's all right. I'm sure of it.'

To reinforce the fact, they heard the front door open and Sarah's voice thanking Sam for a nice evening and agreeing on the time to meet tomorrow, then, 'Goodnight'.

Words tumbled from Sarah's lips.

'Oh, Ma, Pa, Laura. Oh, it was ever so nice. We went over to Walthamstow to meet his mother, she's a widow woman. She lives in this house all by herself. Oh, and she is ever so nice. She gave me a hug. Said Samuel, as she always calls him, said Samuel wrote of nothing else in his letters except me. What do you think of that? Then, Sam-as I call him,' and she gave a little laugh, 'he took his Ma and me out to tea. Said he had a beautiful lady on each arm. We went to one of those posh places you know the ones with large tubs of ferns. There was a musical trio playing and we had a pot of tea with its own jug of hot water and milk all on a silver tray and cups with gold bands round the edges. And a whole plateful of cakes lots with cream in them,' Sarah finally paused and sighed. 'Tomorrow he's calling for me at three and we're going to take a boat somewhere, I can't remember where. Oh, it was such a lovely day.'

She drifted out of the kitchen in a dream leaving George and Jane open mouthed.

'Well, what do you make of that? Sounds like wedding bells are in the offing don't you think?' Laura said. 'I do hope so. And I hope, seeing as Sarah is the eldest, I hope she marries before I do.'

Sitting in Mrs Sawyer's parlour the following afternoon. Laura was acutely aware of the contrast with the woman Sarah had described yesterday. In the months since that first tea party, there had developed an uneasy truce between Mrs Sawyer and Laura. They both spoke to Eddie but not to each other; not directly that is. Laura would say to the room at large that it was hot or cold or wet or fine as the case may be and it was good to be indoors having a cup of tea. Mrs Sawyer only addressed Eddie.

She had turned it over and over in her mind as to why Mrs Sawyer didn't like her. Would she had liked her if she worked in an office like Violet? She thought not. No woman would ever be good enough for her son. Yet she must have realised he would want to marry some time.

When taking Laura home Eddie never made a comment on his mother's behaviour; no excuses. Nor did he ask Laura to overlook his mother's snubs. He would hold her arm and give it a squeeze and say, 'It's been a grand afternoon, Laurie.'

Today, he surprised her.

'I've worked it out, he said. 'My apprenticeship ends 15th May 1914. I'll be certificated on the 25th. We'll be wed on the 27th of June.'

Laura laughed. 'Don't you think I should be consulted about the date?'

'But you don't have any special dates, like being certificated. I know it's three years hence still it's best to have it settled.'

'That's not very romantic, Eddie, just deciding on your own like that,' Lara said lightly but was hurt at his blunt statement.

He never said if he had mentioned the date to his mother.

It was December before Sam was granted further leave but he kept up a steady correspondence during that time. When he came to call on Sarah a few days before Christmas, he came in his soldier's uniform. George had answered the door but it was some time before they entered the kitchen.

'Jane, dearest, what do you think? Sam has been promoted to Corporal.'

Shoulders back, muscles flexed, Sam, proudly displayed his stripes.

'Oh, that is so clever of you, Sam.' Sarah's eyes glowed.

George cleared his throat. 'And that's not all. Sam has asked for our daughter's hand in marriage,' George said. 'What do you say, Jane?'

'Well,' Jane hesitated. 'Sarah is not twenty-one. But they can be considered betrothed.'

Sam vigorously shook George's hand and was undecided whether he should shake or kiss Jane's hand. He did neither. Instead he saluted her and turned to Sarah. Her beautiful complexion was enhanced by a deep blush. He reached into his pocket and took out a neat box and offered it to her. Sarah's eyes danced as she opened the lid and saw the dark red ruby perched on a golden bridge surrounded by small pearls. Sam took her left hand and placed the ring on her finger.

It was a marvellous Christmas holiday especially as

many workers were granted Friday off as Christmas Day was on a Saturday and Boxing Day on Sunday. One thing marred the happy festivities: news of the death of Great Aunt Laura; the last link with the past. Laura was most upset at the loss of her namesake. She also had a feeling of guilt of neglecting the old lady. Great Aunt had done so much for them. Laura's earliest happy memories were of running around Clarke's farm, basket in hand, searching for hen's eggs. And watching the birth of Rosie. Later, when she was temporarily blinded, getting Great Aunt to read word after word from the dictionary - and being cross when she left out words she could not say. When was the last time she had seen Great Aunt? Laura couldn't remember. Now she was gone.

After the gay celebrations of Christmas with shops and markets brightly festooned and displaying fir trees draped with tinsel and coloured balls, New Year was an anticlimax. It was back to the usual grind. Everyone hated it but, much as she tried, Laura couldn't get the practice stopped. The New Year's Day ritual had to be endured. At eleven forty-five Johnson would sound the bell. Benches had to be wiped clean and work neatly placed on view. Five minutes later, the doors were flung back and the Board of Directors entered led by two Garsten brothers. Johnson would call: 'Workers!' - and all would stand as if in military review. The visiting group would pass up and down each line, uttering: Prosperous New year' to left and right.

'Miserly old bastard,' someone muttered. 'prosperous for the bosses.'

'It's Leap Year this year,' Kate whispered. 'I think I'll pop the question to old man Garsten.'

Laura pulled a face as she looked at the grey haired, sickly faced old man with the drooping gingery moustache.

'Better to be an old man's darling then a young man's slave,' Kate giggled, causing Johnson to frown sternly at her.

Some of the Board members were now so tottery on their feet, it took more than ten minutes to walk around the factory floor. The workers saw their well earned hour's break dwindle to fifty minutes At last the inspection was over and the workers hurried away from their benches.

There was a commotion in the street outside.

'What's up?' Kate asked.

'Can't yer see! Look!'

Laura edged her way through and stared, like everyone else, at the sky. Above the roof tops on the opposite side of the road, spirals rose up; smutty fragments drifted down onto the pavements. The acrid smell filled her nostrils and choked her lungs. A sudden explosion sent another ebony cloud belching upward. She heard someone say: paint factory. Her heart froze. Soon she was racing across the road and darting through back alleys. Passers-by stared as she dashed along and, as she reached the mouth of the road, the fire tender hurtled past. She pushed against a stream of people hurrying away from the disaster.

'Get back you damned fool,' a man shouted. 'Can't yer see the place is burning?'

She leant against a brick wall as the human tide swept past her. How long she stood like that she wasn't sure. Something nagged in her mind and she looked again at the burning structure; her eyes scanned to the neighbouring building focused on the giant lettering: Jantsen and Nicholson. It was unscathed.

'Wotcha, Sis. What you doing here? Come to look at the blaze?' Georgie asked.

The sound of his voice gave her relief, she hugged and kissed him.

'Here, give over, Sis.'

'Someone said it was the paint factory.'

'No. It's the feather curling place, two doors up. Of course, they have to use candles to do the job.'

The crowd roared. They turned to see the last remnants of the fragile timber structure swallowed up by enormous flames and so take the lives of several girls.

All night Laura's dreams were filled with fires. Smoke pervaded her nostrils and lungs until she gasped for air and awoke. It wasn't time yet, but she got up. She tip-toed along the passage into the welcome warmth of the kitchen In the dark she held her hands out to the stove and tensed as she realised someone was behind her. Then she heard her mother's stifled sob.

'Ma! Ma! What is it? What ails you?' Laura was beside the hunched figure in the rocking chair. 'Georgie wasn't hurt yesterday. None of us were. What is it? Tell me, Ma. Let me help.'

'Nothing you can do,' Jane mumbled.

In all their troubles of the past, Laura had never seen her mother cry, not really cry; mostly a grim squeezing of her eyes. Now tears streaked her face.

'Do you know how old I am, Laura? I'm forty-one years old. And I'm going to have a baby.'

'A baby!' Laura repeated in astonishment.

'Yes, a baby.'

'But that's wonderful,' Laura said gleefully. 'Honestly, it is. It's nothing to cry about.'

'It's another mouth to feed. I shan't get thirty shillings for the child. That's only for the likes of those whose men folk contributed regularly to the sickness benefit. Your Pa's wages were never enough to feed and house us. It's only since you three have been working that things got better, But Sarah and you, you'll both be married soon and have your own families,' she said peevishly. 'I don't want a baby at my age.'

'Ma, don't say that.'

Jane grasped Laura's arm. 'I'm frightened.'

'But why, Ma?' Laura laughed. 'You had three babies before.'

'I'll tell you something. Promise me you'll never repeat it. Not to anyone, you understand.'

'Yes, I promise.'

'I love your father so much, Laura. But I did a terrible thing. Years ago, when you were little, about five. I found I was with child. We already had you three, your father had just been taken on again after weeks out of work, we couldn't afford another child. I found someone who took it away from me before it was born. Do you understand?'

Laura's face was puzzled. 'I think so.' A terrible thought occurred to her. 'You're not going to do it again, are you?' she asked terrified.

Jane shook her head. 'But it was a great sin and I wonder if I shall be punished for it.' She was silent for a moment; she looked up into Laura's face. 'Forgive me, Laura.'

She was startled by her mother's words. 'It's not for me to forgive...'

'No, child. Forgive me for the way I've behaved to you. I know you have a special place in your father's heart. Sometimes, I've resented that. Because I wanted all of his love. Forgive me. I should like us to be friends before... before it's too late.'

Laura was moved by her mother's words. 'Of course, we are friends, you daft thing,' she said softly.

Jane raised herself out of the chair. 'I'll brew some tea.'

Laura stood close by her mother. 'Don't worry about money, Ma. I'll feed and clothe the little one. I shan't be marrying for a couple of years and even then I should be able to make clothes for the child. It'll be all right, I'm sure.'

When Jane broke the news to George he was delighted; the thought of being a father again put a lift in his step. Jane couldn't bring herself to tell the others and left it to George. Young Georgie grinned and blushed. It brought back painful memories to Sarah and she took the news quietly.

Sam's letters arrived so frequently, the postman said he was wearing out his shoe leather walking up to Number Four. On her birthday, Sarah received a card with real satin roses which even had a scent.

Laura pondered on what her mother had told her and been somewhat disturbed, not because of what she had done but because it might have an effect on this unborn child. Now she wondered how things would be for Sarah when she married and wanted a family. When they lay in their bed that night. Laura gently took her sister's hand.

'Have you told Sam of your experience?' she whispered.

She felt the body beside her stiffen.

'Have you said anything to him, dearest?'

Sarah made no reply.

'You'll have to tell him, my dear, dear sister,' Laura pleaded. 'You have to.'

Sarah's body shook. 'No!' she said in an anguished cry.

'It wasn't your fault, dearest.'

'Why should I tell him? He'll never know.'

Laura held her close, remembering the secret gossip of the factory girls. 'But he will know, my sweet one. He will know on your wedding night. Don't let him find out then. It would be too cruel for you both. You must tell him now. He loves you very much, Sarah, he'll understand.'

She cradled the sobbing Sarah in her arms.

'I can't tell him, Laura. You must do it for me.'

'No, dearest, it's not for me...'

'Please, please. Write to him'

'No, not in a letter.'

Laura thought I must see his face when I tell him.

'When he next comes home on leave, Sarah, I'll arrange to meet him and tell him if that's what you want me to do.'

'Yes, I want you to do it.'

It was a task Laura was not looking forward to. She rehearsed and rehearsed in her mind what she would say; it all sounded sympathetic but how would the news be received? Tobias and Sam arrived on their doorstep last June, they went together to the event at the Town Hall but since that time Laura had not exchanged a word with Sam. What was he really like? She didn't know. Ma and Pa had spoken to him and George thought he was a fine fellow. Sarah, of course, was head over heels in love with Sam. He had to be all right. He was due for leave in April, Sarah said. Laura wondered about trying it out on Eddie but Eddie already knew of Sarah's experience and could not react as one hearing it for the first time.

Sarah continued her correspondence as before. The weeks passed and too soon it was April.

As they came out into the Spring sunshine for their hour's break, Kate linked arms with Maisie and walked beside Laura.

'We never got a squeak out of her last week,' Kate complained to Maisie, 'Cos she was doing some fancy job for the bosses.'

'It was for Mr Garsten, the eldest brother, Mr Johnson said. Laura had to put something, a moonogram, I think you said on all his cases and bags as he was going on an ocean liner.'

'Well, it was me wot was going to propose to the old codger,' Kate laughed, 'not that I could do a moonargram or whatsit. But now this week, she still don't say nothing to us, do you?' Kate gave a hefty push of her elbow into Laura's side.

'I don't mean to shut you out, friends. I've got to meet someone tonight and it won't be easy what I've got to say to him'

Kate stared at her. 'Yer don't mean to say yer gonner break with Eddie? After all this time!'

'Oh, no! She wouldn't,' Maisie said with a whimper.

'No, you goose.' Laura took their arms. 'It's another young man and that's all I'm going to say.' She paused. 'Except I'd like you to wish me luck.'

After work that evening they walked together to the station. Laura and Sarah were the first to part company as Kate and Maisie went on to the tram stop.

'Here!' Kate said. 'Look at them headlines.'

They stared at the placard as the news boy called: 'Read all about it. Titanic sank two twenty this morning.' The liner on its maiden voyage had struck an iceberg and sunk.

'Here,' Kate said again. 'That was the ship Old man Garston was on. Johnson had a picture of it. Looked ever so funny with four funnels sticking up.' She nudged Maisie. 'Just as well I never wed him I might've been on it, too, for the honeymoon,' she laughed. She looked at Laura. 'Cor! What a bleedin' shame! All them suitcases and bags you done for him. Gone to the bottom of the sea now. Ta'ta.'

They hurried off but Kate turned round.

'Best of luck,' she called.

In their room, Laura waited behind the curtains. As soon as she saw the figure turn the corner, she ran out of the house and stopped him just by Number One's gate.

'Miss Laura,' Sam said. 'It's nice to see you. What are you doing? Let go of my arm.'

'Please, Sam. I must talk to you and it's better if we walk somewhere.'

'It's Sarah, isn't it?' He pulled away as if to go back.

He stood facing her. 'What is it? Is she hurt?'

'No, she isn't hurt, Sam. Please may we walk. Let's cross the road.'

She led the way and he followed, dejected and forlorn. When Laura stopped she realised where she was. Unknowingly, her feet had led her to the horses' watering trough – her first rendezvous with Eddie – and her spirits lifted.

'I know what it is,' Sam said. He looked at her with brimming eyes.

'I don't think you do, my dear friend.'

He was taken aback by her tone and kind words. He blinked back the tears. They squatted on the edge of the stone trough; she was on the corner facing him. 'Three years ago, on her seventeenth birthday, Sarah and a young man went out together. She came home in a very distressed state. Her clothes were torn and there were scratches over her lovely face and down her neck and chest.' She paused to observe Sam's reaction. She continued quietly, 'The man had violated her body.'

Sam's hand went to his mouth. His face was ashen.

'My father was prepared to do murder but our first concern was for Sarah. She was utterly broken. We feared for her sanity and that she might've taken her own life. By the merciful Grace of God, she lost the baby. After the evil was swept from her body, she began the long climb back to life. Since that dreadful night, she had not been out with a young man until you came along. She loves you so very much and longs to be your wife but it's important you should know of her condition. She was too frightened to tell you herself, frightened you would reject her.'

A groan escaped his lips. 'Oh that poor dear darling girl. Oh my sweetest Sarah. Such a delicate flower.' He stood up. 'I must go to her. She will see me won't she, Miss Laura? I thought your news was that Sarah rejected me! She will marry me, won't she, Miss Laura? Please tell me. Her, er, experience, won't stop her from marrying me, will it?'

Laura reached up and kissed him. 'I'll look forward to welcoming you as brother-in-law, dear Sam. Go on, run ahead. Go to her.'

He was soon out of sight.

By the end of Sam's leave, Laura wasn't surprised to hear they were making wedding plans.

'I should like to be married in the month of June, Sarah said. 'It's always supposed to be lucky if you do. So we'll be wed June of next year.'

Laura smiled. That would be nice; Sarah and Sam in June 1913 and she and Eddie in June 1914. It had worked out perfectly. Time enough to make Sarah's trousseau before completing her own.

When she met Eddie, she delighted in telling him the news.

'It will be such excitement,' Laura said. 'Think of it, we'll be able to see what goes on at Sarah's wedding so there won't be any surprises for us,' she laughed.

'Well, I thought perhaps, you'd changed your mind about me.'

She was puzzled. 'What do you mean?

'What's that you've got pinned to your coat?'

Laura glanced down. 'I'd forgotten about that. It's a paper rose. They were selling them in the city this week; it's a new charity for hospitals and nurses and they call if Alexandra's Rose day. Isn't it a nice idea. They say Queen Alexandra chose the twenty-sixth of June because it was the day she arrived in England.'

'I thought another man had given you a token.'

His brusque tone startled Laura until she looked up at his face and saw it crease in merriment. She joined in the laughter.

'How is your Ma, Laurie. Is she keeping well?'

'Well enough but she is so big. Poor Pa has to sleep on the floor, there's no room for him in the bed. She is fretful for the time to pass.'

They strolled along hand in hand.

'Won't it be grand, sweetheart, when we have our own family,' he said softly, stoking her palm. 'I think three. What say you, Laurie?'

'Yes, three would be nice but I shall be happy with whatever blessings the good Lord sends.'

By the second week of July, Jane was suffering real discomfort. She couldn't stand or sit or lie down for more than a few minutes at a time.

'Shall I ask Mrs Walters to come over and sit with you Ma,' Laura asked.

'It'll be a day or so yet, girl, so no need to inconvenience folks. I'll be all right. Go on. Off to work, now'

Each morning, Laura asked the same question but Jane was adamant.

'Leave me be, girl,' she said angrily and pushed Laura out of the door.

As she moved back toward the kitchen, she experienced the first stabbing pain. Squeezing into the rocking chair, she glanced at the new marble mantel clock George had proudly bought last Christmas: ten minutes past seven. An hour later she struggled to the front door. A schoolboy was kicking a tin along the kerb.

'Here, lad! Run down to Number Nineteen and tell the lady there that Mrs Stringer wants her.'

'Nah! Why should I? Go yourself, missus.'

'If you don't fetch her you'll have to deliver the baby,' Jane shouted.

The boys eyes popped wide open as he surveyed the bulging figure in the doorway. He turned and ran like a hare.

Leaving the door wide open, Jane shuffled to the bedroom and heaved herself onto the bed. It was seventeen years since he had given birth to Georgie. She racked her brain to remember but another violent pain shook her body and she lay exhausted. Throughout the morning she floated between waking and sleeping; pain and relief. Mrs Walters was bustling in and out of the room; other neighbours came to help. Sometime later Jane thought she saw the midwife.

When the shutters were pulled across the market entrance, closing business for the day, George hurried away. He wondered whether it would be quicker to get the train; it was a tedious journey by tram. But it would cost an extra copper or two for the train, so he made his way to the tram stop. It rattled and jolted along and at the junction a new driver took over adding to the travelling time. It was nearly a quarter past three when he turned into Burgess Road.

The door was open and he heard voices coming from their bedroom. A cold fear swept through him. His feet were like heavy stones, he could not move. The voices stopped. Only an eerie silence filled the house until moments later it was broken by an irritated wail, followed by a babble of sound. He pushed open the door. As he entered the midwife turned about and thrust the small bundle into his arms.

'Here's your little daughter, Mr Stringer. A scrawny little scrap for all her mother's size.'

George gazed down at the wrinkled shrimp pink face topped by a mass of black hair. He tickled the baby's chin and screwed up eyes opened for an instant to reveal coal black eyes. He gently carried the baby back to the bed and put it into Jane's arms.

'How are you Jane?' He looked at her drawn face.

'Glad it's all over,' Jane murmured.

'Best delivery I've had for ages,' the midwife said. 'So fast and easy.'

'We didn't have to do anything to help her, did we?' Mrs Walters said. 'Very lucky you were, Mrs Stringer.'

'Now she needs rest,' the midwife said and shooed out the other ladies. 'Just a few minutes, Mr Stringer. Here let me have the baby.'

She scooped up the small bundle and placed it in the wicker cradle.

It had cost a shilling in the junk shop. After brushing it thoroughly, Laura covered the inside with a fine cambric edged with white lace and made a wadding mattress to match.

Jane's head rested against his shoulder as George perched on the edge of the bed. With a towel, he gently patted the perspiration from the sandy freckles across the bridge of her nose. Her eyes flickered open.

'We shall have to think of a name for our dear little girl, my dearest wife.'

'Grace is a nice name, don't you think?'

'Yes, I do. There's a novice working with Sister Anthony at the hospital, got a very nice name: Jessie. What do you say to that 'Grace Jessie Stringer.' George rolled the words off his tongue.

'They go nicely together, George, but I think the other way round.'

George looked as pleased as Punch. 'If you really say so, Mother, then it shall be Jessie Grace Stringer, born this Tuesday, the 16th of July Nineteen Hundred and Twelve. I'll get it registered proper like tomorrow.' He leaned down and kissed her. 'I love you Jane Stringer,' he whispered as she drifted off into sleep.

Unlike her previous pregnancies, when she had to be up and working the next day, this time she was pampered. Her two daughters insisted on taking care of the baby and made her stay in bed for over a week.

Before going off to work they made sure she had every-thing to hand and left the door on the latch for Mrs Walters or the midwife to call in to attend to Jane and the baby during the day time.

'I've made a jug of lemon barley, Ma. It's here on this box.' Laura moved to stand beside the bed. 'I've heard several members at the Mission call their parent Mum. I should like to call you that, too. Would you mind if I said Mum instead of Ma I think it sounds nicer. Especially as you are a new mother again.'

'I don't mind what you call me, girl. I Just hope we can manage.'

'Now, don't go over that. Mum. I told you I would take care of little Jessie. I promise you I always will.'

On Saturday afternoons, Laura would put Jessie in the bassinet and push it all the way to the park. She talked to the baby, described everything she saw and Jessie gurgled in reply. By December, the baby had put on weight and was a healthy robust infant. Jane, once she was active again, shed her excess weight.

On the Sunday before Christmas, they gathered in the kitchen. Sam and Sarah sat with their backs to the window; Eddie and Laura backing onto the range. George was one end of the table; Georgie sat alongside his father next to Sarah and Jane at the other end with the bassinet beside her. George poured a glass of port wine for everyone.

He raised his glass. 'Its been a grand year. Good health.'

'Good health,' they chorused.

'And we've a wedding to look forward to next year. To Sarah and Sam,' George raised his glass again.

Sam stood up. 'If I may take the liberty, sir, I should like to propose a toast to Laura and Eddie. Their mar-riage soon to follow.'

Sarah nudged Georgie. 'When are you going to bring home your girl?'

'I haven't got a girl,' he protested.

'We saw you mooning over a pretty little thing with ringlets, didn't we Laura?'

Jane leant back in her chair and looked around at the family gathered there.

Yes, they were very fortunate. She smiled to herself. Not all luck was bad.